A History of
Magic and
Witchcraft
in Wales

T0322363

A History of
Magic and
Witchcraft
in Wales

Richard Suggett

First published 2008
Reprinted 2008, 2011, 2024

The History Press
97 St George's Place,
Cheltenham, Gloucestershire, GL50 3QB
www.thehistorypress.co.uk

British Library Cataloguing in Publication Data.
A catalogue record for this book is available from the British Library.

ISBN 978 0 7524 2826 0

Typesetting and origination by The History Press Ltd.
Printed by TJ Books LImited, Padstow, Cornwall

CONTENTS

About the Author

Richard Suggett was educated at Penarth Grammar School and the Universities of Durham and Oxford. His publications in social and architectural history include a study of the architect John Nash (1995) and *Houses and History in the March of Wales* (2005), a study of medieval houses in context. He is currently an Investigator at the Royal Commission on the Ancient & Historical Monuments for Wales, based at Aberystwyth, and an honorary fellow of the University of Wales Centre for Advanced Welsh and Celtic Studies.

I

WITCHCRAFT IN WALES

It is a commonplace to say that historians struggle to hear voices from the past, especially when writing about popular culture. It so happens that there are some very insistent voices demanding to be heard on the subject of witchcraft in Wales. The documentary history of witchcraft in Wales begins with a dialogue between two Welshmen published about 1595 and ends three hundred years later with a conversation between two Welshwomen published at the turn of the twentieth century. This conversational form was absolutely appropriate to the discussion of witchcraft. Witchcraft was inseparable from discourse, the interchange of words and ideas, rumour, and raised and hushed voices. Some of these raised voices have been preserved in the legal record. Wales has abundant legal records, a bureaucratic consequence of the Act of Union, and this study has tried to make the most of them. In the legal record the different voices of accusers and accused are preserved. The voices are usually mediated through the written word in English and Latin, it is true, but the voices are still there to be heard. Sometimes the authentic vernacular words of an accusation have survived: '*Witch wyti, a myfi a'th profia di yn witch*' – 'You are a witch, and I will prove you a witch'. It emerges that witchcraft was intensely oral – a matter of words or ways of speaking and their interpretation. The historian of witchcraft in Wales – and, indeed, witchcraft anywhere – has to begin by retrieving lost ways of speaking and reconstructing an obsolete vocabulary that classified those associated with the supernatural.

Witchcraft studies have become central to the historiography of late medieval and early modern Europe. The subject is intrinsically fascinating but analytically elusive. At the theoretical level there has been an invigorating dialogue between historians of witchcraft and social anthropologists about the rationality and social relevance of witchcraft beliefs. The dialogue has been interrupted, but its legacy has been closer semantic attention to the categories of belief. At the empirical level, a great deal of archival rummaging has gone into establishing when, where, and how many suspected witches were formally prosecuted in numerous legal jurisdictions.

Although many areas still await investigation, or have suffered archival losses, the map of European witch-hunting can be provisionally drawn. It is now clear that witchcraft persecutions peaked around 1580–1630, but the dynamic of prosecution shifted from a sixteenth-century continental centre to the margins of Europe in the seventeenth and eighteenth centuries. There is however little agreement as to how the considerable geographical and chronological differences in witch-hunting should be interpreted.[1]

Witchcraft studies are important because accusations were inseparable from situations of conflict, power, and social control; indeed, studies of witchcraft tend to expand to become histories of social relations in the early modern period. The symbolism of the 'witch' figure provides a revealing negative image of destructive aspects of society, the opposite or inversion of the 'ideal' society. At the sociological level, the analysis of witchcraft accusations and prosecutions has revealed a great deal about mechanisms of social control and the coercive role of the state. But was witchcraft, to cite some recent competing explanations, in the final instance really 'about' the growth of individualism, a crisis in gender relations, or the state-building process?[2] The tendency to explain witchcraft by making it an epiphenomenon of closely-defined relations of domination makes it difficult to account for conceptual change, that is, what happens to witchcraft beliefs over time. The challenge of witchcraft studies is to integrate both the conceptual and social dimensions of belief, and to extend analysis to the periods before and after the classic witchcraft trials which have engaged the attention of most specialists. The immediate purpose of this study is to establish the pattern of witchcraft prosecutions in Wales, to fill in one of the blank areas on the far western side of the map of European witch hunting, but also to deal with the issues of the transmission, reproduction, and transformation of belief.

Evidence

The evidence relating to witchcraft in Wales is complicated in an interesting way by numerous references to Welsh occult beliefs in English literary and historical sources. Elizabethan and Stuart divines and politicians frequently referred to the religious ignorance of Wales. Religious radicals in the south of England perceived Wales, Cornwall, and the north as 'dark corners of the land', in need of illumination by preaching and the light of the gospel. These were places where 'God was little better known than amongst the Indians', the House of Commons was told in 1628, and prayers were little more than spells and charms. In Wales, a Presbyterian, John Lewis of Glas-crug, in *Contemplations* published during the Civil War in 1646, condemned the 'swarm of blinde superstitious ceremonies that are among us, passing under the name of old harmless customs'. Cromwell himself is supposed to have said that the common people of Wales were 'but a seduced ignorant people'. Religious ignorance implied superstition, and superstition included not only the practices of a residual Catholicism but also magic and witchcraft.[3]

The supernatural powers attributed to the Welsh were a popular literary trope. There was perennial interest in the insinuating appeal of prophecies, and the Welsh were regarded as having a special expertise in interpreting prophecy. There was some fascination with the particular character of the half-diabolic Merlin: 'Some Incubus or Spirit of the night / begot him then, for, sure, no mortal did it', as a character puts it in *The Birth of Merlin.* In Shakespeare's dialogue between Hotspur and Mortimer in *Henry IV, Part I*, Hotspur complains that Glendower's stories of the dreamer Merlin and his prophecies are 'skimble-skamble stuff / As puts me from my faith'. Shakespeare's Glendower, 'that great magician', famously claims that he can 'call spirits from the vasty deep' and tells Hotspur, 'Why, I can teach thee, cousin, to command the devil'. There is of course humour in the dialogue with Glendower, but (as Katharine Briggs pointed out) 'there is meant to be some truth in his claims, for on his command music sounds from the air as it might have done for Prospero'. Shakespeare's treatment of Glendower as a magical Welshman had deep historical roots. The poet-chronicler, John Hardyng, described how Henry IV's three campaigns in Wales had been frustrated by dreadful weather raised by magic:

> The king had neuer, but tempest foule & raine
> As longe as he was ay in Wales grounde
> Rockes & mystes, windes & stormes euer certaine
> All men trowed, yt witches it made that stounde.[4]

This was not retrospective poetic license. A contemporary chronicler records that the tempests that disrupted Henry IV's campaign against Glyndŵr, nearly killing the king on one occasion, were indeed attributed by some to Glyndŵr's sorcery: 'There were many that supposed this was do[ne] be nigromancy, and be compelling of spirites.'[5]

The Welsh fortune-teller was a partly comic, partly serious literary stereotype, but in sixteenth- and seventeenth-century England there were some larger-than-life Welshman of braggadocio type who could have stepped off the Elizabethan or Jacobean stage. One may instance Evans, the astrologer, and Arise Evans, 'the Welsh prophet'. John Evans was an 'excellent wise man' who had 'study'd the Black Art' and subsisted chiefly from the sale of antimony cups supposed to counteract poisons. He instructed William Lilly in astrology, and according to his distinguished pupil was the most saturnine person he had ever beheld, as well as a quarrelsome debauchee who usually sported some injury. In Wales the quaintly-named Arise (=Rhys) Evans, a prognosticator and sometime critic of Lilly, was shut up in a chamber by family and neighbours in Wrexham in 1634 because of his dangerous discourses about the monarchy, but in England during the Civil War and Commonwealth his prognostications and visions found a ready audience. He rebuked Lilly and other astrologers for their erroneous predictions and reliance on a false Merlin. 'The true British Merlin', he maintained, 'cannot be translated into English or any speech verbatim, nor cannot be understood but by some few Welsh-men which had the traditional rule to understand it from hand to hand ever since Merlin's time.' Evans reported a claim that the 'Book of Merlin' would be 'out of date and no use' by the end of 1657 (if interpreted using a 'golden number' of twenty-eight years). Nevertheless, in 1659 he called upon Englishmen to stop despising the Welsh and to heed their prophesies, 'that ye may as Britons be made partakers of the blessing with us'. Evans lived long enough to rub his scrofulous nose in the hand of Charles II (whose restoration he had predicted), and Evans's apparent cure was attributed as much to his remarkable personality as to royal thaumaturgic powers.[6]

English men and women of the sixteenth and seventeenth centuries certainly regarded Wales as a place where black and white witchcraft flourished, so much so that English charmers might claim some sort of Welsh influence. As early as 1528, Margaret Hunt confessed before the Commissary of London that she had used various charms to cure lameness, the ague, sores, and harm caused by the envy or malice of enemies. She declared that these charms involved the recitation of prayers learned in Wales from one Mother Emet. Sometimes a Welsh connection was attributed to those accused of witchcraft in England; a popular account of the Lancashire witches suggested that a Welsh witch had corrupted honest English folk. Mother Cuthbert became a witch after accepting an invitation to revel and feast with many other women, who were entertained by the 'antic dances' of familiars cavorting to the homely accompaniment of gridiron and tongs. Taking Mother Cuthbert aside, the host asked 'how she liked their cheer and sport?' 'Very well', she answered, but desired to know more of her new companions. Naming herself Mother Crady, the host revealed she was 'a witch of Penmure [Penmaenmawr], a great Mountain in Wales, and the rest were her country-women of the same faculty.' The Welsh witch 'being desirous to have her of her fraternity' had provided the entertainment to show that she might always live 'jocund and merry' as a witch. Mother Crady gave Mother Cuthbert some magic ointment and an imp, 'a little thing like a mole'. The chapbook recounts the pranks of Mother Cuthbert as she took magical revenge on those who had injured her.[7] The woodcuts illustrating the text are unusually sprightly and informative. They show Mother Crady and her Welsh companions at a 'witch-feast' dressed in gowns and high-crowned hats. This was, it seems, the old-fashioned costume of the Welsh countryside, which had its origin in urban styles of the seventeenth century. The Welsh, or rather stereotypes of the Welsh, may have had an enduring influence on depictions of the witch-figure in popular literature, especially in children's stories: it has been suggested that the traditional costume of the witch favoured by the illustrators of fairy-tales is the cloak and tall, broad-brimmed hat of Welsh peasant costume.[8]

In Wales there were many magical and natural wonders, some the subject of ballad and pamphlet. Sometimes these marvels were brought to England. Human wonders from Wales exhibited in London included a Montgomeryshire woman who sprouted a horn from her forehead, and a Denbighshire super-centenarian, aged 130 and more, who acquired a second set of teeth in her dotage among other strange accomplishments, and was regarded as the 'wonder of her age'.[9] On other (mainly literary) occasions Englishmen sought out Welsh marvels. A chapbook account of Jack the Giant-killer published in Shrewsbury has Jack seeking out conjurers as well as giants in Wales, and breaking the enchantment of a beautiful woman possessed by devils whose familiar regularly transported her to Lucifer. Jack travels over hill and dale and through primeval woods to outwit a two-headed giant who was dissembling rather than fiery: 'for he was a Welsh giant, and what he did was by private and secret Malice, under the false Shew of Friendship'. A fierier giant named Thunderdel travelled down from north Wales to kill Jack, uttering the immortal words, 'Fee, fau, fum, / I smell the blood of an English man ...' After killing Thunderdel, Jack successfully challenges 'Galigantus' who, helped by a conjurer, had enticed many knights and ladies into his enchanted, mountain-top castle, where by magic art they were transformed into sundry shapes and forms.[10]

In real life, as opposed to fantasy, English men and women sometimes travelled into Wales seeking consultations with Welsh enchanters and soothsayers. Richard Gough, the historian of the Shropshire parish of Myddle *c.* 1700, preserved an entertaining story about a parishioner, Rees Wenlock, who rather sceptically consulted a Welsh wise-woman about a lost cow only to be thoroughly disconcerted when she revealed her knowledge of his own nefarious activities. English men and women continued to consult Welsh conjurers throughout the eighteenth century, and in the nineteenth century they were frequent visitors to a notorious cursing well in north Wales presided over by an infamous conjurer, Jac Ffynnon Elian.[11]

It must be emphasised that literary accounts of magic in Wales were an expression of English attitudes towards the Welsh rather than a record of actual practices in Wales. It is of course an anthropological commonplace that neighbouring peoples may attribute to each other all sorts of horrible propensities. But the general associations that upland areas have with remoteness and backwardness are an enduring trope. It has been claimed that the witch-craze was associated particularly with the highlands. It is impossible to resist citing Hugh Trevor-Roper on the highland origin of witch-hunts where the 'thin mountain air of the mountains breeds hallucinations, and the exaggerated phenomena of nature ... easily lead men to believe in demonic activity.'[12] Admittedly Trevor-Roper was referring to mountainous areas in continental Europe, but there is a lingering metropolitan perception – a residue of the religious debates of the sixteenth and seventeenth centuries – that the upland areas of Britain were not only remote but also backward and superstitious. These dark corners of the land preserved traces of an 'old religion' in curious customs like the sin-eater, famously one of the remains of gentilism ('gentiles' = heathen or pagan) recorded by John Aubrey and kindred intellectuals, the forerunners of folklorists. As Aubrey put it,

'The Britans imbibed their Gentilisme from the Romans; and as the British language
is crept into corners: sc. Wales, and Cornwalle: so the Remaines of Gentilisme are still
kept there, which customes (no doubt) were anciently all over Britain and Gaul: but
the Inundation of the Goths, drove it out together with the Language.'[13]

Some Welsh intellectuals conceded that for historical reasons their less well-edu-
cated countrymen were prone to superstition and credulity. David Williams, the
radical educationalist and founder of the Literary Fund, considered that the ancient
Cambrians had been so enervated by magic and superstition that they had allowed
the war-loving Saxons to overwhelm them. 'Irritability, indecision, and credulity'
remained peculiarities of national character. This credulity had its origin in the historic intermixture of Druidism and Christianity in Wales, and was still expressed in
'traditional apprehensions of invisible spirits' which gave rise to that 'extravagant
sensibility' for which the Welsh had long been remarkable.[14]

The idea that customs and superstitions were relics of ancient, pre-Christian
beliefs has been influential, and informed Margaret Murray's discredited thesis about
witchcraft as an old religion. Nevertheless, the curious continue to look for pre-
Gothic mystery and magic in Wales. Indeed, the intoxicating associations between
'magic' and 'druids' and 'Celt' are so contemporarily resonant that it may seem surprising to discover that Wales did not suffer greatly from witch-trials.[15]

Prosecutions

There was not a witch-hunt in early-modern Wales. The evidence from surviving criminal records is quite unambiguous on this crucial point. L'Estrange
Ewen, the pioneer in these studies, concluded after studying a small selection of
the relevant records that 'sorcery either was not a prevalent practice or that it did
not greatly perturb the Welshmen'. More recently, a review of the range of seventeenth-century evidence for a single Welsh county (Flintshire) lends support
to Ewen's view.[16] My own exhaustive examination of the Welsh assize records,
while adding more than twenty cases to those found by Ewen, confirms that there
were relatively few prosecutions for witchcraft in Wales. The thirty-four surviving cases for which details have survived involved the prosecution for witchcraft
of forty-one suspects between 1568 and 1699. Acquittals were high; indeed, many
cases were thrown out by grand juries and never reached trial. Only eight ver-
dicts of guilty are recorded, and these resulted in judgments of death on five
convicted witches in three cases in 1594 (Denbighshire), 1623 (Caernarfonshire),
and lastly in 1655 (Anglesey).

Trials began relatively late in Wales and were essentially a seventeenth-century
phenomenon (Fig. 3). There was a scattering of indictments towards the end of
Elizabeth's reign, and formal accusations continued at a slow rate until the mid-seventeenth century when ten persons were indicted during the Commonwealth

between 1655–8. Only ten further cases are recorded between the Restoration and the end of the century, and these prosecutions all ended in acquittals. Half of these cases were concentrated in a final flourish in the 1690s. The last trial for witchcraft occurred in 1694 (Cardiganshire) and the last bill of indictment was rejected by a Pembrokeshire grand jury in 1699. The dates of the last execution (1655) and the last trial (1694) for witchcraft in Wales are part of a broader European pattern of decline in the second half of the seventeenth century, although trials and executions continued well into the eighteenth century, especially in parts of northern and central continental Europe.[17]

The low rates of witchcraft prosecutions in Wales are not attributable to the defective survival of criminal records. The records of indictments for three of the four circuits of the Welsh Courts of Great Sessions are more complete than their English assize counterparts; only north-west Wales has substantially lost its criminal records.[18] Quarter-sessions records have survived less well, but it is unlikely that cases of witchcraft were tried before these courts because justices of the peace referred indictments for serious felonies to the Great Sessions for trial. Were prosecutions a sensitive index of popular anxieties about witchcraft? This has been held doubtful. It is more probable that the level of prosecutions reflected the concerns of those in charge of the legal process rather than the intensity of accusations at the local level, indictments 'forming the tip of an iceberg of unascertainable dimensions.'[19]

However, in Wales an excellent check on these otherwise concealed accusations is provided by the extensive survival of the civil records of the Great Sessions which include actions for slander brought by those accused of witchcraft.[20] Slander actions were brought for damages and related to seriously-intended accusations of witchcraft rather than 'mere vulgar abuse'. The words complained of were certainly spoken openly and publicly (as the common form expressed it), and these verbal confrontations could be the first step in the process leading to formal prosecution.[21] As it happens, the number and chronology of slander cases very closely matches the pattern of formal prosecutions (Fig. 4). The thirty-nine actions for slander show that there were not vast numbers of serious accusations that were never translated into prosecutions. Moreover, the distribution of these slander cases tends to reinforce the chronological pattern of indictments. There were few sixteenth-century actions for slander, and most cases were brought in the seventeenth century. When slander cases are added to prosecutions a pattern of accusations is revealed which begins towards the end of the sixteenth century, builds to a mid-seventeenth-century peak, but declines thereafter until a second but smaller peak occurs in the 1690s. In the early eighteenth century there are several slander cases but no indictments for witchcraft.

Even when witchcraft prosecutions and cases of slander are combined, the relatively low level of accusations and the lateness of prosecutions make the contrast between England and Wales quite striking. The greater number of Welsh prosecutions actually occurred after the Elizabethan period when the majority of prosecutions in England on the Home Assize circuit had already taken place, with over seventy executions in Essex alone. The intensity of prosecutions in Essex was exceptional, for reasons which are not fully understood, but the comparison is still revealing between the combined Welsh counties and the small area covered by the Palatinate of Chester (whose justices also served north-east Wales) where some fifty persons were accused of witchcraft or related offences between 1560–1711, eight of whom were executed.[22] The contrast is all the more striking since, after the Acts of Union (1536 & 1543), Wales and England shared the same legal and administrative machinery. Wales had a national system of assize circuits in the Courts of Great Session with centrally-appointed judges who administered the common law in each of the Welsh counties (except Monmouthshire) twice a year. When we compare the English and Welsh situations the differences in the pattern of prosecutions are not readily explicable in terms of different judicial systems. There were however obvious differences between Wales and the regions of England in language and culture. Before we can begin to analyse the pattern of Welsh witchcraft accusations and prosecutions, it is first necessary to know how witchcraft was conceptualised in Wales.

A Welsh Anti-Witchcraft Tract

Fortunately, ideas about witchcraft in Wales at the time of the first prosecutions are colourfully presented in a late Elizabethan anti-witchcraft tract, generally known from its running-title as *Dau Gymro yn Taring*, or 'Two Tarrying Welshmen'. The author, Robert Holland, a Welshman from Conwy, was a Cambridge graduate who had spent a decade as a schoolmaster and curate in rural Cambridgeshire following his ordination in 1580.[23] Holland returned permanently to Wales as a beneficed clergyman, appointed rector of Prendergast, Pembrokeshire, in 1591. Pembrokeshire was a strikingly divided county linguistically, but Holland moved easily between the two cultures, writing (and presumably preaching) with equal facility in English and Welsh. His first literary production as minister of Prendergast was an English metrical Life of Our Lord, published in 1594 to benefit 'such as have delight to be reading and singing of Ballades and other English meters, by giving them better matter to read and sing'.[24] A little later, about 1595, Holland published an anti-witchcraft tract specifically to warn his Welsh-speaking countrymen about the dangers of witchcraft and magic. Like other entertaining but didactic tracts designed for popular consumption, Holland's text takes the form of a dialogue, and it was probably intended to be read aloud much as his metrical history was composed to be sung.[25]

The tract begins with two Welshmen, Tudur and Gronw, meeting on a mountain 'far from their homeland'. At first Gronw is afraid that Tudur is a charmer who will bewitch him. Tudur assures him that he does not know that skill or 'art' (*celfyddyd*), and they fall into a discussion about witchcraft. Gronw (presumably Holland) is described as a knowledgeable man who has travelled, read books, seen and heard many things which Tudur (representing Holland's countrymen) is anxious to learn, he says, for the sake of his country. The dialogue is partly structured by the citation of numerous proverbs. As Gronw puts it, it is said that every proverb is true: *a gwir meddant hwy yw pob dihareb.*

The two Welshmen discuss the meaning of the proverb, *bwrw cath i'r cythraul*, that is 'to throw a cat to the devil', which Tudur had read in a book of proverbs.[26] He wonders what was in the mind of the person who first thought of the saying. This proverb, Gronw maintains, refers to offerings made to the devil by ungodly people, and he explains it by relating some sensational tales of diabolic sacrifice and witches' familiars which, he says, he had heard last winter in 'Albania', that is (ostensibly) Scotland.[27] Gronw had stayed in the house of a respectable old gentleman who often had a houseful of neighbours (husbands, wives, and young people) and their custom on long winter nights after supper was to sit by the fireside relating tales to pass the time agreeably – a situation familiar to all Welsh people, of course. When their conversation turned to sacrificing to the devil, Gronw was alert to listen to everyone's story. Many of the storytellers knew of people who had grown rich through sacrificing to the devil. One had heard of a rich man from 'our country' who sacrificed a wether sheep and a fattened bullock every May-day Eve. He explained (responding to Gronw's questions) that the man would take the animals to a secret place, and the devil ('or something of that kind') would seize them and they would never be seen again grazing on the mountain. Sometimes he sacrificed a beast by throwing it over a crag to break its neck. It would be difficult, the storyteller concluded, to share between the poor in ten years the sacrifice that was made to the devil on one occasion.

The conversation moved closer to home. 'Good God', exclaimed a young girl sitting in the corner by the chimney, 'is it perhaps by worshipping the devil and offering him sacrifices that one of our neighbours became so rich?' His beginnings were as 'weak' as his ancestry (so her mother said) but within a short time he amassed 'an empire of wealth'. Now, she asked, 'Who in the country is as wealthy as he?' Gronw pointedly asked if their neighbour would be 'throwing a cat to the devil' on May-day Eve? The girl's mother then had her say. The gentleman in question had indeed had a bad name for associating with the devil 'and giving him many a fine bullock'. Moreover, she had often heard from her father (when she was 'the age of that chatty one over there') also a great traveller, of another wealthy man who lived overseas, somewhere between Brittany and Scandinavia, who offered sacrifices to the devil in the same way as their neighbour. The fireside companions produced more tales about 'throwing the cat to the devil'. A young man living near another storyteller had married a rich old widow but he began to lose cattle from a disease. To avert disaster he tied a live horse to a post and burnt it to cinders as a sacrifice. However, no lasting good came from it because before he died he was barely worth the value of the sacrifice. See, said everyone, how true the proverb is, 'The devil is wicked even to his servants': *drwg y ceidw diafol i was.*

Then another woman rose to tell her tale (it is interesting that the storytellers stood to tell their tales, demanding the attention of the fireside group) and introduced the subject of witches' familiars. She remembered an old neighbour who would always have a rat feeding in her lap; many wondered that the rat was so docile. A servant once watched her through a spyhole feeding the rat, and to his amazement saw the rat had changed into a huge form or 'image', and that his mistress was feeding the devil. The company then turned to Gronw – as a learned man – asking if it was true that the devils go to men and women who call themselves charmers, wizards, soothsayers and the like (*swynwyr, rheibwyr, daroganwyr*), and appeared to them in a guise easiest for them to keep, e.g. cats, mice, or frogs, and were used by them to avenge themselves on others and to steal what they fancied. 'Too true', replied Gronw, who 'without mentioning what he had read' described how he himself had heard an old witch (*hen reibies*) and her daughter confess in the hearing of many good men that they had kept the devil for a long time in the various guises of a cat, mouse, or flea, and sometimes a badger, whatever form was convenient. They gave the devil drops of their blood at different times, and the old woman had dramatically shown some spots on the floor made by blood dropping from her breast. 'She should be burnt!' exclaimed one of the company. Too true, agreed Gronw, but explained that the witch was allowed to live in the hope that she would change into a good woman.

It is obvious from that, agreed the fireside companions, that there is some relationship between the devil and some of the old women who are reputed to charm and bewitch. And yet, added one, it is said that some astrologers, conjurers, and enchanters perform their crafts through knowledge and reading books. The charmers are simple (illiterate) old fools who know about herbs and have learnt a good lesson in charming people and helping man and beast. By now it was getting late, and some of the company were beginning to doze. Gronw had the last word before they all retired, maintaining that although charmers and diviners might appear helpful they were really ungodly people who obtained all their information and knowledge with the devil's help. The following day Gronw bade farewell to his host and set off for home where he longed to be.

At this point the dialogue becomes more earnest and didactic. Tudur implores Gronw to tell him everything left unsaid about these godless people. Tudur knows of a person to whom many people come from far away to get charms for man and beast. He has known the sick healed after being charmed, and others visit charmers for information. Gronw emphasizes that it is just as well to go to the devil himself as to consult the people who gain their knowledge from him, and quotes Scripture to show that God's word not only condemns charmers and diviners but those who consult them.

Tudur exclaims that he never thought that the devil had so many crafts. In a fascinating but rather opaque passage, Tudur says that he and his countrymen are already opposed to certain customs. We are against, he says, pulling or dragging children between double fires, or through an arch, or turning them on the blacksmith's anvil, or laying them at the edge or hopper of a mill, and many other like 'tricks' or customs. These rituals must have been rites of passage performed to protect children from the devil and other spirits, but their significance is obscure and it is interesting that there are few other references to these customs.[28] Holland's attack on magical specialists may have followed an earlier, undocumented Elizabethan reform of popular custom in Wales.

Tudur has a last attempt to justify the respect that many of his countrymen have for magical specialists. Soothsayers, astrologers, and prophets were highly respected by the best gentlemen and freeholders throughout the country, he says. Most charmers, both men and women, do a lot of good for man and beast, and Gronw claims that his countrymen could not be without them. Tudur is unimpressed and responds censoriously: 'Well, that's the way to cast the cat to the devil', he tells Gronw. Many people are praising those whom God commands us to shun, he continues, but concedes that there are differences between magical specialists and their techniques: 'wizards (*rheibwyr*) and the like have taught some how to sacrifice, as the charmers (*swynwyr*) have taught others to pray.' Nevertheless, those who associate with them are lost, and will have the same end as Saul, unless they can find the grace to shake off the devil and repent.

Gronw having had his say proposes to leave, but Tudur pleads with him to stay a little longer 'for the sake of the country I come from and the country I live in'. If Gronw can demonstrate that God commands the complete destruction of wizards, charmers and the like from the midst of his people, then Tudur will accept that they should no longer welcome them. Gronw, citing scriptural authority, convinces Tudur of their evil nature, and is gratified to see Tudur shaking with fright after hearing about God's judgements on these ungodly people. Tudur asks if such things have continued from generation to generation, and Gronw cites the Biblical examples of Pharoah's soothsayers, the witch of Endor, Simon Magus ('a great charmer') Theudas, Elymas, and others who had come to a bitter end. Finally, Tudur asks the 'burning question', what should the common people do when there are witches and wizards in their community? He has heard that drawing blood from a witch or wizard gives protection provided neither man nor beast has been bewitched. Gronw condemns this as a base remedy: the devil has taught people to do wrong for wrong. Gronw emphasizes that no-one should attempt to destroy witches and wizards unless they have the authority to punish them and other evil people. He assures Tudur that those who oppose the devil through their faith shall be rid of him and that no wizard will harm them.

Gronw concludes by emphasising that the common people must listen to God's word, read the Scriptures, and pray often and faithfully. In a final passage, Tudur complains that this is easier said than done, explaining that the clergy do not take pains to read and show God's word to their people, presumably through catechisms and other manuals. As for preaching, Tudur has never heard one sermon in

his parish church and, moreover, the Bible is too expensive for a poor man to buy
and keep at home. God only knows, he concludes, the condition of the common
man is perilous. Gronw responds by urging Tudur to buy 'this little book' – presumably *Dau Gymro yn Taring* itself.[29] The price is small enough for the benefit to
be gained from its frequent reading as well as from prayer. It will bring delight to
the soul but will also shield the body from 'the devilish darts of wizards, charmers, and enchanters, and the like evil men'. Indeed, copies of Robert Holland's
little book must have been read and re-read until they were in tatters. At least,
no printed copy of the first edition has survived, but it was reprinted after the
Restoration in the 1681 edition of *Canwyll y Cymru* ('The Candle of the Welsh'), a
very popular collection of hymns by an Anglican divine, and widely circulated in
the eighteenth century in some seven subsequent editions published between 1725
and 1766.[30]

Robert Holland's tract was a Welsh recension of the Protestant genre of
anti-witchcraft writing in English, which emphasised the diabolical nature of
both witches and charmers and the spiritual dangers of consulting apparently
'helpful' cunning-folk. There were many points of contact with the tracts of
the Cambridge demonologists, including the presentation of the differences
between clerical and popular views on witchcraft in the form of a dialogue. 'Two
Tarrying Welshmen' is closest to George Gifford's *Dialogue concerning Witches*
(1593) in terms of its accessibility. By contrast, Henry Holland's *Treatise against
Witchcraft* (1590) although cast in the form of a dialogue was rather academic and
his worthy interlocutors, Theophilus and Mysodaemon, do not have the same
appeal as Robert Holland's tarrying Welshmen or George Gifford's villagers,
Samuel and Daniel. Robert Holland's tract was written entirely in the vernacular, and he refers only to the Scriptures which were available to all (apart from
a single citation from Eusebius). In places Holland like Gifford reports contemporary magical practices in an almost ethnographic way, but Holland was also
something of a cultural broker. It is clear that Holland intended to introduce
a Welsh audience to anxieties about witchcraft current outside Wales. This is
broadly suggested by the deliberate setting of his dialogue outside Wales and specifically by the Scottish context of Gronw's tales. It is possible that Holland's
anti-witchcraft tract had been prompted by the trials of the North Berwick
witches (1590–2). In a celebrated incident in the published account of the trial,
Agnes Tompson confessed to raising a storm by casting a christened cat into the
sea. However, little if any of the specific detail in *Newes from Scotland* (1591) finds
its way into Holland's dialogue between the tarrying Welshmen.[31]

Holland's tract was not really concerned with repeating sensational details
of cases of witchcraft and maleficium found in the pamphlets of the day. It is
possible that Holland's intended audience preferred to hear first-hand experiences. At one point Holland's mouthpiece, Gronw, although a learned man,
carefully says that he refrained from telling the company in Scotland what he
had read about familiars, but describes what he himself had heard 'with his own

ears' from an old witch and her daughter. One wonders, of course, if there is an autobiographical reference here to Holland's Cambridge years. Holland is primarily concerned with emphasising the notion of the pact with devil, an idea popularized by the Protestant demonologists, by discussing the act of sacrifice – of throwing the cat to the devil. The consequence of the pact was not only the acquisition of malefic power, the ability to harm through diabolic means; another dramatic consequence was sometimes the sudden acquisition of wealth or power. Holland's storytellers knew of neighbours and others who had mysteriously grown rich. They also knew of neighbours who had sacrificed animals for the sake of their other stock. The Faustian theme was widespread, but the immediacy of the accounts of animal sacrifice suggests that Holland was describing a customary propitiatory practice, although there are few other references to this type of appeasing ritual in Wales.[33] These pacts involved men, but Holland is also anxious to introduce the idea of the pact in the form of familiar spirits who feed from blood sacrificed by (female) witches. These witches did not get rich through sacrifice but used their familiars to revenge themselves upon those who had offended them, and make depredations upon their neighbours.

The Vocabulary of Witchcraft[34]

Holland, like the other Cambridge demonologists, was concerned to emphasize the everyday dangers of consulting cunning-folk, who might be popularly regarded as 'helpful' but were really as wicked as witches because they acquired their knowledge from the devil. Holland is introducing novel material to a Welsh audience, and the vocabulary he uses is of very great interest because it permits some understanding of Welsh occult categories at about the time of the first prosecutions for witchcraft in Wales. It is helpful to summarize this information in a table (fig. 5) but it is difficult to convey the overlapping nature of the semantic fields of the various categories. The term *dewin*, for example, was an inclusive category which might refer in different contexts to God, prophets, diviners, the magi, and perhaps any persons associated with more than ordinary human powers, including wizards.[35] However, the various terms tended to fall into one or other of two groups distinguished by the presence or absence of divine inspiration. Specialists in the first group were generally male and ranged from prophets and interpreters of prophecy of high status to the slightly prescient who might use external aids for divination. If persons in this group were mainly inspired, those in the next group – charmers and conjurers – lacked divine inspiration and mainly relied on the petitionary technique of prayer. Charmers, both male and female, however, possessed the faculty of soothsaying in addition to their specialist knowledge of salves and the characteristic use of prayer. Charmers were generally beneficial to man and beast but they were also thought capable of inflicting harm.

Figure 5 ranks occult specialists according to their relative status. At its head are the prophets and interpreters of prophecy of high status. They were, according to Tudur, 'highly revered by the best gentlemen and freeholders throughout the whole country'. Gronw has condemned them, citing Scripture, and Tudur concedes that he has been 'blind' to their connection with the crafts of the devil. Tudur had not thought that God's word was against them, thinking they were good men because they magnified His greatness. Who were these prophets? There is plenty of evidence to show that early-modern Wales was awash with prophecy but it is difficult to identify individual prophets apart from those who had careers as prognosticators in England. Numerous prophets were household names, but by the second half of the sixteenth century they were all legendary or historical figures: Myrddin (Merlin), Taliesin, and many others, including several poets. Although prophets were historical figures they were very much alive in the sense that prophecies attributed to them were widely circulated and because there were places and structures associated with them. Taliesin's 'bed' or grave (*Gwely* or, latterly, *Bedd Taliesin*), a chambered tomb, was a well-known feature of the Cardiganshire countryside. In later seventeenth-century Carmarthen a house in Priory Street was solemnly shown as Merlin's birthplace. Elsewhere in the town Merlin's oak was carefully tended because of the prophecy that Carmarthen would stand only as long as the tree.[36]

Prophets may have been regarded as divinely inspired but secular prophecy was dangerous because it was always ambiguous and related to political events. The Tudor dynasty was widely regarded as fulfilling prophecy, the king identified with the *mab darogan* or son of prophecy, but the Tudor administration in Wales looked on prophecy with increasing disfavour. The government's concern about prophecy was understandable because of its association with rebellion, and rebellion, as the state well understood, was worse than the sin of witchcraft. The very serious revolts of 1549 had been buoyant with prophecies. In Wales, less than a generation before, the revolt of Rhys ap Gruffydd, which ended in 1531 with his execution, had been encouraged by a prophecy that played upon the significance of the raven as his family badge. Interest in prophecy was potentially dangerous and seditious and carried harsh penalties. The state's concern about prophecy was reflected in several mid- and late Tudor proclamations, instructions, and statutes. Legislation (1541–2) passed between the first and second Acts of Union made it a felony to make predictions based on the interpretation of names, badges, and coats of arms. Less than ten years later, a new Act (1549–50; renewed 1565) imposed severe penalties on those who circulated 'fond and fantastical prophecies' which stirred up disorder or rebellion. Instructions (1550) from the Council in the Marches gave the new Welsh justices a policing role. They were to make diligent search for 'tellers of newes, berers of tales, secrete whisperers of the kynge or the counsaille' and 'purveyors of blynd and false p[ro]phises'.[37]

The prophecies of Merlin and Taliesin were enduring. At country gatherings in north Wales at the end of the sixteenth century it was alleged that the traditions of these prophets, as well as Welsh saints, were recited. So addicted were the Welsh to the prophecies of Merlin and the 'fond fables' of Taliesin that an aspiring Cardiganshire sheriff promised to bring Sir Robert Cecil 'such volumes of prophecy' as would make a memorable bonfire in London. There can be no doubt that there were numerous volumes of prophecy in circulation, primarily among the gentry, some of whom no doubt had the reputation of being skilled in interpreting prophecy as well as adept at astrology.[38] There was no shortage of predictive rumours. Magistrates were certainly aware of an opaque 'babble of the base sort' which included speculations about the death of the monarch, rumours concerning great figures of the realm, and reports of visions seen in the sky. Some of these rumours were probably spread by vagabonds and low-status minstrels.[39] It is however extraordinarily difficult to identify named prophets or seers of high status in the sixteenth-century historical record. By the time that Holland wrote in late-Elizabethan Wales they belonged to the past, and continuity with the past had been broken by the collapse of the bardic order in Elizabethan Wales.[40]

Interpreters of prophecy may have included conjurers, who, according to Robert Holland, were high-status occult practitioners who performed their crafts through knowledge and reading books. The primary meaning of conjurer was one who could invoke and exorcise spirits.[41] More broadly, the conjurer was a magical specialist who used special formulae (invoking a higher authority) to summon devils, compelling them to say or do what he commanded. There were several key references to invokers of spirits and their books in different vernacular versions of the Bible.[42]

Although there are numerous references to conjurers in sixteenth-century England, and the word was adopted by Protestant radicals as a term of abuse for recusant priests (who might perform exorcisms), it has proved hard to identify any suspected conjurers in the Welsh record.[43] In an important passage, Holland implies that conjurers were of declining importance in Wales, and places them in the past. Tudur specifically says 'we do not hear so much about magicians (*hudolwyr*) and conjurers (*consyrwyr*) these days'. Moreover, 'it is not necessary to go to them for information, the charmers or cunning-men and -women (*swynwyr a swynwragedd*) can do this.' Cunning-folk were growing in importance in post-Reformation Wales (as will be shown in Chapter 4) and they were among Holland's principal targets as being little better than witches, deriving their knowledge from the devil. Conjurers were much talked about in Wales but there may have been few actual practitioners; conjurers like prophets were probably primarily historical or legendary figures. Nevertheless, the idea of the literate conjurer with his powerful books appealed to the popular imagination, but it was only after the repeal of the witchcraft statutes that cunning-men openly cultivated a reputation for being conjurers, able to call and command devils, and possessing secret books of magic (Chapter 5).

There remains the category of the witch. Holland uses the term *rheibiwr* (male) and its female correlative *rheib[i]es* to convey the notion of a maleficent witch. They are not particularly common words at this period and remain somewhat obscure categories, but it is clear that *rheibio*, 'to bewitch', retained the etymological sense of 'to plunder' or 'despoil', from the Latin *rapio*, and had semantic associations with greediness and excess.[44] *Rheibwyr* appear to have been conceptualised as predatory in a quasi-physical sense, consuming and destroying their enemies' substance. The survival of several charms or prayers against witchcraft (*rac raib*) from the end of the fifteenth century establishes some antiquity for the notion as well as an association with the evil power of the eye. One late-fifteenth-century prayer against witchcraft is glossed *sswyn rrac llygadynn*, that is 'a charm against the evil eye'.[45] *Llygad-dynnu*, literally 'to pull with the eye', meant 'to bewitch', but referred specifically to the idea that witchcraft might be exercised through a look as a kind of fascination. The verb appropriately rendered the Vulgate's *fascinare* in the 1567 Welsh New Testament (and subsequent translations) but required *rheibio* as a reinforcing gloss, possibly because *llygad-dynnu* was by then losing its literal meaning: *A Galatieit ynfydion, pwy a'ch llygatdynawdd* [margin: *ribodd*] *chwi*, 'O foolish Galatians, who hath bewitched you?'[46]

Charms against witchcraft followed the same general form as other protective prayers or *loricae*. One charm introduced as a good prayer against sorcery and the hurting of men and cattle invokes the blessing of the Father, Son, and Holy Ghost, all the saints, male and female, of heaven, the heavenly angels and archangels, the Blessed Trinity, the Blessed Lady Mary and her Lord Son born on Christmas Day. The invocator says: 'I bless thee (making the sign of the cross) and your men and your cattle and all that you have'. A similar protective charm, attributed to the end of the fifteenth century, is more specific. After the sign of the cross has been made, Christ's name is invoked to repel 'every sort of fiendish (literally, unspiritual) misfortune, both from above and below the earth, from the devil of an envious and evil-hearted man who has bewitched the cattle and their owner'. There is a final appeal to the Virgin Mary, the male and female saints of heaven, the virtues of their breasts, and the virtues of the five heavenly places. These protective invocations might be recited with other prayers or written down. When used as written preservatives, the charms were placed over a doorway or threshold, the vulnerable entry into a house or cowhouse. A Latin charm dating from the earlier sixteenth century, written on a strip of parchment, is actually endorsed 'supra ostium', and was intended to protect the livestock of David ap Rees ap Jankyn ap Llewelin of the lordship of Denbigh from devilish sickness ('*morbo diabolico*'). Presumably the charm was placed over the beast-house doorway when the cattle were brought in for the winter. It is clear from contemporary documentation that the literate specialists who devised these written charms included priests.[47]

These charms or prayers seem to have been intended for protection against witches or sorcerers who looked on destructively from afar. Late-medieval poets sometime referred to this destructive look from an unknown enemy. Most notably, an elegy by Tudur Aled (fl.1480–1526) described the mysterious death of Tudur Llwyd of Bodidris, near Ruthin, who died after a skirmish from an apparently slight wound to the cheek that resembled a mere needle. According to the poet, Tudur Llwyd was 'the pride (*drych*, literally 'mirror') of the fair, valiant, spirited' but 'an evil eye over there saw him!: *Drygolwg draw a'i gweles*! Central to the notion of the evil look (it is clear from a comparative perspective) was the recognition that the possession of those qualities on which men prided themselves (a good bearing, strength, bravery, and so on), as well as the possession of wealth, might well offend those lacking them. The destructive sentiments of envy and anger were characteristically expressed through the eyes of the aggrieved and might (with the devil's assistance) destroy what gave offence.[48] A satire by Gruffudd Hiraethog (d. 1564) likened the action of a cat stalking a cock-thrush, which it killed, to the operation of the evil eye. The sharpness of the image derived from its accuracy. Like the innocently provocative bird unwittingly caught in the unblinking and deadly stare of the cat, it was difficult in a status-conscious society for the well favoured to avoid attracting the malign attention of the evil eye. As the poet said of the thrush, 'It will not turn out well but badly, [for] he whom the evil eye may see'. Sometimes, when praising a patron, a poet would express the wish that no eye (or heart) that does evil should see his patron, as when Tudur Aled sang to Robert ap Rhys, a chaplain at the Tudor Court and beneficiary of the sale of monastic lands, whose worldly success may well have prompted envious looks.[49]

Tudur Aled initially attributed the unexpected death of his patron to the evil eye but acknowledged that there were other possible explanations for the misfortune. Tudur Llwyd may have died because of mischance (an accident), or from poison, or because God wanted to take him (because He loved him). However, as Tudur Aled's poem shows, sorcery could explain misfortune when death was strange and unexpected. In an elegy to Siôn Gruffudd the elder of Chwaen, Lewys Môn (d. 1527) similarly describes how Anglesey was shrouded in coldness like the Alps after the double death of father and son from the same (unspecified) mischief, which the poet attributed to the evil eye. 'All evil eyes were to be had yonder', says the poet, 'a place [from where] to bewitch us greatly': *Llygaid drwg oll a gaid draw / a lle'n rhybell i'n rheibiaw*. More broadly, the surprise and unfairness of the death of the virtuous and generous could be likened to an act of sorcery or plunder (both meanings are present and interlinked in the poetry), although it was the living suffering the loss who were pillaged or (metaphorically) bewitched. 'Alas Rhiwabon, you have been bewitched!': *och Riwabon, fo'ch rheibiwyd*, exclaimed Lewys Môn after the death of Siôn ab Elis Eutun. 'Haven't we been utterly bewitched?': *Oni'n rheibwyd ni'n rhybell?* Tudur Aled bitterly asked after Tudur Llwyd's sudden death.[50]

Sorcery in late-medieval Wales, as in many other cultures, was conceptualised as akin to an act of consumption which plundered and destroyed the victims' substance, rather like the ravening of wolves with which *rhaib* was sometimes associated. Sorcerers like wolves lived beyond the bounds of the society they ravaged, and were placed outside all community, including Christian society as a whole. According to one prayer against *rhaib*, the envious man who practised sorcery had an evil and excommunicate heart and had rejected the Catholic faith. 'May the cross of Christ be to the benefit of a Christian ... against bewitchment', hoped Gruffudd Hiraethog.[51]

The sorcerer was essentially a faceless outsider, but we must note a few hints in the early-sixteenth-century legal record that suggest that some tried to hire the destructive services of sorcerers. A remarkable complaint made by the bishop of St Davids about 1500 alleged that his enemies, Thomas Wyrriot, a Pembrokeshire gentleman, and his concubine, whom the bishop had excommunicated, had hired a sorceress to kill him. The bishop imprisoned Tanglwst ferch William but she escaped to Bristol where she 'hyred a woman called Margarett Hackett, which was practized in wychecraft'. She returned to Pembrokeshire with the hired witch where they made 'ij ymages of wax' intending to destroy the bishop. Not satisfied with this, they sent for another unnamed sorceress who 'hadd more connyng and experiens' and made a third wax image. The bishop survived to make his complaint against them in the Court of Chancery.[52] The idea that sorcerers were available for hire was present in the earliest surviving slander case relating to witchcraft, also from Pembrokeshire. In 1551 William Johnes of Haverfordwest accused Maud Steven, 'housewife' (a respectable householder), of giving a third party, Margaret Baldwyn, witch-money ('the wyche money') as payment 'to be wyche my kyne so that my sarvant can make noe butter nor chese this twenty dayes.'[53] It is chronologically revealing that this mid-Tudor action, with its special accusation of payment for sorcery to a third party, predates by a generation subsequent slander cases which concerned direct rather than indirect accusations of witchcraft.

The system of occult classification in Wales was evidently not static. Holland himself draws attention to the declining importance of some specialists, the conjurers (*consurwyr*) and magicians (*hudolwyr*). The term *hud*, the magic of the Mabinogion, was certainly weakening having acquired pejorative connotations of juggling and deceit; persons termed *hudol* in the mid- and late-Tudor legal record were invariably entertainers rather than occult specialists.[54] Clearly the presence of loan-words from the Latin (*dewin, rheibiwr*) and newer borrowings from the French or English (*consuriwr*) reflected historic shifts of meaning. The introduction of a new loan-word – *wits* or *witsh* – directly borrowed from the English 'witch', appears to have had a considerable semantic impact, and the conceptual difficulties connected with the borrowing are apparent in the early usages of the term.

The first example of the noun 'wits', with other grammatical forms, occurs in William Salesbury's 1547 black-letter Welsh–English dictionary: '*wits dewim=wraic a Wytche*'. The apparent oddity of this entry (which includes the misprint 'dewim' for '*dewin*') is explained by Salesbury's intention to provide the Welsh interpretation of English words. The Welsh head-word *wits* is followed by an explanatory expansion (*dewin-wraig*), which corresponds, to the English lemma 'witch'. Salesbury defines *dewin* as 'a soothe sayer' and has added the qualifying *gwraig* or woman. Salesbury was a cultural broker who was not without a sly misogyny, and it is revealing that in this early usage he has clearly identified witches with women.[55]

The semantic difficulties surrounding the notion of witchcraft are clearly seen in the problems encountered by the Welsh translators of the Bible and their revisors who attempted to provide an accurate but idiomatic version in the vernacular. The translators generally avoided words (*gwiddon, gwrach, hudoles*) associated with mythology and the magic of *hen chwedlau* or old wives' tales.[56] However, they frequently employed terms associated with charming where the English translators had used 'witchcraft' or 'sorcery'. A revealing instance occurs in Salesbury's 1567 *Testament Newydd* where the word *cyvaredd* 'charm' is used to render the verse 'for by the sorceries were all nations deceived' (Rev.xviii.23), but is marginally glossed with the explanatory *wiscreft* or witchcraft. Significantly, the crucial imperative 'thou shalt not suffer a witch to live' (Exod.xxii.18) did not receive a consistent translation. The term *rheibes*, used in the translation of 1588, was discarded in 1620 in favour of the imprecise *hudoles*, although both terms, it may be noted, were female.[57] The 1620 Welsh translation of the Bible tended to follow the English Authorized Version, but the choice of Welsh words in contexts where the English '(be)witch' or 'witchcraft(s)' occurs was essentially inconsistent, and clearly illustrated the difficulties of conveying the notion of witchcraft in Welsh beyond terms connected with charming and soothsaying.[58] The influence of the Bible is apparent in the Welsh language terms for witchcraft favoured by the prose-writers, translators, and lexicographers of the period who tended to exclude recognizable English loan-words from their texts. But it is revealing that these literary forms were not used in the spoken language. Actions for slander clearly show that the loan-forms '*wits*' or '*witsh*' were almost invariably used in colloquial speech in the seventeenth century when making accusations of witchcraft.[59]

The linguistic evidence suggests that the structure of popular occult categories was changing in sixteenth-century Wales. In particular, the loan-word wits had a range of associations not formerly conveyed by the Welsh terms connected with charming, soothsaying, and sorcery. *Rhaib* (sorcery) seems to have conveyed the notion of faceless and faithless enemies associated with the evil look from afar, or amoral sorcerers who could be hired to inflict injury, but it remains a somewhat mysterious category. The borrowing of the English word 'witch' and its related forms suggests concern and interest in a new form of witchcraft. There were indeed cultural brokers who were prepared to tell the Welsh people about this new type of witchcraft which lay within rather than outside the community. Holland's tract was a discussion of witchcraft beliefs by an intellectual, essentially a dialogue between a Protestant cleric and his people, concerned to deploy an authoritative interpretation of the nature of witches and the dangers of apparently helpful magic.

There was certainly a new, popular concern about witchcraft in later sixteenth-century Wales. A Welsh *cursor mundi* poem of *c.* 1600 included witches among many contemporary ills seen by the poet in a revelatory dream on St Lucy's Eve. Witches populated the dream alongside many other sinful oppressors, finding poetic description alongside cheating tradesmen, despicable usurers and contemptible entertainers:

> *Yr oedd yno lawer o witsys*
> *wedi darfod vddyn ddewis*
> *diawl yn feistyr vddyn*
> *er cael drygv da a dŷn*
> *yr oedd rhai kynn gyfrwydded*
> *ag i medren godi kythrelied*
> *a chymysgv yr awyr*
> *a gwnevthvr drwg heb fessvr.*[60]

(There were many witches there, having chosen the devil as their master, so as to harm man and beast. There were some so expert that they could raise devils, and create storms [literally, mix together the air], and do evil without limit.)

The poet has included witches among all those deceivers who were 'wolves in sheepskins'. Witches were now neighbours rather than unknown enemies outside the community. It is fortunate that documentation relating to the earliest witchcraft accusations has survived, and that these new beliefs and the circumstances of prosecution can be contextualised very fully, sometimes with surprising results.

The First Execution: The Case of Gwen the Daughter of Ellis (1594)

Documentary sources of the sixteenth century tend to flatter the importance of the wealthy and literate who by and large produced them. But occasionally the voluminous Tudor legal record can brilliantly illuminate the lives of the poor and obscure, giving them a retrospective significance because of their involvement in events that sharply reveal the conflicts and 'mentalities' of the period. This chapter reconstructs from legal documents the life story of Gwen ferch Ellis (i.e., Gwen, daughter of Ellis), which in other circumstances would have remained hidden from history. Gwen struggled with the vicissitudes of life, acquired a reputation for healing and charming and with it a little prosperity, but came into conflict with those more powerful than she was. Gwen's life tragically ended on the gallows. She was prosecuted for witchcraft at a time when there were numerous trials of suspected witches in parts of England and Scotland, and when Protestant demonologists were calling in sermons and in print for the punishment of witches. Gwen's case reveals the nature of popular magic in late-sixteenth-century Wales, and shows how a charmer and soothsayer could become redefined as a witch. Gwen ferch Ellis was in fact the first person executed for witchcraft in Wales, and her case has some unexpected connections with Elizabethan writers on demonology.

Gwen and Her Accusers

Who was Gwen ferch Ellis? Gwen first emerges from the historical record in June 1594 when the bishop of St Asaph committed her to Flint gaol on suspicion of using witchcraft.[1] The assize judges subsequently sent Gwen to Denbighshire in the expectation that witnesses would offer evidence against her at the next sessions. As in many cases of witchcraft, there seems to have been no question of bail and Gwen languished in gaol until her trial in October 1594. In other circumstances Gwen ferch Ellis would have lived a life of utter historical obscurity, and there are no documentary references to her beyond the legal record. However we know a surprising amount about Gwen from the record of her examination on 12 June 1594 before William Hughes, bishop of St Asaph and a staunch upholder of the Elizabethan religious settlement. The bishop questioned Gwen about her early life, asking how she earned her living and why she was suspected of charming. Gwen's clear and unambiguous responses suggest she was not over-awed by the encounter. She was stoical about the family tragedies in her life, proud of her expertise as a healer, and confident that her skills benefited her neighbours.

Gwen was about forty-two years old, perhaps a little older, when she was arrested in 1594. Her life had spanned Elizabeth I's reign, but she was born about 1552 and would have had memories of the Catholic Wales of Mary Tudor and experienced the subsequent religious conflicts of the Elizabethan reformation. Gwen's exam-ination revealed a dislocated childhood, geographical mobility, and successive marriages. By her own account, she was born in the parish of Llandyrnog, within the prosperous Vale of Clwyd, Denbighshire. Her father's full name is not recorded, and he may well have died when Gwen was a child because, aged five or six, she was sent to Yale to live with an uncle, Harry ap Roger. Gwen remained there for the next fifteen years until she married one Lewis ap David ap Gwyn. Their life together was brief. Gwen's husband died after only two years of marriage. Gwen, a young widow, subsequently married Lewis ap David ap Gruffith Gethin, otherwise Lewis Gethin. Her second husband was a miller, and in 1588 Lewis and Gwen lived at a mill near Llaneilian-yn-Rhos. After eighteen years of marriage Gwen was wid-owed for a second time. In midsummer 1592 Gwen married a third husband, John ap Morrice of Betws-yn-Rhos, near Abergele, and settled in her husband's parish. Nothing more is heard of Gwen's husband during her examination, imprisonment and trial.

Gwen explained to the bishop that she made a living by spinning and making linen cloth for sale in the markets, as many other women did. Gwen also had a special skill – she made medicines ('plasters and salves') for sick beasts. She charged nothing for these remedies, but they became her chief source of maintenance. Those who used Gwen's medicines usually paid her in kind, giving her wool, corn, cheese, or butter for her trouble. It was at this point that the bishop asked Gwen if she had ever used witchcraft or charming to help or hurt man or beast? Much would depend on her answer.

Gwen replied without evasion that in addition to salves, drenches, and plasters, she had used charms for the past ten years. Many came to her for assis-tance, and she had helped sick men, women, and children, as well as sick beasts. Last Whitsuntide she had used charms to help a sick child (whose name she did not know) from Llechwedd-isa in Caerhun, Caernarfonshire. Gwen's reputation evidently extended well beyond her immediate locality as Caerhun is some fifteen miles from Betws. Gwen was asked what words she used when charming, and how she had learnt them. Gwen replied that her sister, Elizabeth ferch Ellis, who had died sixteen years ago, had taught her how to charm. The bishop insisted on hearing the actual words Gwen used when charming. Gwen responded by reciting in Welsh the following charm, which translates as:

> In the name of God the father, the son, and the holy spirit of God,
> And the three Marys, and the three consecrated altars,
> And the blessed son of grace,
> And by [literally, on] the stones, and by [on] the herbs,
> To which the son of grace [Jesus] bestowed their virtues
> In order that they should defend thee, the sinner who suffered adversity,
> As Christ [himself] defended [you].
>
> In the name of the Father, the Son, and the Holy Spirit,
> Against adversity above wind, against adversity below wind,
> Against adversity above ground and below ground,
> Against adversity of [the] middle of the world,
> And against adversity in [any] place in the world,
> God keep you and preserve you from a wolf of a man,
> From the evil thing of hell [Satan].
> I take thee to be a child of God,
> And a follower of Christ and an heir
> to the kingdom of heaven.[2]

Gwen's charm was written down verbatim in the otherwise English document, but her fluent recitation proved too much for the bishop's clerk who left her other prayers or charms unrecorded, merely noting that she had uttered many other words and 'tediouse sentences'.

For the historian this charm is a fascinating and rare survival of the oral religious culture that lay outside orthodox Catholicism and Protestantism. The charm is essentially a petitionary prayer for God's protection, but it has some unusual elements, which may have deep historical roots. The characteristic address to the Trinity is followed by an invocation of the three Marys of the New Testament (the Virgin Mary, Mary Magdalene, and Mary Clopas, who were present at the Crucifixion),[3] the three altars (of uncertain significance), as well as an appeal to the virtues of God's creation, which included the herbs and special stones used by Gwen and other healers. There is a comprehensive appeal for protection against all types of blight and deliverance from the evil thing of hell (Satan) and his embodiment on earth, the wolf of a man. The idea of the wolfish man has Continental, especially central European resonances, and is present in Irish sources, but the wolf-man was probably not thought of literally as a werewolf, a person capable of transforming himself into a wolf.[4] Here the idea seems to be that predatory and vengeful neighbours were aspects of Satan, and present like ravenous wolves on the boundaries of community. To understand the contemporary force of the simile we must remember that wolves may still have roamed parts of upland Wales in the sixteenth century, or would have been a recent memory. As events were to unfold, Gwen might have been saying the prayer for her own protection.

Gwen had a long-standing reputation as a charmer, but the incident that precipitated her arrest and imprisonment was rather different from her regular use of salves and spoken charms. Gwen also used written charms or prayers, including the text of St John's Gospel, widely regarded as a preservative. A written charm had been discovered in the parlour at Gloddaith, the Caernarfonshire house belonging to Thomas Mostyn, head of one of the principal families in north Wales, and a justice of the peace in two counties. The Mostyn family were so powerful locally that a proverb reminded that even Mr Mostyn had a master: '*Mae meistr ar Meistr Mostyn*'.[5] The charm found at Gloddaith was regarded with much suspicion because it was apparently written backwards, and in the inverted world of witchcraft beliefs was therefore thought to have destructive rather than protective uses. Gwen was closely examined about the paper: had she brought or sent it to Gloddaith? Gwen had heard that such a written paper had been found at Gloddaith but knew nothing more about it. However suspicion had fallen on Gwen because of her association with Mistress Jane Conway of Marle, near Conwy, who seemed to have had some differences with Thomas Mostyn. Gwen admitted that she had obtained two copies of St John's Gospel from Mrs Conway, apparently written by her son. A further written charm was found in Gwen's purse when she was examined before the bishop. Gwen also conceded that once, about two years before, she had remained all night at Gloddaith when Mr Mostyn was away from home, although she did not explain the circumstances. The implication seems to have been, although it was not actually stated, that Mistress Conway had employed Gwen to bewitch Master Mostyn.

Suspicion had fallen on Gwen soon after the discovery of the charm. Gwen claimed that some friends and neighbours advised her to leave the district ('to get herself owte of the waie') because Mr Mostyn would have her punished. This was sound advice but Gwen imprudently remained in Betws, presumably because she felt she had done nothing wrong, and was duly arrested and taken to Flint gaol. Gwen's house was searched, and two artefacts were discovered which were regarded with deep misgivings: a brass or tin image of Christ rising from the dead, and a bell without a clapper. Gwen told the bishop that she had been given these objects by her late sister (who had taught her how to charm) but denied using bell and image when charming. However these interesting artefacts do reveal the connection between the prayerful world of charming and pre-Reformation religious practices.

On 12 June 1594 Gwen's examination was signed by the bishop and marked by Gwen with a cross as a true record. A month later, on 10 July, Gwen was questioned further about her involvement with Mistress Conway. The final record of Gwen's examination was communicated to the assize judges, Richard

Shuttleworth, chief justice, and Henry Townshend, second justice of the Chester circuit. The procedures that were to lead inexorably to Gwen's judicial murder had been set in motion. On 12 July the judges issued a special commission from Flint Castle empowering named Denbighshire magistrates to examine witnesses who were prepared to prove the matter of witchcraft against Gwen. Some weeks later, on 30 August 1594, two justices of the peace assembled interested parties at the parish church of Diserth (otherwise Llansanffraid Glan Conwy), where witnesses were sworn and examined. This must have been a dramatic and excited assembly of witnesses and officials since it was the first case of its kind in northeast Wales, and the accusations made there would become issues of life and death at Gwen's trial. No doubt some of the participants would have known of the sensational pamphlets reporting witchcraft trials in England, which placed special emphasis on the relationship between witches and their familiar spirits in animal guises. Revealingly, some witnesses were to claim that Gwen had a familiar or devil through which she worked her mischief.

Seven witnesses, five men and two women, had their examinations recorded by the clerk. Their depositions related to events that had happened up to six years before. The most serious allegation, on which Gwen was subsequently indicted, was made by Elin ferch Richard of Llaneilian-yn-Rhos, a widow aged about sixty. Gwen's second husband had worked at Elin's husband's mill. In 1589 it so happened that the witness's son, Lewis ap John, fell out with Gwen and had struck her. Shortly after the quarrel her assailant mysteriously became quite frantic. Neighbours said that Gwen had avenged her injury by causing Lewis ap John's madness, and furthermore it was believed she could make him recover – if she wanted. Elin pleaded with Gwen to help her son, saying that she herself would ask Gwen's forgiveness and make amends for the injury her son had done. Gwen was alleged to have said that if only Elin had come sooner she could and would have helped her son, but now it was too late as Lewis ap John had only a short time to live. Elin believed her son had died on the very day predicted by Gwen.

Other witnesses reported disturbing encounters with Gwen and attributed to her a vengeful personality. Gruffith ap Hugh of Betws described how his widowed mother had lost an ox in summer 1592. They went to Gwen for information about the missing beast, and promised her a quantity ('hoop') of rye if she could tell them where the ox had strayed. Gwen said that the ox was in Gwytherin, but after searching there the beast was eventually found miles away in the upper part of Llansannan. Gwen was therefore denied her reward, and Griffith heard that she was discontented. Sometime later, about the feast of the Ascension 1593, Gruffith's brother, David ap Hugh, lay sick. Gwen went to him and gave him a medicinal drink but also charmed him with some salt. Soon afterwards David became very sick, and told his brother that the drink had done him no harm, but maintained that the charming or sorcery with the salt had harmed him and would be the cause of his death.

It is clear that Gwen had a considerable if somewhat ambiguous reputation for charming and soothsaying, and that many consulted her for cures and for information. In 1591 William Gruffith ap William of Betws, bailiff of the hundred of Is Dulas, aged about thirty, as a Christmas diversion, resolved to test Gwen's reputation. One may suppose that this sort of teasing was an occupational hazard for charmers and soothsayers and might sometimes destroy or enhance their reputations. An unnamed Arfon soothsayer, who discovered lost things for others, was ridiculed when she failed to find her own cauldron which had been deliberately hidden under her bed to test her skill.[6] In this sceptical spirit, the bailiff sent word to Gwen that he and some companions intended to come and drink in her house, adding mischievously that if she had any skill in soothsaying she would be able to predict when they would arrive. Without any further warning, William and four companions arrived one evening at Gwen's house and peremptorily demanded some drink for money. Gwen, not wanting these uninvited guests in her house, resolutely set her back against the cellar door, but one Robert Evans (Evance) roughly thrust her aside with his left arm. Gwen warned that she would avenge any injury done to her, and then instructed her maid to fetch some drink. The drink was brought and consumed, and then Gwen herself fetched more in a large jug ('stondart'). When this vessel was set before the bailiff and his companions they spied with growing consternation a great fly moving on top of the drink. This fly seemed bigger and uglier than other flies, and they became convinced that it was Gwen's demon ('divell') or familiar. The company were frightened but sufficiently self-possessed to try and scoop up the fly with their mugs. The fly evaded capture and eventually the contents of the jug were emptied onto the floor, but strangely the fly – said to be as large as a bumblebee – could not be found.

After this confrontation Gwen ominously said that she would be even with the bailiff and some of his companions. Within a fortnight Robert Evans had mysteriously broken the very arm he had used against Gwen. More dramatically, the bailiff's wife lost the use of her limbs and lay sick for a long time. In desperation she sent for Gwen, who told her she would be able to help her and ease the pain – if she had faith in her ('if she would believe Gwen'). One evening the bailiff came home and was outraged to find Gwen not only in his house but standing by his child's cradle. The bailiff was prudently taken to one side, allowing Gwen to leave the house quietly. Later the bailiff demanded to know from his wife, who still lay in her sick bed, 'Why that witch ('witche') was in his house?' Gwen, the charmer and soothsayer, was now openly and publicly termed a witch before some of her neighbours.

Gwen was arraigned at the Denbighshire Great Sessions in October 1584. Three indictments were laid against Gwen: for bewitching Robert Evans by breaking his arm; for bewitching Lowri ferch John ap Ieuan, the wife of the bailiff of Is Dulas, who had lost the use of her limbs; and for murdering Lewis ap John by witchcraft (Fig. 8). The grand jury seems to have had doubts about this last indictment because although it is boldly endorsed as a true bill ('*billa vera*') the faint prior endorsement '*ignoramus*' (we take no notice [of this bill]) can also be made out.[7] The jury's hesitation was understandable because the Elizabethan Act (1563) against witchcraft had made death by bewitchment a felony punishably by hanging; the penalty for the first offence of wasting or laming a person was imprisonment and the pillory. The grand jury were evidently persuaded – possibly coerced – into finding a true bill for the greater offence, and Gwen was indicted on a matter of life or death.

Gwen and the Demonologists

It was odd that the event which had precipitated Gwen's arrest – the discovery at Gloddaith of a written paper believed to be a witchcraft charm – had faded from investigation. As the case developed, there seems to have been a diversion of interest, perhaps deliberately encouraged, away from the gentry families initially involved in the case to accusations of '*maleficium*' by Gwen's neighbours.

When questioned by the bishop of St Asaph, Gwen had denied leaving the charm at Gloddaith but she did admit that she had obtained written prayers or charms from one Mistress Holland otherwise Jane Conway of Marle. Jane Conway seems to have taken an interest in Gwen's expertise, and had discussed some of her affairs with her, revealing some of her 'sorrows' to Gwen during the Christmas holiday at Marle in 1592. Jane evidently felt financially wronged by Thomas Mostyn, although the details are obscure. She pressed Gwen (presumably as a reputed soothsayer) for information about Thomas Mostyn. She asked Gwen about Mr Mostyn's money or gold; Gwen replied that she did not know about his affairs. Jane Conway then told Gwen that Mr Mostyn had sent his money to Mr Kyffyn, but the horse that had carried the cash had been hurt. Gwen intimated that she did not know how the horse had been hurt. Jane Conway further said that Mr Thomas Mostyn was a sickly man, and asked Gwen how long he would live. Gwen replied that she could not tell.

Gwen was subsequently examined in gaol by three prominent Flintshire justices of the peace (John Hanmer, Roger Puleston, Simon Thelwall), apparently on the instructions of the assize judges, about certain recent conversations concerning Jane Conway, Gwen confessed that she had been assured that Jane Conway would not leave her in want. But lately two women strangers had come into the gaol, telling Gwen that Jane Conway was angry with her because she was afraid that Gwen had 'told more of her than was the truth'. Gwen also affirmed that the details of her earlier examination taken before the bishop were true in every particular: Jane Conway had discussed Thomas Mostyn with her, and she had given Gwen copies of St John's Gospel written by her son. Gwen denied leaving a written charm at Gloddaith, but damagingly added that she had seen something similar in Jane Conway's prayer book. Another active witness, present when the constable had searched Gwen's house, described how (apparently on his own initiative) he had questioned Hugh Holland, Jane Conway's son, about the writing found at Gloddaith suspected of containing words of witchcraft. Hugh Holland was asked whether the charm was in his handwriting, and whether he had written the charm found in Gwen's possession at the time of her examination before the bishop. Hugh Holland utterly denied writing the suspect text found at Gloddaith, but confessed that he had copied St John's Gospel out of an old book and had either given the text to his mother or had left it in the old book in his mother's house.

This evidence made a damaging situation potentially very dangerous for Jane Conway and for her son. Who was Mistress Jane Conway? She can be identified as the widow of Hugh Holland of Conwy from a pedigree registered with Lewys Dwnn in 1597 by their son, Robert Holland. The Hollands of Conwy were prosperous landowners, merchants, clerics and lawyers who were related to many influential families in north and west Wales, as a genealogy compiled by George Owen shows. Their family motto, still inscribed on Hugh Holland's splendid monument in Conwy parish church, was '*Fiat pax, floreat iustitia*', 'Let there be peace, let justice be done'. The Hollands were blest with numerous progeny in the sixteenth century. Jane was the mother of a large and interesting family of eleven surviving children, the last born when she was aged forty-eight or more.[8]

Two of her sons, Robert and Henry Holland, were Cambridge graduates who had pursued clerical careers in East Anglia after ordination at Ely in 1580.[9] Robert Holland was none other than the author of *Dau Gymro yn Taring*, the anti-witchcraft tract examined in the previous chapter. The Holland brothers served country cures near Cambridge during the 1580s; Henry was appointed vicar of Orwell, while Robert was licensed curate and schoolmaster at Dullingham (1580). It was relatively common for young Cambridgeshire curates to augment their stipends by teaching in a village school before they were beneficed.[10] The Holland brothers were inspired by the Calvinist sympathies of some of their university contemporaries, especially the theology of William Perkins, and the 'practical divinity' of Richard Greenham, parson of Dry Drayton, a 'model Puritan' parish less than ten miles from Henry Holland's Orwell, and coincidentally the family home of George Gifford, the demonologist. One way or another, the principal late-Elizabethan Protestant demonologists (Gifford, the Holland brothers, Perkins) were all associated with Cambridge and a group of parishes within five miles of the university town.[11]

Henry, while parson of Orwell, published *A Treatise against Witchcraft* (1590; Fig. 6). His Treatise was dedicated to Robert Devereux, second earl of Essex, a Cambridge contemporary who had extensive interests in south-west Wales and may have been an occasional patron of the Holland brothers. It is surely significant that Robert Holland was to name one of his sons 'Devereux'.[12] Robert Holland had found his way to Pembrokeshire by Michaelmas 1589, when he was paid as a preacher in Haverfordwest, a prosperous town with some burgesses of

Puritan sympathy.[13] Holland must have had a friend at Court because in 1591 he was appointed rector of the Crown living of Prendergast, one of the more lucrative Pembrokeshire parishes, publishing his own anti-witchcraft tract sometime after among other edifying publications. This was evidently the end of a difficult period for Robert. In the preface to his metrical *Holie Historie* (1594) he refers obscurely to 'his former miseries' and of having been 'foure yeares or more tossed with sundrie troubles & adversities'.[14]

Robert and Henry Holland were dutiful parish ministers with Puritan sympathies, whose publications reflected the preaching and catechising emphasis of their ministry, and it is of absorbing interest that both should have published anti-witchcraft tracts in the 1590s. To have one demonologist in the family was extraordinary enough, but to have two was a unique distinction. The following diagram sets out the family relationships:

Hugh Holland	=	Jane, daughter of Hugh Conway
of Conwy, esq.,		of Bryneuryn, esq.,
died 1584		married 1543

Henry Holland, MA,	Robert Holland, MA,	Hugh Holland	Eight
c.1555–1603. Author	1556–1622. Author of	of Conwy, named	other
of *A Treatise against*	*Dau Gymro yn Taring*	in depositions	children
Witchcraft (1590).	(*c*. 1595). Rector of		
Vicar of St Bride's,	Prendergast, 1591		
London, 1594			

The Holland brothers wrote their tracts at a time when witchcraft prosecutions were particularly severe in south-east England, especially in Essex, and they may well have had direct knowledge of contemporary witchcraft trials in East Anglia. Intellectually Robert and Henry Holland were influenced by their university contemporary William Perkins (1558–1602), the celebrated Puritan author and preacher, whose *Discourse of the Damned Art of Witchcraft* was posthumously published in 1610. Robert Holland's anti-witchcraft tract was published after Henry's treatise (1590), but the exact date of publication is not known beyond that it was printed 'about 1595' and shows the influence of George Gifford's colloquial *Dialogue concerning Witches and Witchcraftes* (1593).[15]

The Holland brothers' anti-witchcraft tracts were both cast in the form of a dialogue but are interestingly different in style. Henry Holland's *Treatise against Witchcraft* (1590) is a learned tract in English, laden with quotations, engaging with the leading authorities of the day, and aimed at a theologically sophisticated audience. He explains that his Treatise was partly prompted by the 'brutish ignorance' of the common ('rude') people that led them into 'a continuall trafficke' with cunning-folk ('witches'). He was also concerned to repudiate the views of learned sceptics by deploying arguments used by some Continental demonologists. As a consequence, Henry Holland's *Treatise* 'despite its populist intentions and solemn translations of all the Latin texts, has a curiously remote and academic flavour.'[16] Robert Holland's dialogue, by contrast, was urgent and accessible, and written in idiomatic Welsh to inform the people of Wales about the dangers of witchcraft. The dialogue, which possibly draws on actual discussions had between parson and parishioners, conveys the complexity of popular attitudes towards witchcraft and magic, and describes numerous specialists, particularly charmers and soothsayers, some of whom – as the dialogue points out, somewhat ironically as it turned out – were highly regarded by the best gentlemen and freeholders throughout Wales.

Despite the contrasts in language and style there are many points of similarity in the arguments deployed by the Holland brothers. A crucial correspondence, shared with other Protestant demonologists of the period, was the attack on popular magic with the insistence that 'black' and 'white' witches were equally evil. They argued that the apparently helpful nature of some 'good' or 'white' witches disguised their links with the devil. Henry Holland recognized that many people consulted 'wise men' and 'cunning women' because of sickness, losses, and other extremities, but condemned them as ungodly because they did not trust in God's mercy, and devoted a chapter to discussing this fearful sin. Robert Holland has much to say on the same point. He maintains that there was a relationship between the devil and charmers although they appeared to help man and beast. Charmers were ungodly people because they acquired their information and knowledge with the help of the devil. Robert Holland emphasizes that it is just as well to go to the devil himself, as it is to go to the people that serve him and gain their knowledge from him.[17]

Gwen ferch Ellis was clearly a charmer (*swynwraig*) and soothsayer of the type described by Robert Holland who helped the sick and found lost goods. Gwen was modest or circumspect about her abilities. She put it simply to the bishop: 'diverse that have comen to her did beleeve that she co[u]ld helpe theim, and so she beleeved likewise.' One could not wish for a clearer statement that Gwen's authority as a charmer or soothsayer (like all diviners) derived from the confidence of her clients. Many who consulted her believed that she could help men, women and children, as well as sick beasts, and so Gwen came to believe she had the power to do good. Nevertheless, Gwen's reputation was not unambiguous. While she was credited with doing good to man and beast, she was also thought capable of inflicting harm. What should be done in these cases? The Holland brothers and their fellow demonologists were quite clear. They quoted scriptural authority to show that God had commanded the destruction of all witches – helpful as well as harmful – but emphasised that none should attempt to destroy them unless they had the necessary legal authority.

And so it happened. The grand jury, possibly after some coercion, found a true bill against Gwen for murdering Lewis ap John by witchcraft. The supposed victim's mother was the principal witness in the trial that followed. No details of the oral evidence given at the trial have been preserved, but the written depositions perused by the jurors are those now available to the historian. The

trial jury, composed of local gentlemen, also considered the cases of two suspected thieves indicted for grand larceny, one of whom was acquitted and the
other found guilty of the reduced charge of petty larceny, punishable by whip-
ping rather than hanging. This merciful act, which saved the life of the prisoner,
seems to have displeased the trial judge, and the jury were ordered to appear
before the court at the next sessions. However no mercy was shown in Gwen's
case. The calendar of prisoners formally records the trial jury's verdict of guilty
and the judge's subsequent judgment of death by hanging (Fig. 7). This was the
sentence required by statute, and there is no record of a reprieve or pardon. The
sheriff's officers would have publicly hanged Gwen at the end of the sessions
after the judges had been escorted to the next assize town on the circuit.

Gwen's tragedy was that she had been caught up in an incident seen as potentially threatening by an important gentry family. Had her charming been confined
to her neighbours of low and middling status Gwen might never have come to the
notice of the authorities. As it was, Gwen's activities had crossed a significant social
boundary, and her prosecution seems to have been encouraged at different stages by
bishop, assize judges, and justices of the peace. Nevertheless, as the case developed
local tensions and conflicts informed the prosecution, and the prosecutor of the
fateful indictment was a woman, the mother of Gwen's supposed victim. Witchcraft
prosecutions were socially complex events, as Gwen's case illustrates, involving a
dynamic between elite power and popular culture. Although Gwen's prosecution may have been encouraged from above, by the gentry and by the justices, it
could not really have proceeded without the co-operation of witnesses drawn from
Gwen's own community.

And what of the Holland family? They seem to have had a lucky escape. Mistress
Jane Holland had associated with a suspected witch, and there was a clear implication that she had conspired with Gwen to leave a written charm intended to harm
Thomas Mostyn. Moreover, Jane's son, Hugh Holland, may have written the charm.
The execution of Gwen ferch Ellis in Denbighshire seems to have spared Jane from
further investigation. For the demonologist brothers, who not only condemned
black and white witches but also those who consulted them, and emphasised the
special godly responsibilities of the literate, the prosecution of Gwen ferch Ellis
would have been an event very uncomfortably close to home. It would certainly
have threatened the respectable reputation of the Holland family and damaged
the credibility of the clerical brothers whose mother and brother were involved in
the very activities that the demonologists condemned in others. The lesson for the
demonologists was that while it was easy enough to encourage the lawful prosecution of suspected witches, actual witchcraft accusations were difficult to control and
might take unpredictable directions, sometimes even leading to the demonologist's
very door.

Presumably it was a chastening experience for the Holland brothers. Robert
Holland had written complacently in the dedication to his first book, *The Holie
Historie*, that he had found 'a breathing time' at Prendergast after his 'travels' or

travails. The dedication is dated 1 August 1594, but a few months later with Gwen's trial he would have cause again to observe the 'special warnings of the Lord' in relation to his family. The chronology of events suggests that his response was to write *Dau Gymro yn Taring*. It is certain that Holland's anti-witchcraft tract was written after the trial of Gwen ferch Ellis. There is a revealing contrast between Holland's expansive *Holie Historie,* written in English during 'a breathing time', and his Welsh anti-witchcraft tract, which is short (barely 4,000 words), urgent (apparently shorn of the usual preliminary dedication and preface), and direct.[18]

Henry Holland was appointed vicar of St Bride's, London, in the year of Gwen's trial. He had left Cambridgeshire in 1592, following his friend Richard Greenham, the distinguished Puritan preacher and a neighbouring parson, to a London 'lecture-ship'. Holland's Sabbatarianism was expressed in a number of published sermons, but his principal literary work was a laborious, influential, and frequently reprinted edition of Greenham's *Works* in which the dangers of consulting witches and wizards figured among many collected 'godly observations' and 'cases of conscience'. Henry Holland's early death in 1603 was attributed to his exhausting diligence as a minister and preacher of God's word, compounded, it may be added, by his unofficial calling as an 'irregular', unlicensed physician.[19]

Robert Holland's concern for the spiritual well-being of his countrymen, and his continuing Puritanism, was reflected in further publications in the vernacular: a Welsh guide to prayer (1600) and translations of William Perkins's exposition of the Lord's Prayer (1599) and his Catechism.[20] With the accession of James I (a fellow demonologist, of course), Holland translated James's guidance to his eldest son (*Basilikon Doron,* 1599) into Welsh, allowing himself some 'sawcy' or impertinent remarks in an English preface which additionally advised that Prince Henry should acquire 'a taste of the [Welsh] tongue', so that (as 'the Church and common weale grow rich, & the people poor') when the prince became Governor he could listen to his people ('as Mithriaates could doe') without interpreters.[21] The translation of *Basilikon Doron* was published in the year that a new Act (1604) was passed against conjuration, witchcraft, and dealing with evil and wicked spirits. Holland remained practically concerned with godly discipline, and as an official of the consistory court made a presentment at the assizes of habitual absentees from church in his archdeaconry. He seems also to have become the bishop of St David's 'Ordinary', and in that office would have been instrumental in saving the lives of many convicted felons at the assizes by assisting those claiming benefit of clergy to read the neck-verse, a mercy that would not have been available to Gwen ferch Ellis as a woman.[22]

Gwen's Case in Context

Gwen's prosecution would have been a sensational event in 1594, partly of course because it was a case of witchcraft and partly because it involved local gentry families. The case was unusual on other counts. Women were rarely indicted for capital felonies at the Great Sessions, and it was therefore highly unusual for a woman to be put on trial for her life in the Welsh courts. The Court of Great Session was overwhelmingly a male arena with male judges and other officials, male juries, and a preponderance of male prisoners and male witnesses. Statistically women made up somewhat less than ten per cent of prisoners at many sessions and were sometimes completely absent from the gaol calendars. Women made only occasional appearances as prisoners, generally as petty thieves and very occasionally as murderers. Gwen's case was in a special sense an instance of murder.

Was Gwen ferch Ellis in any sense a typical suspected witch? It is useful to try and detect some regularity in the relative status of suspected witches and their accusers, but indictments do not provide an uncomplicated guide to status. Gwen was not a stereotypical witch – elderly, socially isolated, and dependent on the charity of others. Gwen was middle-aged, economically independent, and prosperous enough to keep a maid. Gwen had been married several times, and most suspected witches were married or widowed women with kin. The twenty-four suspected witches for whom some details of status have survived form a miscellaneous group of 'widows' (10), yeomen (5), the wives (6) and daughters (1) of yeomen or husbandmen, and the wives of craftsmen (2). It is not easy with such small numbers to infer any convincing regularities in the statuses of suspected witches and their accusers, and the difficulty is compounded because the 'styles' recorded in indictments are not necessarily accurate. However a clearer profile of accused witches emerges from slander cases brought in the Court of Great Sessions. These actions preserve accusations of witchcraft that were contested at an early stage and were never brought forward as bills of indictment. All thirty-nine cases involved actions brought by women. The dominant pattern found in twenty-five cases (or sixty-five per cent) was for a married woman (with her husband) to bring a slander action against another married woman and her husband (14) or a man (11). Crucially, accusations seem more likely to have been translated into prosecutions when the principal accusers (the prosecutors of indictments) were men and the accused were unmarried or widowed women. The Welsh assizes were very much dominated by men, and women (who certainly made accusations of witchcraft, as slander actions show) may have been inhibited from pursuing prosecutions, or were disabled by the requirement for prosecutors to show serious intent by entering into substantial recognizances. Nevertheless women as much as men had an important if secondary role in witchcraft trials as sworn witnesses for the prosecution.[23]

Prosecutions for maleficent witchcraft began in Wales only in 1595 when Gwen ferch Ellis was indicted at the Denbighshire Great Sessions. The elaborate trial documents testify to the novelty of these late Elizabethan proceedings, and the social complexity of witchcraft cases. The depositions reveal something of the transitional nature of belief at the time. Gwen was a 'helpful' charmer and soothsayer of the type condemned by Holland: she practised charming and was able to give tidings of things lost, but she also had the reputation of avenging injuries. This dual repute seems to have been characteristic of some other women accused of witchcraft in Wales. Maggi and Gwenllian Hir, indicted for witchcraft in 1656, were charmers and 'mumblers' of prayers or charms. Katherine Rees, accused of witchcraft in 1694, was a fortune-teller who threw dice upon a book.

It is interesting that Gwen's case was not actually the first case of witchcraft and magic brought before the Great Sessions. There had been earlier prosecutions involving soothsaying (1568, 1570), bewitching to unlawful love (1579), and enchantments (1589). A Breconshire yeoman was suspected of witchcraft and murder in 1592 but was not indicted. Gwen's prosecution two years later was the first unambiguous case of 'maleficium' or black witchcraft tried at the Court of Great Sessions. After Gwen's prosecution and conviction at the end of the sixteenth century there was a slow but steady trickle of witchcraft accusations in Stuart Wales. Witchcraft prosecutions in Wales were essentially a seventeenth-century phenomenon. Acquittals were generally high but several suspects were found guilty of witchcraft after Gwen's conviction and execution. One must note two other trials that resulted in judgments of death. In Caernarfonshire in 1623 two sisters (Lowri and Agnes ferch Evan of Llanbedrog) and their brother (Rhydderch ap Evan of Llannor, yeoman) were convicted of bewitching to death Margaret Hughes of Llanbedrog in 1622 and laming her sister Mary Hughes, rendering her speechless in 1616. The three accused were all sentenced to death by hanging. In Anglesey in 1655 Margaret ferch Richard of Beaumaris, widow, was sentenced to death for bewitching Gwen, wife of Owen Meredith, who had lingered for two months until she died on the last day of December 1654.[24] It is a pity that the depositions of witnesses do not survive in these cases, but we know from Gwen ferch Ellis's case that accusations of witchcraft were very complex events. The Caernarfonshire case was certainly a cause célèbre in north-west Wales. A letter describes the 'great sture' in Llŷn when Rhydderch ap Evan and his sisters were apprehended on suspicion of witchcraft. The suspects were roughly handled and committed to gaol without bail. Their neighbours regarded them as 'honest people and of good conversation'; a local gentleman 'could not tell how to medle in bussines of that nature' and sought advice from the influential Sir John Wynn of Gwydir.[25]

These tragic cases involving the executions of five accused witches do not amount to a witch-hunt. We must compare the low levels of prosecutions in Wales with the intensity of prosecutions (which varied geographically) in England and Scotland. It has been estimated that in sixteenth- and seventeenth-century England some 500 suspected witches might have been hanged; in Scotland, which experienced several episodes of witch hunting, many more accused witches were probably executed. Welsh witchcraft cases, which involved some thirty-five accusations between 1594 and 1698 and a similar number of slander cases, are negligible in comparison. Nevertheless, the chronology of witchcraft prosecutions within Wales was clearly influenced by the intensity of prosecutions outside Wales. The initiation of prosecutions in Wales falls towards the end of a very significant period of witchcraft trials in southern England during the second half of Elizabeth I's reign. By 1594, the date of Gwen's case, suspected witches had been prosecuted for several decades in increasing numbers on the Home Assize Circuit (especially in Essex) and there had been a steady accumulation of pamphlets reporting and sensationalising witchcraft trials. Witchcraft prosecutions in England became less frequent during the first half of the seventeenth century but sharply increased between 1640–59, particularly as a consequence of the witch hunting in East Anglia conducted by Matthew Hopkins in the late 1640s. There was a corresponding increase in cases of witchcraft in Wales in the 1650s. A steady decline in witchcraft prosecutions in the second half of the seventeenth century occurred in both England and Wales, but a final flourish of Welsh cases in the 1690s may reflect concerns prompted by the intensity of prosecutions in New England. The last witchcraft prosecution in Wales vividly illustrates the transatlantic dimension to witchcraft beliefs. At Haverfordwest in 1699 Dorcas Heddin was indicted for bewitching two sailors on a ship bound for Virginia who were giving her short rations. The devil had appeared to Dorcas and offered to founder the vessel and destroy all the crew, but Dorcas agreed that only those who had 'straitened' her in her allowance of water and other provisions should be struck down with sickness.[26]

Gwen ferch Ellis's prosecution reveals that in late Elizabethan Wales there was popular belief in harmful as well as helpful witchcraft, that witnesses would come forward to give evidence against their neighbours, and that juries were prepared to convict accused witches. The elements for making a witch-hunt were certainly present in early modern Wales, yet prosecutions for witchcraft never became numerous and are barely significant statistically when compared with other felonies. This is difficult to understand given the high rates of prosecution in some other parts of the British Isles. The establishment of the Court of Great Sessions coincided with the first Act against witchcraft (1542), but it took over fifty years before a case of causing death or injury through witchcraft was prosecuted at the Great Sessions. For the most part, popular magic seems to have been marginal to the concerns of the ruling class in Elizabethan and Stuart Wales – unless it touched them directly, as Gwen's case demonstrated. The relative absence of witchcraft prosecutions in early modern Wales suggests that prosecuting witches was not among the priorities of the Court of Great Sessions. This did not mean that witchcraft beliefs were unimportant in Wales. On the contrary, Gwen's case shows that notions of harmful witchcraft were deeply embedded in popular culture. The next chapter attempts to place these beliefs in context.

AMBIGUITIES: WITCHCRAFT, WOMEN, & CURSING

It is somewhat paradoxical that although there were relatively few witchcraft trials in sixteenth- and seventeenth-century Wales, literary sources as well as the evidence presented at prosecutions show that the idea of the witch-figure became deeply embedded in early-modern Welsh society. Although most Welshmen and women were never directly involved in witchcraft accusations, they would have readily recognised the stereotypical witch-figure as presented in stories and folk-tales, and drawn upon in the language of insult. A distinction needs to be maintained between the witch-figure as an imaginative construct and the social reality of actual situations of witchcraft accusation, but both have to be considered in relation. This chapter first discusses the image of the witch-figure before exploring actual situations of witchcraft accusation.

The Witch-Figure

Slander and insult provide an insight into the stereotype of the witch in the seventeenth century. Witches were old – *hen witsh* was a common insult – as well as deceitful. Gwen ferch David of Llanrwst was said to have 'lyed like an ould witche' in 1603. They were also ugly – *witsh hagr* was used as an insult – and might have facial hair; in 1691 Mary John Rheinallt was pursued by her son-in-law who said 'hee would beate the bearded witch to pieces'. Witches were dirty or filthy – *witsh frwnt* used in 1673 was probably a common insult. The gibe 'go[a]tish witch' (*witsh afr*), made in 1613, was perhaps an allusion to the recipient's supposed appearance or smell, possibly a sexual insult, or maybe all of these things. In short, witches were regarded as physically repulsive: *Yr wy ti cyn hylled a witch* ('you are as hideous as a witch') was a proverbial comparison.[1]

These hideous attributes were amplified in the loathsome and frightening imaginative figure of the *gwrach*. The word has come to mean a witch in modern

Welsh, especially in children's stories, but it formerly had a wider range of reference and was applied to many animals or plants regarded as odd or repulsive, certain spiky or prickly domestic objects, and in some places was a name given to the intermittent fever or ague (*y wrach*) which periodically 'seized' many people. When applied to people in the sixteenth century, *gwrach* was a disparaging term for an elderly woman, corresponding to the English 'trot' or beldam. The Conway parson who carefully recorded the burial in 1581 of Eleanor ferch Thomas Gwyneth 'alias *Gwrach* y Gwenniath' was noting the demise of an insinuating beldam, 'the flattering hag', rather than a witch. It is interesting that *gwrach* was rarely used in the language of insult in early modern Wales and never in actual situations of witchcraft accusation. The *gwrach* of the imagination tended to inhabit lonely and desolate places, as many place-names attached to bogs, moors, secluded hollows, isolated habitations, and occasional archaeological sites show. The *gwrach* might emerge from places such as these to frighten people, sometimes in the form of the *gwrach y rhibyn*, a hideous figure with long tresses and yellowed teeth. The *gwrach* exaggerated some of the physical characteristics associated with witches but it was very much a fanciful construct.[2]

Persons actually accused of witchcraft might or might not have been physically unprepossessing, but they were all regarded as morally depraved. Witch and whore, and allied terms, were commonly linked as insults. 'Thou art a witch and a witching jade' were actionable words spoken in Glamorgan in 1607. Calling a neighbour 'witch' and 'fayden' (*maeden*; ironically 'maiden' = whore), and other unspecified 'good terms', was complained about at the Breconshire Quarter-sessions in 1690. 'Old witch, old whore, old gunpowder' was an interesting and litigiously explosive combination of insults uttered in 1627 at Tenby; 'gunpowder' perhaps implied the pox. *Pittan witch boeth*, whore and burnt or poxed witch, were insults uttered in Denbighshire in 1712. Sometimes supposed witches were explicitly accused of sexual predatoriness. Jane, wife of Edward Lloyd, was not only called a wicked witch but upbraided in the open street at Ruthin for being a 'naughty queen yt raisest ye husbands out of their beds from their wives to wander under hedges'. Witches were regarded as sexually deviant. John Lewys very provocatively said to William Griffith of Llanddeusant, Carmarthenshire, 'Thy mother was a whitch & thou hast carnallie dealt with her.'[3] Those who called women witches were also liable to use sexual insults of the grossest kind. In 1653 Lewis Jones of Meidrim and his wife, Elinor, were accused of calling one woman a witch, and saying that several other women were fornicators ('strikers') who used dildos: '*Hen strikers yw nhwy gyd, ag 'n yuso dildoes*'.[4] This last insult, spoken by Elinor, might conceivably imply that the women had rejected men.

In the imagery of insult, witches were outside the sexual control of men. Witches were not respecters of husbands – neither their own nor other women's husbands. Agnes Griffith, indicted for witchcraft in 1618 in Pembrokeshire, was suspected of planning to poison her husband but a watchful neighbour plucked the poison 'out of her bosome' ('I did that indeed'!) and cast it away. Suspected witches might side with women who had been abused by their husbands, although one had to be watchful of a witch's concern. *Cusanu'r witch* (the witch's kiss) was an idiom for overly solicitous clucking and tutting. One day Maggi Hir, a Carmarthenshire charmer, asked Gwenllian Owen, the wife of Lewis Walter of Llangadog, 'what ailed her that her face was blacke and blewe?' When Gwenllian replied that her husband had 'in some measure abused her', Margaret uttered an oath and said that if Gwenllian would give her some part of her husband's codpiece ('either a band-stringe or a pointe') – which symbolized his maleness – she would make sure that he never again abused her. When Gwenllian asked what would happen to him, Margaret simply replied that 'she would make an end of him'. Gwenllian pro-tested (according to her own account), saying, 'Noe, thou shalt have none from me for my husband is father of 6 children, and I pray God to keepe him in health.' Nevertheless, some days later Gwenllian accepted a charm from Maggi – 'a hand-ful of linseed' which she was to scatter at a cross-way near her house where several paths intersected. Gwenllian, presumably intending to injure rather than kill her husband, placed the charmed seed in a little heap to one side of the crossing. Maggi chided her, and Gwenllian inadvertently stepped very near the linseed. 'Oh', said Maggi, 'thou hast spoyled thy selfe', and Gwenllian was afflicted with a great pain in her foot. Gwenllian then blessed herself, saying, 'God blesse me from thee, I see they wayes are not right, I will have nothinge more to doe with thee.' Fifteen years later Gwenllian gave evidence against Maggi when she was prosecuted for witchcraft.[5]

A malevolent gaze accompanied by muttering characteristically expressed the witch's envy and anger. In 1693 a Pembrokeshire justice of the peace reported a whole catalogue of disasters that had followed in the wake of Olivia (Olly) Powell's peram-bulations in Loveston as different things caught her eye and prompted a derisive 'ha'! The narrative of events offered by sworn witnesses seems informed by a story-tell-ing tradition which attributed to the suspected witch tricksy elements from the witch-figure of the imagination. One day Olly Powell spied a new furze-rick. 'Ha!' said Olly, 'yonder is a furs reek where never was one before, but before tomorrow 'twill be upside down.' This accordingly happened to the amazement of all, includ-ing the parson. Olly passed William Nash's house where a rented cow grazed in his garden. On noticing the animal, Olly recited a rudimentary but ominous verse, 'Take a cow at a price, she will be full of lice.' Soon after the cow sickened and was found lying down strangely, head on belly. The sick cow would neither drink nor chew the cud, and after four days 'the flyes began to fall on the cow', settling in 'greate heapes', and eventually maggots ('maggons') covered the beast. Another witness had been sitting by her door, contemplating her old duck with its ducklings 'dibing' in a small pool, when Olly passed by. Olly asked who owned the ducks; the woman replied they were hers. 'Ha!' exclaimed Olly, 'you will have little good of them'. Olly had scarcely gone a hundred yards before the ducks left their pond, fell on their backs and died. 'Her tricks before tryal', a local gentleman noted, 'are nothing to w[ha]t she have since done, by report.'[6]

Witches were creatures of the night who wrought their mischief after dark. When honest folk were safely in their houses at night, with the doors secured, witches wandered abroad like thieves. Suspected witches were therefore sometimes found night-walking. Agnes Griffith, accused of witchcraft in 1619, was regarded as a common night-walker, leaving the house after dark and not returning until day-break. A witness complained that one May night Agnes had lurked at a place called Gelli Oer-nos, prompting 'greate outcries and hoobehoobes' there. Agnes was apprehended on another nocturnal excursion and spent the remainder of the night in the constable's custody until rescued by her husband.[7] Witches made butter and cheese at night (rather than openly in the day as others did), presumably after sur-reptitiously milking their neighbours' cows. A neighbour bought a 'green cheese' cheaply from Gwenllian David for threepence but returned it finding it very unsa-voury, asking why it had been made without salt. Gwenllian, who had neither 'kine, sheepe, nor any kind of cattell', replied that 'it was made after night'. Nocturnal visits from a witch were sometimes revealed by the discovery of 'witches' butter', a kind of gelatinous fungus that appeared where witches had lurked. Margaret Roger deposed on oath that a woman begging at her door had observed a strange substance upon the door-post, informing her that it was 'witchis butter'. Neighbours were consulted, and one prepared a knife with a red-hot blade and thrust it through the fungus into the door-frame, leaving it there for a fortnight. While the knife was stuck in the post Gwenllian David lay sick and implored a neighbour, 'Oh draw the knifes out of my backe and heart'. It was said that as soon as the knife was removed, Gwenllian began to recover.[8]

Witches were not necessarily observed when wandering abroad because they could change shape, sometimes assuming an animal form. Eighteenth- and nine-teenth-century accounts of witches commonly credited them with the ability to metamorphose into hares and other animals, and a belief in leporine trans-formations was certainly present in late-seventeenth-century Wales. When Olly Powell, a reputed witch, concluded her business at a Pembrokeshire coal-works and departed, Henry Phelps told a fellow workman that if he went to the top of a bank near the pit he would see Olly 'run like a hare'. The evidence against Anne Ellis implied that she could change into a cat. A sick child thought bewitched by her 'fell a scriking pitiful' saying, 'Dady the catt was uppon my backe and hath made me bleede'. It was believed that witches could enter houses through the keyholes of locked doors. In 1650 Jane Meredith threw Joan Morris out of her house, saying 'Out of my house witch! I saw thee coming in[to the house] through a hole in the lock three or four times.'[9] Witches were able to invade the most personal of spaces, and might attack people in their beds and babies in their cots. A sworn witness testified that one night after she had bolted her door and the family had gone to bed, Olly Powell mysteriously appeared at her bed-side, asking for bread and for salt. When these were refused, Olly leaped over the woman's sleeping husband and child and lay on top of her, and was so heavy that 'she thought she should have lost her breath'. After a long struggle, the woman

bit Olly's fingers to the bone, and the witch made off scattering some ducks settled at the foot of the bed which set up an 'ugly noyse', but managed to leave the
house as she had entered it – fast-bolted.[10]

Witches were credited with knowledge of sorcery and sometimes used wax
figures to do their mischief. An action was brought in 1589 for the slanderous
accusation made at Llandeilo Fawr, Carmarthenshire, that Anne, wife of William
Vaughan, was a witch and always had 'grene waxe' in her hair ready to use in her
'arte'. The significance of the specific colour of the wax is not clear. Agnes Griffith
was allegedly seen by her accusers three hours after nightfall either sitting or kneeling, 'her heare aboute her eares', with four or five burning candles on the ends of
the fingers of her left hand, and having in her right hand a wire or needle prick-
ing an object kept close in her left palm. The witness claimed knowingly that many
of a neighbour's cattle had died at about the same time. Maggi Hir, suspected of
witchcraft in Carmarthenshire, had shown one witness 'a little image' made of
wood or wax which was full of small holes. Another witness claimed that she was
stricken with great pain after Maggi Hir had borrowed four yards of diaper tape or
hair-lace, having relief only when Maggi Hir returned the lace, which was found
strangely plaited and pricked full of small holes 'like parchm[en]t where bone laces
are wrought upon'.[11]

Witches were supposed to injure the health and property of their enemies in
unusual ways. When animals were suddenly and strangely affected by illness,
neighbours by consensus might decide they were bewitched. Bewitched pigs
ran mad and cattle died mysteriously. Shortly before some bewitched calves
died 'all or most of their heare pilled and fell from their backes'. Harry James's
bewitched cattle were well at nightfall but dead by the morning. When their car-
casses were flayed the flesh was found to be 'like geley'. David John of Llangadog
claimed that his bewitched cow fell sick and then 'went upon her backe aboute
the house and through the partitions in the house', although he did not convince
the grand jury.[12]

Witches were associated with fire and strange lights. In 1655 a Flintshire mariner claimed that he was led to a particular house by Dorothy Griffith, a suspected
witch, who was strangely illuminated as if many lighted lanterns were mysteriously carried about her. He was amazed to see that the marsh behind her 'was soe
covered with fire and light that one might have gathered needles'. Once inside
the house, the candlelight and fire in the hearth made him swoon repeatedly,
one witness reporting, 'his eyes seeming to bee like a flame of fire in his head'.[13]
Strange fires in the Harlech area, possibly the combustion of marsh gas, caused
great consternation in 1694 and were attributed to witchcraft. The fire was said to
arise nightly from a place called Morfa Bychan (where a suicide had been buried)
and travel across the Dwyryd estuary. The fire consumed hayricks but would
afterwards retreat to ground regarded as poisoned and then vanish. The strangeness of the phenomenon made the rector of Dolgellau consider the fire 'was in a
great measure occasion'd by witch-craft'. He supposed that 'a consult of a parcel

of witches mett at that poyson'd ground who might ord[e]r it [the fire] to retreat to them after it had done mischief'. He prayed that if this was so, God would 'make a discovery of them and bring them to condign punishment.' Nobody was ever accused although there were suspected witches in the neighbourhood.[14]

Witchcraft Accusations

Even if the effects of witchcraft were dramatic, identifying and prosecuting a suspect was easier said than done. Nevertheless, many communities might have a small pool of possible suspects. In 1657 Anne Ellis of Penley, Flintshire, was accused of bewitching a child, but she countered by telling the examining justice that 'she hath heard many say that one Jane, the wife of John the thatcher, of Penley, ... not onely bewitched the childe but the father alsoe.' It is apparent from pre-trial examinations that some suspects had gained a reputation for witchcraft long before they were actually prosecuted. Presumably many suspects were never formally accused of witchcraft, and went to their graves as reputed witches. The burial of John ap David alias witch was recorded at Oswestry in April 1598. John's cognomen, almost an occupational surname, belonged to a class of nicknames that bluntly reflected notoriety.[15]

A reputation for witchcraft was generally shaped over many years, and was the consequence of an accumulation of incidents. A consensus of opinion among some (but not all) neighbours was probably needed before a formal accusation was made. The written pre-trial evidence, the sworn testimony of witnesses, often related to incidents that had occurred several years or even a decade or more before a formal accusation of witchcraft. Gwen ferch Ellis was indicted in 1594 for an incident that had happened six years earlier. The prosecutor of suspected witches in Llŷn, Caernarfonshire, accused them of causing sickness 'w[hi]ch hath possesed his howse ... this xviii yeares'. A pathetic note addressed to the Flintshire assize judges explained that Anne Ellis had bewitched the writer, Richard Hughes of Penley, eight years before when a boy of twelve. Since then he had been bedridden, 'full of issues running night and day', and was so sore that he could be 'handled' only by his mother. Hughes told the judges that he was so ill that 'I can nither com[e] nor rid[e] to plead my cause' but had written the letter to 'speake the truth' concerning 'this woman', the suspected witch. Richard Hughes's mother had travelled to the assizes to give evidence against the suspect, but he implored the judges to 'send my mother home soone so as ever you can' as he was in such a pitiful condition.[16]

Confronting a suspect face-to-face and calling him or (more usually) her a witch was an important aspect of a loosely-structured process that could lead eventually to formal prosecution. Eynon Philipes, sworn to give evidence as to the life and character of Agnes Griffith, a suspected witch, began by saying that he had 'hard her tearmed and called a witch to her face by diverse persons'. When

Richard Lloyd's daughter was afflicted with facial paralysis (she 'having her lipp near the ear of one side and the eye of the same side nearer the eye brow then it ought') a physician, Richard Bloome of Carmarthen, eventually suggested that a fortune-teller with a 'pyde eye' had caused the sickness. Bloome advised calling her 'by the name of a witch' whenever they met, even if the place was very public, and he undertook before witnesses to indemnify ('save harmless') Richard Lloyd from the costs arising from a slander action. It was evidently expected that someone verbally abused as a witch might well initiate an action for slander for damages. The strategy might prove expensive for the accused witch but probably pre-empted prosecution. Agnes ferch Maddock of Wrexham initiated four actions of slander against her accusers between 1604–10 and in the end obtained an order from the court for arbitration of the matter. On the other hand, failure to initiate an action for slander might well be taken as a tacit admission of guilt. When Katherine Rees was prosecuted for witchcraft in 1693, it was recalled that although Erasmus Thomas had called her a witch whenever they fell out, she always appeared unconcerned and never contradicted him. In a mid-seventeenth-century case, a witness deposed that she had heard Gwenllian David and Margaret David 'calling one another witch several times'. This should have prompted a flurry of writs, but in this case it was probably an unusual instance of a permissive joking relationship between kin.[17]

What specific situations prompted witchcraft accusations? Certainly, the now-classic situation of charity refusal is present in the Welsh material, and it is useful to examine it closely because of its comparative interest.[18] In 1607 Katherine Lewis, wife of Thomas Bowen of Tenby, labourer, was suspected of bewitching some pigs at Gumfreston, Pembrokeshire. Katherine had called at Elizabeth Browning's house 'having a pot with her' and 'seemed to seeke something'. Elizabeth fetched a dishful of milk, but judging that Katherine's pot was 'full inough' did not give her all of it, prudently asked what else she would have. Katherine asked for some flour, which Elizabeth gave her 'because she feared that Katherine would do her some hurt yf she should deny her for that she was a woman suspected of witchcraft.' Immediately after Katherine's departure two sows 'heavy with pigs' ran about 'in most straundge fashion' casting their litter ('falling their pigs'). The piglets died and the sows languished. Browning and his wife, and all those who saw the pigs, supposed they had been bewitched.[19]

Reputed witches were represented – as in this account – as unreasonably wanting something over and above what was appropriate, but which might be given to them nonetheless because of their baleful reputation. There was consternation when Gwenllian Hir arrived at Gwenllian Walter's house enquiring for the latter's husband. Learning that he had gone away, Gwenllian Hir said ominously, 'I know I must fall out with him at last.' Asked why she must, Gwenllian complained that 'she hadd noe corne of him since the last harvest'. The failure to give, especially something extra or unmerited, could have dire consequences. Henry Phelps, the principal prosecutor of Olly Powell, said that Olly had come to Jeffreston coalworks asking for a measure ('kinterkine') of coal due to her son-in-law. Phelps instructed the coal-sorters ('riddlers') to give her a sack of coal but Olly boldly desired 'a stone of coal over measure'. Phelps responded with rough humour, 'Poore wrech [neither] thou nor thy horse are ... able to carrey more, but inless thou wilt run [on] all four[s] & help him'. Olly went away muttering, as she was wont to do, and within the hour Phelps was 'taken all over his body w[i]th stiches' and was unable to rest or sleep, and by the fifth or sixth day feared death. Another example of Olly's brazenness was given at her trial. A widow claimed that as she sat by her husband's corpse on the day he was to be buried, Olly made her way through the assembled neighbours and openly told her that 'if she had given her a quarter of her goose w[hic]h she killed ye last Christmas, her husband should have been living & working w[i]th his fellow labourers.' The dead man had 'stood in such dread of Olly yt w[he]n his fellow workemen w[oul]d jest & say there comes Olly, he w[ou]ld fall atrembling all over.'[20]

It seems very probable that some women traded on their reputations as witches, demanding more than was neighbourly, and that some people were more afraid than others of them and tended to give them what they wanted. Anne Ellis of Penley, a poor woman who lived by begging and making stockings, may have adopted this strategy. Many people 'used to give Anne at their doore more than to any other begger out of feare she might doe them or their cattell hurte'. One neighbour, Elizabeth Jeffrey, claimed that she received Anne into her house 'more for feare then love', and was disconcerted by her gnomic utterances.[21] It was said that when Anne was denied meat and drink sickness had sometimes followed the refusal. Susan Adams remembered after a calf had fallen sick that her daughter had refused Anne Ellis's request for some milk, saying 'she could spare not any'. But generally, it was not the refusal of charity as such that was at issue, but rather the unreasonable or excessive expectations on the part of the reputed witch. Anne Ellis had come to Margaret Barnatt's house for relief, which was given her, but it was 'not of the best' and shortly after Margaret's child fell sick. At Olly Powell's trial a witness remembered the veiled threat she employed when coercing something extra from one of her alleged victims, 'Ha, y[o]u must always give sowle [= relish, something extra] to all such expected . . . people as I am & all y[o]u have will doe well'. The carefully reported phrase 'expected person' – '[so] her words was' – here means 'expectant', one who expected to receive something and did not anticipate a refusal.[22]

Reputed witches might also be importunate borrowers, and it was difficult to refuse them. It was inadvisable for reluctant lenders to pretend they did not have the desired item, as they sometimes did, since witches knew what to ask for. When Maggi Hir asked Gwenllian Rees for some money, Gwenllian replied that she had none but Maggi retorted 'she would be the better for it if she gave it', accurately pointing out to the discomfited Gwenllian that she had near enough three shillings about her. Borrower and lender were held in a relationship by the transaction, and the lender might suffer from strange afflictions, especially if the loan had been made unwillingly. Ann Morgan at first declined to lend Maggi Hir her hair-lace (a kind of ribbon for binding the hair) but after enduring Margaret's 'begging and desireing for earnest' eventually relented and gave her four yards of 'diaper tape' from her coffer. Maggi promised to return the hair-lace the following day but casually kept it for six months, and during this time Ann was afflicted with great pains and covered in red spots 'somwhat like flea bitinge'. The pains left her when Maggi returned the hair-lace (which was strangely punctured) and rubbed it on her breast, as she had done when she had borrowed it. Maggi Hir borrowed a pair of gloves from David Thomas Jenkin of Llangadog and kept them for six months. While Maggi retained the gloves, David found he 'could not esc[h]ew or avoide her company' but after she had returned them he could not abide the sight of her. Lending was of course an expression of neighbourliness, and the reluctance to lend evidently revealed the desire not to recognize the relationship.[23]

Suspected witches begged and borrowed from neighbours in the same or adjoining parishes. Suspected Welsh witches were certainly not socially isolated, but accusations generally followed, as in England, quarrels and acts of rejection between neighbours. When requests for trifling loans and small gifts of food were refused, the refusal entailed the rejection of the reciprocities of neighbourliness. It is surely no coincidence that accusations of witchcraft were sometimes made only after a suspect had left a locality and was no longer a neighbour. Katherine Lewis was accused of witchcraft by some of her old neighbours after she had removed from Gumfreston to Tenby. Agnes Griffith was accused of bewitching a former neighbour's cattle only after she had moved to Cenarth from Pontrhydgelli, although there had been 'some variances and debates' between them for many years.[24]

Suspected witches do not seem to have been greatly separated in status from their accusers. The enmity expressed in witchcraft accusations was characteristically a relationship that had developed from conflicts among neighbours rather than between those separated by a status gulf. It emerges from depositions that there was often a long history of enmity between a suspected witch and her principal accuser. Agnes Griffith acknowledged 'variances and debates' with her accuser over many years and conceded that they 'yet doe continew in variance'. Dorothy Griffith of Llanasa, committed to the common gaol on suspicion of witchcraft, complained to the chief justice of Chester that her accuser bore great malice towards her and her family, and that there had been 'spleene and malice' between their two families for several years. A certificate signed by thirty-one neighbours attested that 'we never hard or knew any such malignitie in her nor was she or any of her kyn[d]red to our knowledge ever before attainted with any such suspicion.' Suspected witches were rarely without kin. Olly Powell of Loveston was a poor widow, but her interests were protected by her son-in-law who admonished one of her accusers, saying that 'he should be questioned for what he had done already to Olivia'. Accusations of witchcraft inevitably divided a community; some chose to give evidence against the suspect while others might elect to stand surety for the suspect's bail and appearance. Sometimes neighbours would advise a suspected witch to leave the district to avoid arrest. Two

Flintshire constables apprehended Anne Ellis at Renberry, Cheshire, after she was persuaded by neighbours in Penley to flee, 'being terrified with the apprehension of imprisonment'.[25]

A suspected witch indicted in Caernarfonshire was regarded by neighbours as an honest freeholder of good 'conversation' but – a fatal 'but' as it turned out – he was known to 'beare the malice'. Bearing malice was a besetting vice in early modern Wales that corroded neighbourliness. The desire to be even or to be 'quit' arose from a strong sense of personal worth and a corresponding feeling that insult and injury needed be avenged and that justice should be seen to be done. Witches and non-witches alike threatened to be even with their enemies. But while the non-witch would bide his or her time until the time was ripe for revenge, the witch was revealed because her revenge was swift and mysterious, disaster quickly overtaking her antagonist after the threat to get even. When David John of Llangadog fell out with Gwenllian David's son, she threatened 'to be quit or even' with him, and the very next morning David's cow was sick. After Katherine Rees had quarrelled with David Thomas, clerk, she announced 'she would be quits with him very speedily some other way', and immediately after he fell sick. When Harry James fell out with Agnes Griffith, she declared that she 'would be even with him', and within a week several of his best cattle died suddenly, and so witchcraft was suspected.[26]

Threatening phrases of this type were not peculiar to suspected witches; they were uttered by anybody and everybody who felt wronged in some way. In a revealing incident in 1584 – once again provided by the situation of refusal – Robert ap Edward maintained that he had been accused of child-rape after refusing to give the child's mother some yarn. She had often tried to beg from him and threatened 'she wolde be even w[i]th him', as he always refused her. David ap Ieuan ap Llewelyn complained in 1587 to the Montgomeryshire assize judges that the kinsmen of a suspected felon whom he was prosecuting had made 'threatning speeches', declaring that 'they woulde be revendged upon his goods or body, & yf they missed therof woulde sett his house one fire'. These were the actions of aggrieved men and women, who couldn't allow a matter to rest, but striking at an enemy's body or goods out of malice or for revenge was of course something that witches were readily imagined to do.[27]

The Devil

At one level – that of the witch-figure of the imagination – witchcraft was a complete fantasy, but at another level – that of actual accusations – witchcraft beliefs were grounded in a reality of destructive sentiments of malice and revenge familiar to everyone. It is interesting and revealing that men and women in early-modern Wales who had an utter horror of witchcraft would sometimes concede that some of their own actions had been prompted by the devil. The devil was held responsible for those occasions – which fill the gaol files – when men and women did the unaccountable or the unjustifiable.

The idea that the devil's influence might entail the loss of human self-control through evil makes intelligible a number of cases of bewitchment to love and religion and the attribution of madness to the effects of witchcraft.[28] Apparent irrationality might be attributed to witchcraft; indeed, to be called 'bewitched', with its implications of weakness and irrationality, was as offensive as being termed a witch. John ap Harry complained to the Flintshire assize judges in 1620 after he had been publicly called 'bewiched', with other 'by-names' and lewd terms, in front of parishioners at Caerwys parish church.[29]

Although suspected witches were formally accused of causing several deaths and illnesses, in a number of cases victims claimed no great injury beyond a temporary swooning, which might otherwise have appeared trivial. A mariner claimed in 1656 that he had met a witch at Llanasa, Flintshire, and was led by strange lights to a house where he then 'fell into a traunce and did not knowe what hee did or spoake all that night long till the dawning of the day.' Similarly in 1655 Rees Bowen described how after meeting Maggi Hir, a suspected witch, he was taken with a 'kind of forgetfulness of himself and strangeness not knowing at the instant where he stood', although he soon recovered his senses and went on his way, taking up the burden that had fallen from his back during the trance. More remarkable still were the adventures of a Cardiganshire labourer, Erasmus Thomas, who maintained that he had encountered three witches as he was walking home at dusk after a day's work. They 'struggled with him all the nighte', conveying him from place to place until daybreak when he recovered his senses and found himself outside a neighbour's house much bruised but otherwise unharmed. An interesting aspect of this late-seventeenth-century case is that Erasmus Thomas claimed to have recognized one of the witches, a fiddler's wife, and demanded compensation ('satisfaction') from her several times.[30]

Witchcraft was but a special instance of the devil's influence in human affairs. It was somewhat paradoxical that although accusations of witchcraft were rare, it was supposed that the devil intervened constantly in worldly affairs. Those who committed evil acts frequently confessed they had done so through the instigation of the devil. The devil ensnared people by overcoming their normal sense of morality, prompting them to do evil acts. The effects of the devil's influence were sometimes described as a kind of enchantment or forgetfulness and in that state of dissociation people were 'allured' (as one felon put it) to murder or steal. There are many examples in the examinations of suspected felons – both men and women – but only a selection can be given here. A Denbighshire gentleman confessed in prison to a murder saying 'that the devill did drive hym to come into the house where the fact was done'; Hugh ap William of Ruthin claimed that as he was cutting peat on a mountain 'the devill put into his myned to take and drive [away] six sheep'; similarly when Robert ap John was traversing Berain common he found himself 'possessed and instigated by the divell to drive away five sheep'; the maid who set the fire to her master's barn said there was 'noe reason for it but that the Divill did prick her'; when David Rhydderch was apprehended for theft he became 'sad and pensive' and went quietly with his captors after explaining that 'the Devill had strongly possessed him'; Owen David, asked why he had stolen some cloth from a rack, maintained that 'the Devell was buissy w[i]th him', otherwise he would never have committed 'such an ungraseful fact'.[31]

Suspected felons often maintained that they were 'led' by the devil to a particular place where they committed a crime. They appear to describe a feeling of compulsion (rather like that experienced by some modern shoplifters), but occasionally thieves provided very vivid descriptions of actual diabolic encounters that are more difficult to understand. Sometimes a disconcerting but not disagreeable or monstrous diabolic apparition would lead a man to commit a theft. In 1654 Thomas John, a Carmarthenshire labourer accused of felonious theft, explained to a magistrate that as he was returning from Llangennech fair at night 'some thinges' appeared in front of him 'in the likenesse of 2 men and one woman skippinge and dancing' leading him to a black heifer grazing at the wayside. Thomas John then drove the beast before him, still accompanied by the leaping and dancing apparitions, until he came to Nantyrarian, 'silver stream' or 'stream of money'. There the apparitions left him, 'makinge a noise before and behind him as if a man did strike a table boord very hard with a trencher'. It was a significant moment. Thomas John decided to drive the cow home, and the following day sold it at Llandovery for thirty-four shillings. This moment of temptation was to put him on trial for his life. The tempter of another cattle thief, Ieuan John ap Howell, was agreeably sociable but more obviously diabolic. In 1612 Ieuan confessed to a petty constable that as he was travelling to Narberth fair he met the devil in the guise of a man, that is apart from his 'having two great hornes on his head'. They shared a pot of ale at the fair, and slept a little, but on the way home the devil persuaded Ieuan to steal a fat cow, promising to save him from hanging for the theft. As it turned out, this was an empty promise.[32]

The devil was a persistent tempter, and evidently had no trouble speaking either in English or Welsh or appearing wherever he wanted to. In 1630 a Flintshire gentleman, John Foulkes of Cilowen, was troubled by 'dreames and distracc[i]ons of mind', which he sought to drive away by reading the Bible. Eventually an 'apparic[i]on or vision' in the form of a man with a black beard appeared in his bedchamber telling him in Welsh (as the justices carefully noted) that 'this woman which lieth in bedd with thee will in few daies take away thy life.' In the morning Foulkes told his wife about this ghastly messenger, and she protested spiritedly that she bore him no malice, 'What, do yow thinke that I would doe yow any harme? I am not such a Jew.' The black-bearded man appeared again, convincing Foulkes that his wife intended to kill him and remarry. The following day Foulkes murdered his wife with her 'batting-staff' as she sat 'pleasant and merie', 'spinning upon a little wheele and singing'. The dreadful deed done, Foulkes recovered himself and set off for St Asaph, resolving to place himself in the custody of the bishop or another magistrate.[33]

It is apparent from some examinations that occasionally felons felt themselves pursued by the devil. The examination of Robert ap Hugh ap Ieuan ap William before the Council in the Marches had to be abandoned after the suspected thief suddenly wept and beat his breast, 'cryeinge upon God to deffend hym from ii Devills in the lykenes of ii greate black doggs w[i]th whyte longe teeth and ffyery tonges.' The next morning Robert's responses to questions were so unreasonable that further examination was stayed. Robert proved to be a turbulent prisoner, breaking a strong lock and going among the other prisoners with a knife. At his trial he maintained a rigid silence, refusing to plead, and as a consequence may have suffered the terrible punishment inflicted on the maliciously mute of being pressed to death.[34]

Claims that crimes were instigated by the devil have a frequency and consistency that attest to the popular belief in a constant and provocative diabolic presence in society. The idea seems to have been that the devil was able to overcome people's wills through their lack of grace and provoke them to murder, steal, and abuse their neighbours. A Montgomeryshire housebreaker explained that he was prompted to enter a house by the instigation of the devil 'for the want of Gods grace, the gyde of all good accions'. Those who lacked God's grace were vulnerable to the assaults of the devil. A Pembrokeshire woman explained that she drowned her children because 'she wanted grace'; similarly another Pembrokeshire woman explained that she abandoned her base child 'in regard she wanted grace'. Those lacking sufficient grace found the devil's temptation irresistible, and a crime was inevitable. When the remains of stolen flesh and tallow were discovered in Hugh ap Rees's house in 1625, he simply said sadly, 'It is a thinge that wold be, for the Divell did tempt him to do hit', and could only ask his neighbours to pardon him.[35]

Those who habitually led anti-social lives might perceive themselves as already damned. They were not witches but behaved as if they might be. John Stonne, accused of many crimes and misdemeanours in 1648, publicly 'dranke a health to ye divill in a heathenishe and barbarous manner'. He often abused his neighbours, and when asked to forbear would rise up in a choler saying, 'he had butt one soule and that was damned long before, and what cared he for that.' Those who led evil lives might start calling upon the devil, cursing themselves and others in his name, wishing that he would carry away their enemies. Lawrence ap Evan, a Pembrokeshire husbandman, 'daily threatened his neighbours with cursing and terrible oeths' in 1634, including the idiosyncratic, 'The devill rott off his arms'. This type of cursing might become habitual for some but was utterly repugnant to most people. A Cardiganshire servant-maid described how she had left her place within a week, 'and would not for a world serve in such a house' again, because of her new mistress's prophane cursing. She often heard Katherine, wife of David Lloyd of Llanfihangel-y-Creuddyn, 'in a most wicked manner offer her husband unto the divell'. Moreover, she would unpleasantly disturb her servants' meals: 'her manner was to curse the meate, and wishe it might proue their poison, if they did not worke sufficiently for it'.[36]

Some (compounding their evil) even persuaded others to call upon the devil, and the consequences could be appalling. This seems to have been the import of a rather elusive case from late-Elizabethan Montgomeryshire. Lawrence Harryes of Llangurig confessed to having murdered his wife because, as he said, he was weary of her 'odious life'. She had beaten him on the night before the murder, but Lawrence described a further strange 'unkyndnes' that had arisen between them: 'she went about to entize him and allure him to say c[er]ten words in worship of the dyvell'. At length she persuaded him to repeat certain blasphemous words. As a consequence (so it seems), the morning after Lawrence killed his wife with an axe ('hatchet glave'), inflicting a single mortal blow to the head. Lawrence claimed not to remember the event since he was 'allured', presumably by the devil, and was 'not in his p[er]fect memory in the aforenowne', but recalled that his wife did 'at divers tymes request him to kill her'. Lawrence confessed to having killed her, though instigated by the devil, and at the assizes was found guilty of murder.[37] Confessions of diabolic temptation were not really in the nature of extenuating excuses. They did not save a felon from the gallows – they merely testified to a suspect's weakness and lack of grace, and the truth of the view sometime formally incorporated in an indictment that a felony had been committed 'without the fear of God and by the instigation of the devil'.

Speech Acts and Witchcraft: Blessing and Cursing

Protection from the devil and against injuries and misfortune generally were sought in appeals to God for His grace. A late-sixteenth-century account of popular religion ('superstitious practices') in Wales establishes that the routines of daily life were constantly punctuated by blessings and petitionary prayers from getting up and leaving the house in the morning to shutting the windows at night. *Rhad Duw ar y gwaith*: 'God bless the work' and similar salutations were common greetings between neighbours. If anything untoward happened, the characteristic saying was to the effect, 'You have not crossed yourself well to day'. Those who succumbed to the temptations of the devil were urged to bless themselves. In moments of extreme danger and temptation, Welsh men and woman called upon God and the saints for their protection, and blessed themselves by making the sign of the cross.[38] Some affecting instances of this are preserved among the examinations in the gaol files. The words and action of a poor Montgomeryshire woman in extremis, uttered in a moment of panic as she desperately tried to conceal the remains of a stolen sheep in a mire, were recorded in evidence against her in 1584. Catherine ferch Rees 'tooke up her hande and blessed her sealfe', saying '†*Du a Mayre am degludie*', that is 'God and O[u]r Lady save me from shame', the symbol indicating that she had made the sign of the cross.[39]

The importance of blessing was exactly complemented by the importance of cursing. In Wales (as in Ireland) there was a strong medieval tradition of religious

cursing by clerics.[40] Literary and legal sources testify to the continuing importance of spoken curses of different type in late-medieval and early-modern Wales,
and the poetic tradition of satire had maledictory elements. There is evidence
for a pre-Reformation tradition of collective, ritualized cursing in Wales that
offended Protestants as blasphemous. 'In the marches of Wales', William Tyndale
observed in the early sixteenth century, 'it is the manner, if any man have an ox
or a cow stolen, he cometh to the curate, and desireth him to curse the stealer;
and he commandeth the parish to give him, every man, God's curse and his.'[41]
Ritualised communal cursing involving priests did not survive the Reformation.
Post-Reformation cursing was highly individual rather than collective, and
without a sacerdotal aspect, but not all private curses were equally effective.
Maledictions by person placed in certain situations were regarded as particularly
solemn and effective: deathbed cursing (discussed below) and parental maledictions were especially powerful. The felicity of a parent's blessing, sometimes
solemnly given to a kneeling child, was matched by the horror with which a
parent's curse was regarded. When John Lloyd ap Richard of Sutton Green said
that his mother and brothers should be hanged if they had their deserts ('right'),
his mother 'fell down on her knees and cursed him'. David ap John of Broniarth
repudiated an attempted reconciliation with his son, John David, by falling upon
his knees and cursing his son and daughter-in-law, afterwards saying 'John David
was the Divels sonne and not his sonne, and that he hadd no p[ar]te of hime.'
Cursing by the poor was also regarded as potent; indeed, so much so that the
poor might be hired for their maledictory potential. In 1612, according to a Star
Chamber allegation, twenty paupers sat down to a mock feast at Soughton, near
Oswestry, at the invitation of a Welsh versifier, and afterwards fell down on their
knees and 'lifting up their hands to heaven' cursed their host's enemies.[42]

Numerous dramatic cases of ritualised cursing are reported from the Welsh
Marches, but it was not so much that 'ritual cursing was a particular feature of the
Welsh Border country', as Keith Thomas has suggested but, rather, that such characteristic Welsh behaviour was inevitably conspicuous with the juxtaposition of two
cultures in the March. Cursers in Herefordshire and Shropshire, usually with Welsh
names, were regularly presented at the ecclesiastical courts. A particularly revealing
confrontation occurred in 1617 when the churchwarden of Westhide, Herefordshire,
complained that Joanna Powell had cursed him 'in Welsh language, kneeling down
upon her bare knees and holding up her hands, but otherwise the words he could
not understand.'[43]

Numerous presentments for cursing and scolding were made in the Welsh
courts throughout the seventeenth century, particularly against women, especially in the latter part of the century when there were occasional multiple
presentments of scolds by grand juries.[44] Indictments for barratry, the habitual
maintaining of quarrels, are scattered throughout the legal record. Katherine
ferch Edward of Ruthin, 'a dayly disturber, curser, and vexer of her neighbours', was indicted several times as a barratrix in 1622, and, as she persisted in

'scoldeinge, curseing, and disturbeinge the neighbours', a warrant was issued for her good behaviour. A number of different speech acts are referred to here. Legal terminology, especially the offence of barratry, certainly did not reflect popular distinctions between ways of speaking, although the longer presentments might differentiate between obviously different opprobrious speech acts. Alice, wife of Robert Mule of Llanfwrog, did 'usually braule and scould with her next neighbours, as namely with Robert ap David, his wife, and others', but on one occasion did 'fall downe upon her knees and curse Robert ap David'. Cursing was not scolding, although the terms were sometimes conflated in legal documents, and some scolders were evidently also cursers. Scolding generally involved a public and prolonged face-to-face harangue, which was might be reciprocated, sometimes accompanied by emphatic gestures. Cursing was a more formal and ritualized public demonstration of outrage than scolding, and the object of the malediction did not necessarily witness the event.[45]

Formal cursing was a petitionary prayer addressed to God, by those who considered themselves wronged, for retribution on the wrongdoer. The malediction was often delivered in a kneeling posture of supplication with the hands upraised to heaven. Occasionally women intensified the drama of the curse by baring their breasts in an additional emphatic gesture of insult and protest. Cursers generally called for the destruction of a wrongdoer's person or property. Katherine, wife of Oliver Rees ap Humffrey, was presented at Machynlleth Court Leet in 1655 for cursing a neighbour 'by prayeinge and wishing with her lifted handes towardes heaven that he shold not be worth an yearleinge sheepe.' Similarly in 1613 in Pembrokeshire, Elizabeth Harris, wife of William Walter of Trevrane, yeoman, fell upon her knees 'in an outrageous manner' and prayed that the curse of God might fall on Jane Walter, trusting to 'see the daie that Jane should not be worth a cowe or a cawlffe.' In 1681 Elizabeth Parry fell down upon her knees and cursed Elizabeth ferch Richard, wishing God would send 'wild fire' from heaven to consume her house. Lucy Richards was 'a common curser of her neighbours' in Welshpool in a 'most dangerous and dampnable sorte'. She had prayed that Jeffrey Lloyd's house might be 'burned over his heade', that Lewis Reynolds 'might be hanged in jubbettes as one Ellis was', and that his fate and the fates of his friends and kinsmen 'might be an example to all the world', and those who harboured or maintained him might not prosper.[46]

Welsh cursers often favoured punishment by the destructive but cleansing power of fire, as some examples will have already suggested, but there was an uncomfortable association with the concealed act of the arsonist. Eleanor Owen of Morton Anglicorum, said to be a woman of 'turbulent and unquiet carriage', reviled and reproached her neighbours, frequently cursing them and their cattle. One Sunday she cursed Kenrick David's livestock 'wishinge that the cattell were on fyer'. On another occasion she 'scowlded at' Robert Davies when he was grafting fruit trees, and then cursed him 'wishing him and his worke on a light fyer'. In 1670 the wives of Edward Jones, cobbler, and Peter Lloyd, gent., met in the open street at Wrexham, and the cobbler's wife fell upon her knees cursing Lloyd and his family, hoping before long to see all his houses on fire. Lloyd apprehensively kept watch night and day to prevent any fire, and petitioned the justices of the peace for help in reducing a danger to the whole town of Wrexham.[47] Fire was regarded with particular horror in the timber-framed towns of the Welsh Marches, where there had been some catastrophic fires in the sixteenth and seventeenth centuries.[48]

In most instances cursing was reported in English-language presentments, but the uncompromisingly comprehensive nature of ritualised cursing becomes apparent when the actual Welsh words of a malediction are given. In 1684 Jane, the wife of Edward Lloyd of Llanynys, Denbighshire, in a dispute about her home, cursed her opponents, saying, '*melltith Duw ir neb a ddelo i'm tu /i/ om anfodd*' ('the curse of God on anyone who comes into my house against my will'), and solemnly prayed that her enemies would never prosper: '*Na chaffo byth gam rhwdd, na byth rhwydeb nag iechyd a gymero nhu i*' ('He who takes my house shall never have an easy step, prosperity, nor good health').[49] The ritual curse was not intended to smite its victim with immediate death but to punish the recipient with a life strewn with difficulties and disaster, and the curse could be visited on the descendants of the offending person. The idea of prolonged punishment is clear in the rhythmic and incremental curse attributed in nineteenth-century sources to the 'Llanddona Witches', and said to have been a common imprecation:

> *Crwydro y byddo am oesoedd lawer;*
> *Ac yn mhob cam, camfa;*
> *Yn mhob camfa, codwm;*
> *Yn mhob codwm, tori asgwrn;*
> *Nid yr asgwrn mwyaf na'r lleiaf,*
> *Ond asgwrn chwil corn ei wddw bob tro.*

(May he wander for ages many; and at every step, a stile; at every stile, a fall; at every fall, a broken bone; not the largest, nor the least bone, but the chief neck bone, every time.)[50]

A curse made from a death-bed was particularly solemn. A dying person brought to an untimely end often 'left' his or her death on those who had inflicted the mortal injury. There was no question of forgiveness for the perpetrator; the death would cry out to be avenged until punished by God. Edward Hughes, churchwarden of St George (Llan Sain Siôr), Denbighshire, was reduced to such 'disquiett and sicknesse' by the 'tormenting language and threatnings' of the parson's wife that he solemnly cursed her on his deathbed. Five witnesses were able to testify that 'he had left his death upon her and his curse and [the curse of] his three children upon the p[ar]sons wife.' Some of the dying man's solemn words were recorded in Welsh: "*yglanastra i ar Mrs Williams yn fyw ag yn farw*', that is 'My curse on Mistress Williams in life and in death.' This seems to have been a customary formula with '*g(a)lanastra*' having the meaning of a death crying out for revenge. In 1689 a dying Denbigh glover named his assailant and solemnly declared, '*fynglanastra /i/ am plant a fo arno fe*', that is 'May my curse and my children's be upon him'.[51] Death might come too quickly to allow time for formally 'leaving' a death, but sometimes corpses bled in the presence of their murderers in a mute but dramatic appeal for justice.[52]

The gendered aspects of cursing need emphasising. Men might sometimes curse other men, but these cases seem to have been rare and involved, significantly, parties of greatly differing status. In 1658 a Glamorgan labourer, Thomas David ap David, cursed a gentleman, Robert Jones of Llanfair, by 'falling upon his knees and saying, I pray God the curse of God fall upon thee and they children'. But men rarely – if ever – formally cursed women, except in the special circumstance of the situation of death when 'leaving their deaths'. Women tended to curse other women; it was therefore especially noticed when a woman, like Lucy Richards of Welshpool, was an indiscriminate curser of her neighbours 'as well men as women'. Cursing was at its most dramatic and dangerous when crossing boundaries of age, gender, or status. This inevitably occurred because cursing was interlinked with notions of justice and the concern to punish wrongdoers. Cursing was therefore often a weapon of the socially and physically weak against the strong, particularly women against men, and sometimes dramatically so.[53]

The ritualised cursing of Baron Lewis Owen and the Earl of Pembroke by poor women deprived of their sons by these harriers of thieves and outlaws entered Welsh oral tradition and was remembered long after the events. Lord Herbert of Chirbury preserved a family tradition about the cursing of the Earl of Pembroke in 1468 when he and his brother (Sir Richard Herbert) were sent by Edward IV to quell disorder in north Wales. On Anglesey the Herberts captured seven brothers, the perpetrators of 'many mischiefs and murders'. Pembroke 'thinking it fit to root out so wicked a progeny' commanded that the brothers should all be hanged. The mother of the condemned men upon her knees implored Pembroke to spare one of her seven sons at the very least. Pembroke could make no distinction between the brothers, finding them equally guilty, and commanded that they should all be executed together. The aggrieved mother carrying a rosary ('with a pair of woollen beads on her arms') went down on her knees and cursed him, 'praying God's mischief might fall to him in the first Battle he should make'. The following year a pensive Richard Herbert reminded his brother of this curse on the eve of the disastrous battle of Edgecote. A similar curse followed the capture of a large number of outlaws and felons ('above four score') by Lewis Owen in the lordship of Mawddwy. The mother of two felons pleaded with Lewis Owen to spare one of her sons. When Owen refused, the mother solemnly cursed him baring her breasts, saying 'These yellow breasts have given suck to those, who shall wash their hands in your blood.' Not long after Lewis Owen was murdered by the infamous 'Gwylliaid Cochion Mawddwy', the red-headed bandits of Mawddwy.[54]

Formal cursing seems to have irrevocably altered the relationship between curser and cursed, especially when gender and status boundaries were crossed, and set in train events that could lead to mortal tragedies. A nuanced Flintshire case shows that when a woman cursed a man, he might respond to verbal aggression with physical violence . In 1584, after a dispute over a water source, William Lewis confronted Marsli ferch Thomas, asking 'why she and her children dyd use to curse hym and hys m[aste]r?' Marsli responded gnomically, 'Yf yow deserve yt God send yt yow, otherwise yow shall not nede to care', and again fell on her knees and cursed those who did her wrong. Marsli's husband, fearing that William would harm her, openly declared he would beat her, although William declared grimly he would 'be quyte' with her another time. Marsli's relatives sought to protect her by informing a justice of the threat, but later Marsli was killed by William when their altercation was resumed in an alehouse after she had rejected a piece of bread and cheese offered, perhaps ironically, by him.[55]

The formal invocation of God's wrath was not easily disregarded. A seventeenth-century presentment refers to the 'greate greefe and extreme terror of all the heerers' of a curse, and it was not unknown for those who had been cursed to die. An eighteenth-century chancellor of Bangor diocese was said to have been driven to an early grave by the implacable cursing of an excommunicate, Dorothy Ellis (Dorti Ddu) of Llannor, who lay in wait for him outside the churchyard, 'raising her clothes and falling on her bare knees, cursing him frightfully with all her strength'.[56]

Those who frequently resorted to cursing might acquire a reputation for witchcraft, especially when cross-gender cursing was involved. In 1674 at Llandegla, Denbighshire, John Parry did 'curse and banne' Mary, wife of Thomas Lloyd, who subsequently fell dangerously ill and died within a month. Parry, a man of 'lewd conversacion' and a night-walker, confessed to a neighbour that his 'divelish and inhumane thoughts' had caused seven of Edward ap Evan's cattle to run mad. Anne Ellis of Penley, Flintshire, indicted for witchcraft in 1657, seems to have been tormented by her neighbours' children. When taxed with cursing Richard Hughes, a boy who suddenly became crippled, Anne responded, 'Why did he pisse downe her chimley?' The boy denied that 'he did make water downe her chimney in her meat', but he claimed that nonetheless Anne had 'most heinously ... pray'd God that I might go lame and that my nimblenesse might be slackened'. Later, as he was playing stool-ball, he felt as if a sword had been run through his thigh, fell down and was bedridden afterwards. Anne Ellis also became unappeasably angry after Margaret Hughes and other small children had entered her house while she was away and eaten some of her bread. A neighbour pleaded with Anne 'not to curse the children nor do them any hurt', but Anne did not respond beyond muttering to herself, and one of the children fell sick having 'a great lump of the bigness of a hen's egge' under her arm, 'continueing in great paine skeriking, crying and lying upon her face trembling'. In Pembrokeshire Elizabeth, wife of Rees David ap Ieuan of Llandysilio, was an habitual curser who was suspected of witchcraft after she had furiously chased two trespassing calves out of her husband's corn 'bitterly cursing them', after which they died in a strange manner. Shortly after she cursed a straying pig, which expired the same night. The owner of these animals was a poor man, and 'much greeving at the losse' accused Elizabeth of witchcraft, asking 'why she bewitched his sow to death?'[57]

There were significant correspondences between witchcraft and cursing. Cursers like suspected witches were generally (but not exclusively) women and, moreover, cursing and witchcraft accusations occurred in similar social situations, generally following the quarrels between neighbours. In Wales, where there was little elaboration of witchcraft beliefs in the forms of images, charms, and familiars, the connection between cursing and witchcraft was all the more marked. Keith Thomas has drawn attention to the close association between witchcraft and cursing, and the puzzle that a suspected witch might have invoked God's curse. Thomas Cooper, writing in 1617, clearly expressed a paradox familiar to contemporaries in both seventeenth-century England and Wales: 'When a bad-tongued woman shall curse a party, and death shall shortly follow, this is a shrewd token that she is a witch' even when 'invocating upon her bare knees (for so the manner is) the vengeance of God.'[58]

A petition sent to the Denbighshire justices of the peace in 1670 reveals the highly ambiguous nature of cursing. The petitioner, Sarah Poole, described the manner and effect of several ritual curses made by her neighbour: 'Elizabeth Parry came not long ago to my house ... and scandalised me with most filthy and uncivil language and likewise kneeled down upon her knees and cursed me, whereupon I fell suddenly sick and so continued for seven days.' Some years before, Elizabeth had come to scold Sarah 'about some triviall occation', and Sarah asked her to refrain lest she woke her child. Elizabeth responded, 'The Devil bless him and thee also', whereupon 'the child fell sick and dyed before nine o'clock the same night' and, Sarah continued, 'I myselfe fell sick and soe continued three years after'. On another occasion, it was alleged that Elizabeth had said to a woman milking, 'The Devil bless the work', and at these words 'the cow fell down upon her and nearly smothered her'. The inversion of witch and ritual curser is readily apparent in this account: Elizabeth Parry who had formally invoked divine retribution or God's curse was accused of uttering its opposite, the devil's blessing.[59]

Witchcraft appears to have been conceptualised as a form of cursing, whether a malediction was formally spoken or inwardly thought. It is consistent, therefore, that witchcraft – even when a formal curse had not been uttered – was considered relieved by the conceptual opposite of a curse: a blessing formally uttered by the reputed witch over her alleged victim. Those who believed themselves bewitched almost invariably sought out the suspect to obtain a blessing. When Henry John James of Diserth, Flintshire, was suspected of bewitching some oxen, their anxious owner sent for him so 'that he might bless the oxen, conceiving thereby that his charm if he had any would cease.' Persuaded by the entreaties of a local curate, Henry 'prayed God to bless them' and afterwards (according to witnesses) 'the oxen began to mend daily'. Again, after several calamities had followed the 'muttering and curseing' of the reputed witch Olly Powell of Loveston, Pembrokeshire, one of her supposed victims confronted Olly in a harvest field and she was forced to go on her knees and say 'God bless him', whereupon it was said 'he was perfectly well to the admiration of all present.' The owner of a sick cow also forced Olly Powell to say 'God bless ye cow' and she added, for good measure, 'God bless him and all that belongs to him within and without'. Similarly, Anne Ellis, a formal curser from Flintshire, was persuaded to bless cattle and several children she was thought to have bewitched. She placed her hand in a benedictory gesture on one bewitched child, saying 'God bless thee, thou shalt mend after this'. Sick children blessed by Anne recovered – as was 'known to all the neighbours' and others further afield. Thomas Addams of Northwood, Shropshire, who kept a 'good house which hadd often releived' Anne, sent for her when he had a sick child, but under the pretence that he needed stockings knitted. When she arrived, Addams asked Anne 'not to take it ill that he sent for her [for a blessing] for that he hard shee had bewitched many persons'.[60]

Other methods of counteracting witchcraft involving attacks on a suspected witch's property or person were not unknown in Wales. These attacks seem to have been rare but they could be brutal. In 1673 Cicely Holland, 'a very aged, weake and impotent person', said to have been a hundred years old, was found beaten and burnt to death sometime after she had confessed to William Alloway that she had formerly done him 'some hurt in his goods'. Alloway, his wife, and two servants had assaulted Cicely with a poker and brands, burning her about the face, particularly in the eyes and tongue where (one supposes) it was thought that witchcraft was expressed through the evil power of the eye and through cursing. Alloway's wife also cut off a lock of Cicely's hair and burnt it in the fire. The practice of overcoming a witch by drawing her blood, evidently a task of some difficulty, seems to have informed another Pembrokeshire murder, although witchcraft is not specifically mentioned. In 1631 Elen David was violently assaulted in a dispute over a hedge and cried out in Welsh to this effect, 'Oh you have broken my bloode, Oh he hath killed me'! Her assailant, not seeing any blood, replied, 'O whoore, witch, is thy bloud white bloud?' before plucking her by the nose and saying that 'it was noe great matter to kill such an ould witch or jade as shee was'. Cicely's attacker demanded to see her blood, but 'noe blood seemed to distill or issue from her.'[61]

When a case is fully contextualised it seems clear that scratching or burning a suspected witch was generally a kind of reserve strategy, undertaken only after the suspect had refused to pronounce a blessing. When Anne Ellis refused to come and bless the sick John Birch, one of his daughters took some thatch from the suspected witch's house and burnt it under his nose and he recovered. Again, when Olly Powell refused to bless a sick child and cursed him instead, her accuser said he would have some of her blood. After much struggling and 'faire words' she put out her hand and bade him do his worst but 'he should have no blood of hers'. He took a nail from his pocket and thrust it twice into the flesh between Olly's thumb and forefinger, but only after much squeezing managed to force out an 'inconsiderable' drop of blood. 'Gett thee gone', responded Olly,

'for before thou wilt be att home thy child will be well.' Elizabeth Browninge
sent for Katherine Lewis suspecting that her pigs were bewitched. The supposed
witch and her husband eventually arrived (but only after several messengers
had been sent to fetch her), and Elizabeth Browninge told her that 'she had don
hurt to her sowes [and] wished her to do them good agayne'. Katherine Lewis
promptly fell upon her knees 'cursing and railing', uttering several great oaths,
saying (according to her accuser) that 'she had but a life to lose and yf she were
not a witche her selfe she would cause them that should do it.' This would have
been a remarkable admission of guilt, but the servant-maid's account of the confrontation between suspect and accuser seems more plausible than her dame's.
According to the maid, Katherine Lewis fell on her knees and made a solemn
conditional self-curse, 'and wished she might never enjoy any thinge yf she did
any hurt unto them'. This did not satisfy Elizabeth Browninge, who told the suspect that 'she would have some of her blood'. At this point Katherine's husband,
who carried a hay-fork, intervened, saying gravely 'yf thowe take her bludd I
will have thyne for it, for I thought of such a matter before I came hither.'[62]

It was of course with understandable reluctance that suspected witches pronounced
their blessings, for they were taken as admissions of guilt. After giving her blessing
under duress, Anne Ellis could only protest that she had not done any hurt 'but hop-
eeth she hath done good for that God's blessing must doe good [when given] by those
that have power and grace to speak it'.[63] The idea of cursing was interlinked with
notions of justice, and it is clear that different assessments of the curse's justification
led to accusations of witchcraft after formal cursing. Apparently successful maledictions could be explained alternatively as justifiable curses or unjustifiable bewitching.
From the standpoint of a suspected witch, curses were a justified response to injustice;
but from the standpoint of the accuser the reputed witch's malediction was an unjus-
tified response to a relatively innocuous offence. Paradoxically, as Keith Thomas has
observed, 'it tended to be the [suspected] witch who was morally in the right and the
[alleged] victim who was in the wrong.'[64] It is apparent from the Welsh evidence that
'cursing' and 'bewitching' were the alternative interpretations of the same conflict
situation by the author and recipient of a malediction, and the active or performative
nature of blessing and cursing as speech acts was an inseparable part of the definition
of witchcraft.[65] The logic of Welsh witchcraft was this: a curse has been pronounced;
as everyone knows God permits curses to work where there has been injustice. But in
this particular case (as the recipient of the curse sees it) there has been no injustice but
the curse has worked. The efficacy of the curse can therefore be attributed only to the
devil. By this logic of inversions the witch's curse is undone by another performative
speech act. The suspected witch was forced to utter God's blessing over the alleged
victim. In this way formal cursing was redefined as witchcraft.

4

'SWARMS OF SOOTHSAYERS AND ENCHANTERS': MAGICAL SPECIALISTS AFTER THE REFORMATION

Protestants reformers were outraged by the 'swarmes of southsaiers and enchanters' infesting late-sixteenth-century Wales. John Penry, the Puritan, an almost exact contemporary of the demonologist Robert Holland, uncompromisingly urged in 1587, citing Leviticus, that they should 'die the death'. Protestant radicals argued that charmers and soothsayers, despite their apparently helpful magic, were as bad as witches: they derived their power from the devil and should be punished accordingly. But although there were many magical practitioners – indeed, 'swarms' of them – they were rarely prosecuted in the secular courts in Wales. The reluctance to prosecute probably arose as much from the difficulty of demonstrating diabolical association as from popular regard for cunning-folk. Many thought that wise-men and wise-women performed useful if not indispensable services. As Tudur says in Robert Holland's dialogue, 'As for cunning-men and cunning-women (*swynwyr a swynwragedd*) we cannot be without them, they do a lot of good (at least most of them do) for man and beast'. But there were some complex issues. Protestant reformers often attacked magic and superstition in terms of a residual Catholicism. John Penry was particularly forthright in condemning soothsayers and charmers who had (he claimed) 'strocken ... an astonishing reverence of the fairies into the harts of our silly people'. From this proceeded, he fulminated, the 'open defending of Purgatory and the Real presence, praying unto images & with other infinit monsters'.[1]

The Protestant attack on magic was inseparable from an attack on Catholic ritual, doctrine, and forms of worship. Clergy of the new order condemned priests of the old order as magicians, and there was always anxiety on the part of radical Protestants that the Counter-Reformation would make some headway in Wales. However, there was acknowledgement also that there existed outside the institutional framework of the church a popular religion, neither fully Catholic nor Protestant, that drew upon pre-Reformation beliefs and practices and also attributed helpful, positive qualities to soothsayers and charmers and other magico-religious specialists. Popular religion was essentially practical rather than doctrinal, and charmers and soothsayers have to be understood in relation to the popular Christianity in early-modern Wales that was concerned with the vicissitudes of everyday life, saving the body for the present as well as the soul for the future.[2]

Practical Religion

Protestant reformers regarded the medieval church in Wales as magical and super-stitious. Bishop Richard Davies, the Elizabethan translator, in his heartfelt prefatory 'letter to the Welsh people' in the 1567 New Testament, sweepingly declared that there 'still flourished and reigned all manner of falsehood, idolatry, excess, super-stition, charms and incantations'.[3] Many religious images and places of pilgrimage had been destroyed, and with them the physical focus of much petitionary prayer, but frequent and polemical references to 'superstitions' within Wales show that some traditional religious practices were surprisingly resilient. Alongside the official reformed religion there existed a popular religion which maintained many tradi-tional practices, especially in relation to protective prayers, continuing adherence to the cult of the holy well, and respect for the saints. A landscape full of place-names commemorating the saints and their actions functioned as a kind of memory surface for the retrieval and reproduction of the traditions of the saints. The well-cult was impressively resilient despite the destruction of some notable wells that had attracted many pilgrims. St Winifred's Well at Holywell survived the Reformation and retained a reputation for miraculous cures (including the relief of witchcraft) that was exploited by the Counter-Reformation clergy.[4] However, visiting St Winifred's and other saints' wells and chapels was not necessarily a recusant activity, although sometimes it was. Offering at wells was a clandestine action undertaken by many Welshmen and -women who by the late sixteenth century would not have called themselves Catholics. Holy wells in Wales remained the focus of much pop-ular religious activity, and some would have renewed significance in the eighteenth century.[5]

Reform marginalised many aspects of practical religion from the institutional framework of the Church, as many clerics must have recognised. The special status of priests as the ordained intermediaries between their parishioners and God and the saints, as the celebrants of the sacrifice of the Mass who administered the other sacraments, sole dispensers of absolution, and with a special knowledge of effica-cious prayers, and the ability to write them down as protective charms, was much reduced.

Occasionally an Elizabethan cleric acquired a special reputation as the magical protectors of his flock. The powers of Syr Water (or Sir Walter), a Monmouthshire parson, were so great that he routed a devil that had taken refuge on a rock and threatened the town of Usk with a great flood – or so an Elizabethan poet claimed in a remarkable poem apparently addressed to the living cleric. During the tempest Water with relics and pyx called and faced down the devil, apparently using charcoal (possibly to draw a protective circle) during the exorcism. Syr Water is described in extravagant terms as a miracle-worker and binder of devils, and the poet compares him with Simon Magus and other Biblical and legendary figures. Exorcisms had a significant place in post-Reformation religious propaganda, but the exorcism at Usk was not exploited in this way. It seems probable that Syr Water was a religious conservative, and that for poet and people the exorcism at Usk demonstrated in a traditional way the power and sanctity of their priest.[6]

There are occasional, revealing glimpses of the more routine magical activities of unreformed mid-Tudor clerics in Wales. The steward of Elfael lordship complained *c.* 1540 that the parson of Aberedw, Radnorshire, 'for lucre of money' charmed sick horses, cattle, and other beasts, as well as children. The parson, it was said, 'work-ith writynges' – presumably protective prayers – which were set over the doorways of beast-houses, made holy water 'without any salte' for the animals and prepared prayers or charms ('writynges') to hang about the necks of children who cried in their sleep. Remarkably, a few 'writings' of this type have survived; they are in Latin and name the person to be protected.[7] The parson of Aberedw was consulted daily by people from the surrounding district, some travelling up to twenty miles for a remedy. In this case charming was explicitly associated with other unreformed activities. The parson was also accused of not observing the King's injunctions (1538) concerning the recitation of the Articles of Faith, and failing to expunge from missal and breviary the names of the popes and St Thomas Becket.[8]

It became common to associate magic with unreformed religion. An Elizabethan parson of Hirnant, Montgomeryshire, castigated several parishioners for being 'offerers unto wells' as well as 'seekers unto charmers'.[9] Charmers flourished in the context of a popular, practical religion that placed particular importance on prayers as a protection from danger and misfortune, and for relief from illness. A cleric claimed that the continuing popularity of these prayers in eighteenth-century Wales contrived to 'jostle out' of the country the more edifying prayers favoured by the clergy. A few popular prayers have survived from the early-modern period but only because they were collected to show their unedifying character. Prayers invoking the personal protection of the saints were recited in the morning and in the evening. The following 'popish' morning prayer was preserved by Humphrey Foulkes (d. 1737), a scholarly Denbighshire parson and antiquary, who heard it recited by an old man near Bala *c.* 1700 as he had learnt it from his grandmother:

> *Pan godwy'r boreu yn gynta,*
> *Yn nawdd Beino yn benna;*
> *Yn nawdd Kerrig, nawdd Patrig,*
> *Yn nawdd [y] gwr gwyn Bendigedig;*

Yn nawdd Owain ben lluman llu,
Ag yn nessa yn Nawdd Iessu.[10]

(When I get up in the morning [I am] under the protection of Beuno mainly; under the protection of Curig and Patrick, under the protection of the holy and sacred man; under the protection of Owain, the chief banner of an army, and next under the protection of Jesus.)

There are some oddities about this prayer, especially the reference to Owain, and it may not be entirely genuine, but it certainly illustrates the way in which the protection of saints in the late-medieval tradition continued to be invoked in early modern Wales. The invocation of God and the saints was central to a 'creed' repeated at night:

Credo fechan, credo lân, credo i Dduw ac Ifan,
Rhag y dwfr, rhac y tân, rhag y sarphes goch ben llydan:
Cerddais fynudd ac or fynudd
a gwelwn Fair wen ar ei gobennydd,
ai hangel, angel ufudd,
a Duw ei hun yn degdydd [sic; read 'dedwydd']:
ar gwr llwyd a'i wisc wen yn llunio
llen rhwng pob enaid ac uffern. Amen.[11]

(A little creed, a holy creed, a creed to God and John, against the water, against the fire, against the broad-headed red serpent: I have walked a mountain, and from the mountain [*or* up and up] I could see holy Mary [head] on her bolster, and her angel, an obedient angel, and God Himself joyous [*not* 'in ten days']: and the Holy Man with his white robe drawing a veil between every soul and hell. Amen.)

This is a very interesting prayer for protection against misfortune from water, fire, and the devil, imaged here as a red broad-headed serpent. The image of the Holy Ghost drawing a veil between heaven and earth is very powerful. In another version it is Mary who digs a gulf between every soul and hell (*yn tirio lle rhwng pob enaid ac uffern*). A note with the 'little creed' suggests that whosoever repeated the prayer three times before sleeping would be saved from hell.

Prayer was central to popular religious practice, and from prayers we can tease out some of the fundamental themes of popular religion. God had created the world but Satan had rebelled against Him. Mankind seemed to stand between God and the devil and was the site of the conflict between them. The devil was often imaged as a dangerous animal. In the prayer cited above he takes the dangerous but insinuating form of a red serpent; elsewhere (as in Gwen ferch Ellis's charm) he was like a ravenous wolf. The devil was always near at hand provoking people to sin, especially those who lacked grace, and many felons (as we have already described) attributed their evil deeds to the instigation of the devil. Those who led good lives were blessed; those who led evil lives were cursed. The world was unpredictable and people needed protection from the elements, from fire, flood, and famine, and from the blasts and adversities of everyday life which might come at them from anywhere. Life was like a journey or pilgrimage (sometimes imaged as traversing a mountain) which one undertook with the protection of Christ, Mary, and the saints, who through prayer could be appealed to for their protection. The special role of the saints was expressed by naming them in emphatic oaths, and many of the latter were still in common use in the eighteenth century: '*myn Iago*' (by St James), '*myn Mair*' (by Mary), '*myn Elian*' (by St Elian), '*myn lliw Non*' (by St Non's colour), '*myn Dewi a Non*' (by SS David and Non), '*myn yr Allor*' (by the altar), '*myn yr grog*' (by the Cross), '*myn fynghred a'm bedydd*' (by my faith and baptism), '*myn Iesu Gwyn*' (by blessed Jesus), and many others.[12]

In prayer God the Father was never invoked alone but was invariably addressed in the company of Mary and the saints, who were intermediaries between God and His poor people. God the Father was a remote and severe figure who punished people for their sins, sometimes, or so it appeared, quite capriciously. Catholic and Protestant alike might regard natural disasters as God's punishments on a sinful world. The harvest failure of 1585 was followed by the winter which destroyed 'al their cattle wel near, so that now the very sinowe of their mainteinance is gone.' 'This famine is for our sinnes' was Penry's grim judgement. Floods in south Wales in 1607 instilled 'an amazed feare into the hearts of all the inhabitants', who deemed it a second deluge and punishment for their sins. Another dearth in 1612–13 was viewed as further punishment for the sins of the people of north Wales.[13] John Penry observed that his countrymen ascribed 'savadge cruelty unto God the father, because he punished mans sin so severely, even in his son Christ'. They commended Christ but felt distant from the Father: 'I care ... not for the father that cruel man, but the sonne is a good fellowe (*cydymaith da*)' was a remark attributed to a Welshman in 1587, two years after the famine.[14] The '*cydymaith da*' was the good companion who looked out for his fellow travellers. The humanity rather than the divinity of Christ was emphasised; so much so that the oath '*myn cig Duw*', 'by God's flesh', habitually used in south Wales, became a collective term for the people of the south: '*Gwyr Cig Duw*'.[15] At the end of life's journey the dying were visited by the 'ghostly father' or 'God's hand', and the body was left behind as the soul went to heaven or hell. Penry condemned his countrymen for not believing in the doctrine of the resurrection of the body: 'They thinke the soule only shal goe to heaven & not the body also, whence it commeth that they say, they care not what becommeth of the body.'[16] Life was sinful but at death there was the hope that Christ or the Holy Ghost or Mary would intercede for the sinner. As the little creed recited at night put it, 'The Holy Man [Christ] draws a veil between each soul and hell'. Sometimes Mary entreated God to save 'as many of the damned as may bee covered under her mantill: this being graunted al the damned souls shalbe there shrouded and so saved from helfiar.' In the end God was 'bound to save all men, because they are his creatures.' This belief, according to Penry, was 'the cause why our people make but a mocke of sinne.'[17]

Penry complained that Welsh were not interested in the finer points of doctrine; he and other reformers attributed this to the lack of preaching. Some points of the 'high mysteries of salvation' so valued by the reformers were dismissed by the people as 'not beseeming the wisedome of the great God'. Learned appeals to the authority of Peter and Paul in the New Testament met with 'What know we whether they say tru or no?'[18] The people knew about prayers rather than doctrine, and their prayers were not part of the worship of the reformed church but recited and reproduced in the household. John Penry describes how 'Our people learn one of another most blasphemous praiers.' 'Masters of families' would teach them to their households and these prayers were eagerly learnt, the more so because they had an instrumental value and might be addressed to a particular saint whom they thought might be favourable to them and best able to grant their petitions. To the reformers these prayers were painful blasphemies. John Penry claimed that his 'hart bleedeth to think howe these villanies with other ungodly songes are learned of good painfull soules with greediness.'[19]

Charmers and Healers

Robert Holland, the late-Elizabethan demonologist, provides a unique view of 'the swarms of soothsayers and enchanters' in Wales at the end of the sixteenth century, giving some indication of their relative status, specialisms, and sources of knowledge. As we have seen (Chapter 1, above), he divided magical specialists into three categories according to their sources of power. Of highest status were the prophets, astrologers, and interpreters of prophecy, who were 'highly revered by the gentry and freeholders of the country'. Conjurers formed a second category of high status; they performed their craft through knowledge and reading books. Charmers and soothsayers formed a third category. Some had considerable reputations but many charmers were of relatively low status, including (in Holland's words) the 'old fools' who were illiterate but had knowledge of herbs and charms.

In a very significant passage that reveals the changing popularity of magical specialists, Holland's interlocutor says that 'we do not hear so much' about conjurers. 'It is not now necessary to go to them for information or to ask about lost things. The charmers (*swynwyr*) can do this.' The sense of this passage is that charmers had become more important – and therefore more numerous – because of the decline in the significance of conjurers. The perception that charmers were increasing in significance in Elizabethan Wales was probably correct, but it had less to do with the decline of high-status conjurers and more with the hostile attitude of the reformed church to protective prayers, belief in the intercession of the saints, and the magico-religious power of priests. The ritual protection provided by the Catholic Church had been abandoned by the reformed church, but of course the people still suffered from illness, natural disasters, and innumerable other afflictions they wanted to alleviate.[20]

The reformers' attack on clerical magic, and the consequent decline of the clergy's protective role, created a magico-religious space that was amply filled by new specialists (*swynwyr*: charmers), many of whom were women, who offered a similar service outside the framework of the church. The life of Gwen ferch Ellis, examined in Chapter 2, provides a unique account of the background and career of a later sixteenth-century charmer. Gwen had probably known the Catholic world of Mary Tudor but would also have experienced the Elizabethan reaction to Marian Catholicism. She had learnt the words of some charms, essentially prayers, from an older sister who had also given her certain artefacts – an image and bell – that Protestants might associate with the magic of the unreformed church. Gwen's speciality was curing sick children and cattle. An interesting passage suggests that she had some uncertainty about her expertise at the beginning of her career but increased in confidence over time. Acquiring confidence was a somewhat dialectical process; as people placed their confidence in you, so your own assurance grew. As Gwen put it: 'diverse that have comen to her did believe that she cold help theim, and so she believed likewise'. Gwen probably grew into her role as a charmer, and seems to have expanded her field of expertise into soothsaying and finding lost goods.[21]

Charmers had special knowledge of prayers and healing substances. Certain prayers to alleviate illnesses were regarded as so efficacious that they had the effect of charms (*swynion*) and were in popular use. An early-eighteenth-century parson-antiquary noted some of the 'distempers' that were particularly alleviated by these charms: shingles (*eryr*), the stye ('which we call *llefrithen*'), and 'a blast or cavod' (*cawod*), probably a sudden infection. These prayers or charms were in Welsh (with 'some few verses of St John's Gospel in Latin' used against the ague), but he forbore repeating the words considering them 'better forgotten than repeated'. Specialist charmers of course knew many more prayers and charms. Penry describes how literate persons had special access to these prayers in 'ungodly Welsh bookes' which were 'fraught with these Idolatories'. Such was the demand for knowledge about these prayers from the common people, that 'If they meete with any who can write and read, they wil demand of him whether he can teach them ever a good praier against such a disease in man or beast.'[22]

Charmers (*swynwyr*) varied greatly in reputation. It will be remembered that in Robert Holland's dialogue some *swynwyr* are referred to as nothing but old fools who knew about herbs and had learnt a good lesson in charming people. There are occasional documentary glimpses of these illiterate charmers who had regard for the propitious times of the year. In Denbighshire Elizabeth ferch John gathered herbs and flowers on St John's Eve in Midsummer; these plants probably included mugwort (*llysiau Ifan*, named after the saint) which was set under the eaves at Midsummer. Ann Jones cured 'diverse diseases by the gift God bestowed upon her', and her remedies included the use of 'dewe gathered in the moneth of Maye'.[23] Salt was a most important element in the enchanter's apotropaic armoury. The ritual use of salt, thought of as hateful to the devil, was widespread in Europe, and was of course used by priests when preparing holy water. Gwen ferch Ellis referred to salt as 'the holy creature', an expression that vividly conveys the idea that salt became a kind of animate substance after it had been blessed. When Gwen gave salt to a sick client she claimed that it would 'deffende her from all [evil] charmes by the space of yeare and a daye'. Salt was commonly employed to ward off evil and to prevent mishaps. In 1615 some unfriendly neighbours of Elizabeth, wife of Rees David ap Ieuan of Llandysilio, Carmarthenshire, described her use of salt as a charm. When drying oats at a kiln, Elizabeth 'by a kind of sorcerie or enchauntment' would put a certain quantity of salt in a straw bundle in the kiln. 'When the fire did catch on the said wadd of straw, the same with the salt did vehemently burne', and the charm ensured that 'the corne shold be safe in drying from danger of fire'. When asked ('demanded') why she used the charm, Elizabeth said that it was a family practice: 'it was her fathers use and her kinred before so to doe'. Paradoxically the ritual use of salt might be taken as evidence for witchcraft. Elizabeth's custom was taken as further manifestation ('the more to be doubted') of her witchcraft after she had apparently successfully cursed her neighbour's trespassing pigs.[24]

Sometimes Welsh charmers made outrageous claims for the origin of their magical prophylactics and paraphernalia. Margaret David of Llangadog, who was eventually indicted for witchcraft at the Carmarthenshire Great Sessions in 1656, told a client that if rewarded she could cure her husband's sickly sheep and prevent them from dying. First she needed to procure 'water out of the well of Jerusalem mix't with earth from the same'. Two days later she returned with water and earth from the Holy City and a special sprinkler, described as a bone four or five inches long with a forked end. Margaret used the bone to 'cast a little of the water upon each of the sheepe useinge some charme therewith'. Margaret was asked 'what good or virtue was there in that forcked bone', and replied grandly that it was so valuable 'she would not take the best geldinge in Sir Harry Jones stable for that bone'. Margaret's charms were regarded as efficacious, especially in desperate circumstances. On another occasion Rees Bowen was taken with a terrible pain in his left leg, 'abouts the place where he did use to tie his garter' below the knee, and eventually took to his bed 'in a very sadd condition' because of the intolerable pain, his leg 'beinge shrunke and [turn]inge backward and very blacke neere his garter'. Friends thought it would be necessary to amputate and cauterise the leg, but Rees was persuaded to send for Margaret, even though some thought she might have bewitched him. Margaret arrived and 'tooke upp the bed clothes and looked upon his legge', announcing that Rees had indeed been bewitched. Then taking his leg between her hands and rubbing it, she 'mumbled some prayer or charme over it' and the pain began to assuage. From that moment Rees began to recover, getting stronger by the hour, and within three days 'he could goe about the house in and out'.[25]

Charmers flourished in early modern Wales but were in competition with ortho-dox medical practitioners. When sick, one might send for a surgeon, physician, or charmer – the charmer was probably not only cheaper but would also live closer to the patient. When Daniel Evan was injured by a reaping-hook during a harvest quarrel at Llangyndeyrn, Carmarthenshire, in 1652, he first sent for a barber-surgeon from Kidwelly. The surgeon took a hand in curing the wound, but seeing from the patient's swollen legs that he was sick of the dropsy and had some 'impostume', he advised that he had more need of a physician. In the event, after five weeks of sick-ness, Daniel sent for a charmer or enchanter to cure him as he thought he was sick of some 'inward disease', 'called by some the desease of the hart'. The charmer admin-istered something to him, the witnesses did not know what, and was rewarded with 3d. and some oatmeal.[26]

Medical practitioners were interestingly diverse. Physicians, surgeons, apoth-ecaries, and other specialists, sometimes with the occupational surname '*meddyg*', usually practised in the towns.[27] In the countryside some gentlemen acted as ama-teur surgeons patching up minor wounds, perhaps a skill related to the military experience of the gentry class. William Middleton, a Denbighshire gentleman, who attended a wounded man in gaol, was described as having some skill in surgery 'as his father did'.[28] People consulted charmers and mountebanks partly because of a lack of confidence in orthodox practitioners, and partly because they were cheaper and more accessible than the licensed physicians. In rural areas there were often few or no licensed practitioners. The churchwardens of Llandegley, Radnorshire, complained in 1694 that the parish had 'no doctor of physick, midwife, nor chirurgeon'.[29] In this type of situation, presumably the rule rather than the exception throughout rural Wales, charmers and the wander-ing quack-doctors had few competitors apart from some clerics and gentlemen who took an active interest in medicine.

In Elizabethan and Stuart Wales there were still parsons who helped the sick but the prayers and charms of their pre-Reformation predecessors had been replaced by an interest in herbals and the technique of uroscopy employed by the licensed physicians. There is a revealing glimpse of one of these parson-physi-cians in 1606/7. John ap Edward ap Morgan of Llanynys, Denbighshire, had been assaulted, and although he recovered from 'greene and bloudie wounds' he was still 'sore grieved and bruised in his stomacke'. The local curate was requested to take a sample of the sick man's urine ('carry his water') to a neighbouring cleric, Sir Thomas Wiliems of Trefriw, who was also a physician. It was expected that Wiliems could make a diagnosis without actually seeing the patient by scientif-ically examining the urine. The circumstances were explained to Wiliems and he examined the urine, making the diagnosis that John ap Edward's 'grief' was caused by 'bloud congealed and gathered in his breast'. Wiliems confirmed that the patient was unlikely to live, and he died within three days.[30] This case has special interest because Sir Thomas Wiliems, a notable Welsh literary scholar, was suspected of recusancy. It has been suggested that Wiliems was 'an unorthodox practitioner in the old-folk medicine tradition', using, as a contemporary observed, 'ineffectual old simples'.[31] However, Wiliems, despite his Catholic sympathies, was not a priest-physician of the pre-Reformation type who relied on prayers regarded by reformers as charms or worse – that role had been appropriated by charmers (*swynwyr*) who were to be found throughout the Welsh countryside.

People would travel considerable distances to consult *swynwyr* of high reputation. In Robert Holland's dialogue, Tudur observes that he knows of one charmer consulted by many people who came from far away to get charms for cattle and men; in England cunning-folk might attract customers from up to thirty or forty miles away, or so Henry Holland thought. Thomas Cooper considered that 'good witches' were 'rife almost in everie parish' in England, and this was probably true of parishes in Wales.[32] Put another way, it is not unlikely that the number of clergy in Elizabethan and Stuart Wales was matched by the number of charmers (broadly defined). Many charmers were of course relatively humble; the poor curates as it were of their profession. Moreover, there was an unknown number of 'mendicants', that is wandering healers and soothsayers who subsisted by telling fortunes and performing cures. Some of these wanderers made outrageous claims for the origin of their skill and effectiveness of their cures. A hostile but revealing portrait of a late-Elizabethan itinerant physician and surgeon, David Powell of Pennant, Montgomeryshire, has survived. Powell travelled with a portmanteau or 'capcase' on his back 'after the manner of a horse leeche', and carried a little basket containing a urine-viewing flask ('urinal'). Powell claimed to be a perfect surgeon and excellent physician, and in this 'dyvy-lyshe and coseninge sort' wandered up and down the country taking payment in kind (cheese, wool, and 'such odd stuffe') from 'women and silly simple folkes'. He was careful to claim an exotic rather than a supernatural origin for his skill. He had, he claimed, newly returned from Egypt where 'conversinge among the Egiptians', or gypsies, 'he had gotten exquisite knowledge and perfect skyll in the arte and science of phisicke'.[33]

One has to admire the range of skills professed by some of these quack-doctors beyond the cultivation of plausibility ('cosening') attributed to them by their enemies. In 1666 John Chercraft, a colourful and multi-talented personality, escaped from the house of correction at Ruthin, where he had been committed for being 'an idle person', though this scarcely seems possible given his range of skills; presumably it was his lack of a settled abode and consistent trade that perturbed the authorities. He was described as 'professeinge sometimes the arte of writeinge, sometimes the arte of phisicke and chirurgerie, sometimes a piricke [an empiric] maker, a tumbler and juggler, by slight of hand a cheater in his calleinge of phisicke and cyrurgerie'.[34] It is interesting that Chercraft was a scribe or writing-master. Literacy was understandably a prized skill in the fringe medicine fraternity.

Finally one must acknowledge that the peripatetic charmer or soothsayer was sometimes a heartless confidence trickster, moving from one victim to another.

In 1636 Harry Lloyd, a Caernarfonshire 'surgeon and diviner', under pretence of practising surgery or physick was accused of exercising 'wicked and unlawful arts', including 'fortune tellinge, palmistry, common hauntinge & familiarity with wicked spirits in the night time'. These wicked spirits were the fairies, and Harry deluded some clients into believing that he could – for a small fee – arrange to obtain regular supplies of fairy gold. Some confidence tricksters claimed to cure the sick through knowledge gained from the fairies. Ann Jones, eventually indicted for witchcraft in 1634, maintained she could 'helpe diverse diseases by the gift God bestowed upon her.' Her heartless speciality was pretending to cure sick children by conferring with the fairies, and pocketing the money which anxious parents had intended for these spirits.[35]

Love Magic

Charmers, as everyone knew, used charms and prayers which were regarded as doing good – for the most part. However, there was a negative side to the activities of charmers. Charming might be regarded as a type of witchcraft because charms could ensnare and hurt as well as cure. Some wise-women knew how to make love-magic, regarded as closely related to witchcraft, and some were prepared to supply abortifacients.[36] In 1663 Katherine Jones of Minera, widow, was accused of gathering 'savell' and other herbs which were mixed with 'seed stuffe or the like' to prepare a drink which she 'did comonlie give to younger woemen' to destroy their 'unlawfullie conceaved' foetuses. Katherine Jones was also accused of making 'entising powder' intended to provoke infatuation when consumed. The powder, simply called '*swyn serch*' or 'love charm', was surreptitiously administered to a victim, most conveniently in a drink. The effects of Katherine's *swyn serch* could be dramatic and permanent. When given to Anne ferch Hugh Griffith, she forsook her husband and followed another man, 'whereupon shee was divorced from the first, and lives at present with one Robert ap Richard of Trevechan'.[37]

Love magic was regarded as a form of sorcery, and the charmer who prepared it was not unlike a witch. Enticing powder caused that loss of self-control regarded as a characteristic effect of witchcraft and other devilish assaults. A mid-Elizabethan Montgomeryshire allegation shows that those suspected of using love magic could be formally accused of witchcraft. In 1579 David Lloyd ap John ap Ieuan ap Owen of Meifod, gentleman, complained to the chief justice of the Chester circuit that several named suspects had conspired to bewitch, abduct, and deflower his daughter, Margaret ferch David.[38] Instances of abduction (sometimes semi-public or even ritualised events) followed by sex were not uncommon in early-modern Wales, but there was often tension between different assessments of the degree of consent or coercion involved, essentially the difference between rape (a hanging felony) and seduction.[39] In this case, the abductee's father claimed that the suspects had 'by invocation of evil spirits' bewitched his daughter Margaret with 'a fair apple' and a certain powder. Margaret, 'an innocent wench', an undefiled virgin, ate the apple and powder and was immediately 'fired and most devilishly set and bewitched to run away' with John ap Griffith, who subsequently ravished her. Margaret claimed that she had been given the bewitched apple by Margaret ferch David Wyn, probably a cunning-woman.

The physical effects of the love magic, according to the recipient, were surprisingly unpleasant. After only three or four bites of the enchanted apple, Margaret began to feel 'an ache and giddiness' in her head, as well as a 'stitch rise in her right side', and her teeth hurt. She complained of feeling 'very ill at ease', and the cunning-woman produced from her purse a bladder containing a brownish powder lapped in paper, saying it was a remedy that would 'amend all her disease very quickly'. She administered a pinch of this powder but it was bitter and made Margaret's mouth hot 'as though she had been frantic'. Margaret was rescued after three or four days, but the love magic continued to affect her. At the changing of the moon – a significant detail which made Margaret think she had been bewitched – she 'felt herself to be frantic and bereft of her wits' and would remain distracted for one or two days. Moreover, she claimed that six of her teeth had fallen out after consuming the enchanted apple and powder. As for Margaret ferch David Wyn of Meifod, the wife of a husbandman, she prudently disclaimed any skill in witchcraft or sorcery, as did her husband. She denied giving the enchanted apple to Margaret, and claimed that her powder was merely a medicine given to several neighbours who 'had made their moan to her of the toothache'. The powder was nothing more than burnt alum, a remedy recommended by William Gilbert, a respectable surgeon, whom she had consulted about her own toothache. Margaret ferch David Wyn and her husband were apprehended on suspicion of sorcery but they escaped indictment.

Enticing powder was not simply a love magic used to prompt desire in cases of unrequited love – it was a source of power, cynically intended to produce states of reduced rationality and increased suggestibility so that a distracted victim could be exploited and swindled. The powder (possibly the speciality of women charmers) was generally administered by men to women. The real object of Margaret ferch David's abduction and seduction (or rape) was probably the prospect of a dowry of £100 that her father was willing to give 'in preferment of her honest marriage'. After seduction 'honest marriage' was not easy to achieve. Love magic explained some improbable liaisons. When Rheinallt ap Hugh ap Robert of Llanfyllin persuaded Jane Dudley, an old gentlewoman aged about 78, to marry him, her friends were amazed. Eight years before Jane and her husband had pursued a bill against Rheinallt for murdering one of their servants and wounding another. 'Divers of her frendes did vehemently suspect that he had used som unlawfull skill' to inveigle her into marriage. Jane herself was heard to say 'sondry times' that 'she was p[ro]cured by the Devill to entermary with hym.'[40]

Some unscrupulous lovers had the reputation of cynically procuring enticing powder and giving it to more than one victim. Thomas Hughes of

Llanfihangel-yng-Ngwynfa was a serial seducer suspected in 1678 of repeatedly employing enticing powder to take advantage of his victims financially as well as sexually. Three years before he had surreptitiously given Jane ferch Edward 'some inticeing or other inchaunting or bewitching powder' in a posset or special spiced drink. The enticing powder made Jane 'sencless or distracted', and Hughes was able to procure from her a deed purporting to give him all her estate, amounting to some £30. Thomas Hughes fathered two children, which died in unexplained circumstances, and afterwards left Jane destitute and moved on to another victim. Mary Bowdler alleged that Hughes had given her a strange 'shineing' powder, saying that it was 'extraordinary good to be eaten with any meat'. She became suspicious of the powder 'supposeing it to be some bad thing', but Hughes then 'skipped it out of her hands' saying that the mercer who sold it 'had mistaken the powder'. However, suspicions were aroused and Hughes was indicted for witchcraft, accused of attempting to provoke Mary to unlawful love.[41]

Soothsayers

A distinction was maintained between charming and soothsaying although the same person might combine both activities. Gwen ferch Ellis 'did use and practise sowthsaying and charming'. As a charmer, 'diverse have resorted to her for helpe boothe for man and beasts'; as a soothsayer, people consulted her for information, especially 'for knowledge oof things that were lost'. Robert Holland's Dialogue suggests that soothsaying like charming, formerly associated with learned conjurers and astrologers, was becoming a more demotic activity with some quite low-status practitioners who were consulted for information or asked about the loss of something. Holland mentions some of the soothsayers' divinatory techniques: some used the sieve and shears, or a bowlful of water; others could tell who would die within the year by throwing nuts into the fire at Allhallow-tide ('*nos Galan-gaya*'), or with a technique involving water and herbage.[42]

The techniques employed by Welsh soothsayers were by and large akin to those of cunning-folk in England. Divination by interpreting the movement of a sieve and sheers was a technique commonly employed in England, and users of this method in the Welsh Marches were prosecuted in the Hereford ecclesiastical court. The crystal stone or glass, and the humbler dishful of water, were also widely used in England, and a detailed account of its use in late-sixteenth-century Wales has been preserved.[43] Although charmers might also practise as soothsayers there were differences between the crafts. Charming was considered primarily a gift that related to the grace of the charmer; soothsaying was a craft that could be taught and depended on the soothsayer's skill. There was a corresponding difference in the way charmers and soothsayers were rewarded for their services. In Wales, as in England, charmers tended to receive gratuities while soothsayers charged their clients.[44] Gwen ferch Ellis claimed that she did not charge ('exactinge nothinge of anie') for her plasters and salves although she received rewards from her clients, 'they of theire voluntarie wills doe somtymes give her woll, corne cheese or butter for her paynes'.[45] One may note the tendency for women to be charmers and for men to be soothsayers, but this was not a hard-and-fast gender distinction and those skilled in one craft tended to dabble in the other.

Soothsayers seem to have become numerous in late Elizabethan and Stuart Wales and were distinguished from charmers (*swynwyr*) by names equivalent to the English 'cunning-man'. There was a developing and varied vocabulary for soothsayers but *dyn hysbys*, 'wise-man', sometimes *gŵr cyfarwydd*, 'expert man', became the usual terms for a cunning-man. Although the earliest recorded instances of these Welsh terms date only from the eighteenth century, wise-men and wise-women were referred to in seventeenth-century depositions, presumably reflecting Welsh usage.[46] In 1637 a Montgomeryshire farmer announced his intention of consulting 'a doctor or a wise man'; the interesting term 'doctor' meaning a learned or expert man rather than a physician. In 1609 a Denbighshire magistrate or his clerk noted that the owner of certain stolen goods had gone to consult 'a wise man', glossing that this was 'as she termed him'. In 1686 a Gresford spinster was charged at the Denbighshire quarter-sessions with consulting 'one called a wise woman' who undertakes not only 'to give an account of lost goods' but also 'a certayne answer to all questiones yt are or shall be made unto her'.[47]

People consulted soothsayers for information. Soothsayers were able to reveal the truth about particular events in the past or predict certain events in the future in response to direct questions. Wise-men were able to lay open secrets and discover what was hidden or concealed. In particular, wise-men were able to find lost goods, and some were credited with the power to retrieve hidden gold and silver which might be guarded by supernatural beings, including devils and fairies. Confidence in the ability of soothsayers to recover treasure made some the hapless victims of the confidence trickster. In 1636 Harry Lloyd, a Caernarfonshire 'surgeon and diviner', and much else besides, claimed he could make people rich by obtaining money from the fairies. However the discovery of lost and stolen goods and the identification of thieves were central to their activities. Soothsayers did not necessarily give immediate results; they needed time to come to a considered conclusion when consulted about lost or stolen goods, and clients could find this frustrating. When in 1661 Thomas Pierce of Croeseinion, Denbighshire, lost an iron chain, he travelled several miles to consult Elin Coytmore, hearing that she 'did usually give tideinges of things lost'. Thomas urgently wanted to know the identity of the thief, but Elin replied that she did not know at that very moment who had stolen the chain, but promised that 'when shee would bee at leasure, shee would trie her skill'. Some time after Thomas pressed Elin to identify the thief, and Elin repeated that 'shee could not doe it upon a sudden, and desired tyme to consider and shee would doe it.'[48] The techniques used by soothsayers were not inherently time-consuming, but presumably they needed time to gather information so that they could formulate a considered opinion.

Some divinatory techniques involved a dialogue between wise-man and client and would have produced more immediate results. No doubt the wise-man often helped a client to articulate suspicions that were already half formed. The best-known of these dialogic techniques, widely used in England and Wales, involved the use of the divinatory glass or crystal stone.[49] This might involve three parties: the wise-man, the client, and a 'scryer' or crystal-gazer who described things seen in the glass which were interpreted by the client and wise-man. A most illuminating case involving the crystal occurred in 1570 when Hugh Bryghan was examined at Denbigh by the deputy justice of the Chester circuit. Hugh Bryghan was styled of Pentre'r-felin, near Denbigh, but his name suggests a family origin in Brecon. Bryghan seems to have plied his trade throughout Wales, possibly wandering on a circuit. He is surely the Hugh Brichan, then styled of Hereford, prosecuted at the Glamorgan assizes in 1568 for using 'art magic'. Bryghan's speciality was 'to tell tydyngs and declare what becam of goods and cattells stolen, or otherwise lost', using the crystal stone. He had specialized in this form of magical detection for the past nineteen years or so and had learned the art from an uncle, Rees Bryghan. In response to the judge's questions, Bryghan gave further details of his 'scrying'. He denied saying any words, presumably pronouncing a magical formula, before anything was seen in the crystal. He did, however, invoke the Trinity (saying 'in the name of the ffader, the sonn, and the holly goost') and made the sign of the cross over the crystal ('crosse the stoun') before the scryer looked into it. As Bryghan explained, by looking into the crystal the 'vysnamy' ('visnomy' or physiognomy) of a thief could be seen. However few adults, neither men nor women, could see likenesses in the crystal. Bryghan maintained that those best able to see the crystal images were children under the age of twelve who had not yet received communion. This was a dangerous admission of course since it linked successful magic with those who had not received the principal adult sacrament of the Church. The rewards received by Hugh Bryghan were variable: 'of sum iiiid, of sum vid, of sum xiid, and of sum more or lesse.' There seems to have been no fixed charge, and Bryghan's fees presumably varied according to a client's resources and the success of the consultation.[50]

Other techniques for detecting thieves could be directly intimidating, involving a confrontation with the suspect. Jane Bulkley of Caernarfon used a form of ordeal. In 1618 Sir William Maurice of Clenennau, a justice of the peace, sent for her to identify a thief who had stolen cloth from a tenant. Sir William gathered the suspects together and Jane Bulkley gave each of them a piece of cheese to eat on which a servant had inscribed 'such charmes as the said Jane did speake'. Presumably the guilty party would not be able to swallow or digest the cheese. 'The feelings of the guilty party confronted by this sinister lump of cheese may be imagined', comments Keith Thomas on the case, drawing attention to the early medieval procedure of administering the 'holy morsel' to clergy suspected of crimes.[51]

Such was the confidence in the ability of cunning-men to detect thieves, that sometimes the mere threat of visiting a wise-man might induce a confession or prompt the return of stolen goods. Elin Thomas was suspected of arson and theft in 1637, accused of setting fire to her master's barn in Llandinam, Montgomeryshire. While the household were busy putting out the fire, she had broken open her master's chest and stolen gold and silver to the value of £16. Elin, characteristically claiming that 'the Divill did prick her', confessed to these crimes only when her master announced his intention of going to a wise-man 'to inquire howe these business came aboute and who was the cause of it'. Elin confided in a fellow servant that she had not intended to return the money, which she had hidden in a hedge, or to admit what she had done, but her master's threat to consult a wise-man had made her confess.[52]

Sometimes a suspect was directly intimidated by a wise-man. In 1693 John David, a Pembrokeshire farmer, pursued a former servant-maid, Elizabeth, to her new place of service, alleging that she had stolen money from his house at Llanychaer. John David was accompanied by 'a sort of cuning man or conjurer' who tried to intimidate Elizabeth by the 'burning of papers before her'. These papers must have burnt dramatically as some were smeared with oil and one had 'brimston on't'. Elizabeth stood her ground and denied the theft, but her new master turned her out of his service. The high-constable was called and broke open Elizabeth's box, taking away all her possessions, which seem to have been given to John David in compensation for the alleged theft. Elizabeth petitioned the Great Sessions for redress, for she now had no employment and, as she put it, 'had nothing in the world' apart from the clothes she wore. Elizabeth was permitted to prosecute John David for theft but the grand jury rejected the bill of indictment.[53]

Soothsayers helped clients articulate their suspicions and confront suspects. Clients externalized their suspicions and saw (or the scryer saw) suspects in the glass or crystal. One can readily imagine a dialogue between wise-man and client, the latter voicing suspicions confirmed by the interpretation of the crystal. Occasionally, the victims of theft internalised the process and saw the perpetrators in a dream. Cunning-folk could assist the process. An eighteenth-century ballad describes how a farmer consulted a wise-man after loosing some stock, and was given a certain paper to put under his pillow. The paper prompted a dream in which the farmer saw the countenance of the thief. Many clients had suspicions, which hardened into certainties when the suspected thief was seen in crystal or a dream.[54]

Cunning-folk and the Legal Process

Cunning-folk could potentially exercise a profound influence on the legal process because both the victims and perpetrators of thefts consulted them. They located stolen goods and assisted in the identification of suspected thieves. Moreover, according to Arise Evans, it was quite usual for thieves to consult cunning-men or astrologers to learn their destiny. He had heard many a thief say in prison that they would steal and not work because a cunning-man had said they would end on the gallows.[55]

Identifying a thief was a serious business because it became a matter of life and death if the suspect was indicted for grand larceny. It is understandable that the pronouncements of wise-men were often gnomic; it was up to the client to make the necessary connections, tackle the suspect, and bring a prosecution. In 1691 John Evans of Holywell, Flintshire, confidently confronted a neighbour after consulting a 'fortune teller' who had obliquely told him that his cattle had been maimed by a neighbour who lived in a house by a tree whose branches 'laid upon the chymney'.[56] After a wise-man had been consulted, the identity of a suspect usually became widely known. In 1608 the wife of Anthony Burgeine of Holt, Denbighshire, 'reported to div[er]se honest people' that her husband had consulted a wise-man after a burglary 'to learne who had comitted the felonie and what was become of his goods'. The wise-man had shown him in a glass the faces of the thieves, recognized as Lawrence and Thomas Dutton. The wise-man had added the convincing detail that one of the thieves had broken into the house and then opened the door for the other.[57] Those who consulted wise-men in order to identify thieves could themselves risk prosecution, especially if a suspect was wrongly identified. An early-seventeenth-century Flintshire defendant was fined at the Council in the Marches for 'combinac'on and practize to charge the plaintieff w'th fellony by thadvise of a wisard'. In 1686 Eleanor Jones of Gresford, spinster, was bailed to appear at the Denbighshire quarter-sessions on a charge of consulting a wise-woman who specialized in finding lost goods.[58] Anxiety about collusion between wise-man and client must explain Hugh Bryghan's confession that his practise of using the crystal stone to identify thieves was an illusion and deceit done without the warrant or knowledge of the owner of the stolen goods.

There was another side to the business of identifying thieves. A wise-men could help those falsely accused of theft by identifying the real thief. An instance of this occurred in Denbighshire in 1611. Henry Wynne was bound to prosecute a bill of felony against Hugh ap Ieuan of Llanrhaeadr for the theft of money and hat-bands or scarves. The recognisance was brought into the court along with a fascinating letter from one David Robertes, who if not a wise-man or conjurer was an astrologer. Robertes claimed through 'learned arte' ('as well by astronomy as astrologii') to have identified the true thief. He had deduced from a celestial figure some remarkable details of the theft. The stolen goods had been conveyed 'east enclining unto south' a distance of two miles to a 'scatered town'. The celestial figure established that the thief ('malefactor') was 'a big scattering fellowe', aged thirty-two, full-faced with a dark complexion, hazel eyes, thin black hair and brownish beard. He wore a medley-coloured jerkin with brownish breeches, and was said to have been 'a comen gest' in the house where the goods were stolen. This was information of a remarkable specificity. The writer of the letter, David Robertes, then solemnly swore upon 'my lyfe and my credit' for the truth of these assertions, and appealed directly to 'good m[aste]r Harry G[w]ine' (the prosecutor) to remember 'the dreadful day of judgment and the last accompt that there must be delivered', entreating him not to 'slay the inosent bloud of the suspected youth'. David Robertes's intervention was successful. The grand jury rejected the bill and the original suspect was discharged by proclamation at the end of the sessions.[59]

Cunning-folk were ubiquitous but they are rarely identifiable in the legal record. Despite a probable total 'population' of several hundred at any one time in seventeenth-century Wales, very few were prosecuted under the witchcraft statutes. The same was true in England.[60] The demonologists' insistence on the wickedness of white witchcraft was never really reflected in prosecutions for magically finding lost or stolen goods, locating treasure, or provoking to unlawful love, although these activities were specifically prohibited by statute. The difficulty of course lay in demonstrating that there was a relationship between the devil and those who claimed to be charmers and enchanters.

If a soothsayer was apprehended, the best course of action was to claim to be a fraud. When Hugh Bryghan was accused at the Denbighshire assizes of using 'art magic' or conjuration he was closely examined by the deputy justice. Bryghan denied calling on any 'ffammilyer', nor did he keep any stone into which a 'ffammilyer spyryt' had been conjured. He denied that he had conjured at any time, or indeed that he was able to conjure. The judge's questioning about familiars is revealing, since this type of obviously diabolic witchcraft was of most concern to the judiciary. Hugh Bryghan was careful to distance himself from the diabolical aspects of charming. He conceded that he had invoked the Trinity and made the sign of the cross over the stone, but that was all. He admitted that the practice of looking into the stone depended on illusion and deceit, and he promised that he would not thereafter use the stone. Hugh Bryghan's confession was 'read and confessed' in open court at the Denbighshire Great Sessions. Two justices of the peace endorsed the confession, and Hugh Bryghan was discharged.[61] It was probably a lucky escape. Confession of error probably saved Bryghan from the pillory and imprisonment for a year. A second offence (and Bryghan had been apprehended before) carried the penalty of life imprisonment and forfeiture of goods.

There was never a campaign against charmers and soothsayers in the criminal courts, although there may have been attempts to discipline them in the ecclesiastical courts. The pre-1700 Welsh consistory court records have largely disappeared, but prosecutions of soothsayers and their clients in the diocese of Hereford, which extended into parts of Wales, suggest that cunning-folk may also have risked prosecution in the Welsh ecclesiastical courts.[63] Visitation articles in the Welsh dioceses after the Restoration still enquired if there were people who used 'charms, spels, witchcraft' to 'heal and cure men or cattel'.[62] In the later seventeenth century there were fresh attacks on cunning-folk from Anglican religious writers who condemned charmers as ungodly cheats (and perhaps sometimes also as competitors), who by their apparent helpfulness masked the terrible power of the devil. The renewed concern was marked by the reissue of Robert Holland's *Dau Gymro yn Taring* in 1681 (with several subsequent editions) along with a translation of *The Devil of Mascon* ('the Strange but True Narrative of the Chief Things, spoken and acted, by an unclean Spirit at Mascon'), published to strengthen readers in the conviction that there were devils. Holland's tract was reissued specifically 'to stop the common people of Wales from now going (as they usually do up to this very day) to conjurors, charmers, and soothsayers [*consurwyr, swynwyr,* and *dewinesse*] to have their fortune told, and to get information about what they lose, and to get help for their cattle and their men in sickness (or rather to get help from the Devil through these people) and also to stop them from various other damnable habits, which Mr Holant also mentions in this book.'[64] According to one of 'Vicar' Prichard's verses in the same volume, the Welsh people still flocked to soothsayers and enchanters like bees to the vine: '*fel y gwenyn at y gwinwydd*'.[65] Other related attacks on magic included a poetic catalogue 'against some evil habits of people in Wales' added to a translation of the moralising 'Advice of a Father to his Son' (1683). These evil customs included swearing by the Devil, using saints' names in oaths, making the sign of the cross when rising in the morning ('turning their fingers about their noses'), taking notice of omens (especially the screeching of the magpie), as well as resorting to charmers (*swynwyr*) for charms to protect their cattle and possessions against disease and witchcraft (*rhag eu rheibio*), especially on May Eve when rowan was also placed in the growing corn to guard against harvest failure.[66] T.P.'s *Cas gan Gythraul* (1711; 'The Devil's Aversion') was published to discourage the Welsh people from consulting conjurors, and indulging in other superstitions, and instances of divine judgement on those who consulted conjurors and wizards were collected by James Owen in *Trugaredd a Barn* ('Mercy and Judgment', 1687).[67]

Late Stuart concern about cunning-folk had two aspects. There was of course implacable clerical hostility towards cunning-folk who deceived people into thinking that their ungodly services were beneficial to man or beast. However, there was not a call for a campaign of secular punishment of soothsayers and enchanters as illegal and ungodly; this was perhaps a lost cause. Rather, emphasis was placed on the individual's responsibility for his or her own soul by avoiding the temptation of consulting cunning-folk. It was an aspect of the doctrine of providence that required the individual to accept the judgment of God and turn only to those, the clergyman and the physician, authorized by the church to help the sick and not to unauthorized magical practitioners. The vicar of Llandovery, Rhys Prichard, perfectly expressed the doctrine in a series of stanzaic admonitions to the sick.[68] The sick should first turn to the clergyman as disease followed sin. Afterwards, the sick were to send for the physician, for God gives them knowledge to remove illness. The sick were admonished to shun all charmers:

> *Gochel geisio help gan swynwyr,*
> *Yn dy flinder tost a'th ddolur;*
> *Gado Duw mae'r cyfryw ddynion,*
> *Ac addoli gau-dduw Ecron.*

(Never seek help from charmers in your severe trouble and your grief;
Such men forsake God and worship [Beelzebub] the false-god of Ecron.)

> Nid yw'r swynwr ond apostol
> Ffalst i'r diawl, i dwyllo'r bobol,
> Oddiwrth Grist, mewn poen a thrafael,
> I butteinia ar ôl y cythraul.

(The charmer is nothing but a false messenger for the devil, to draw by deception the
people from Christ in their pain and travail, to go a-whoring after the devil.)

However, the unreformed popular religious culture of early modern Wales was
extraordinarily resilient. It is ironic (seemingly an expression of the oppositions
and reversals that characteristically structured popular culture) that those seeking
to reform popular religious culture were themselves sometimes suspected of being
enchanters who 'bewitched' people to their religion. Radical Protestants and field
preachers emerged in the seventeenth century as a category of persons who might
be suspected of witchcraft. The autobiography of the Welshpool Quaker, Richard
Davies (b. 1635), described how it was commonly reported in Montgomeryshire
that the Friends 'bewitched people to their religion' and their neighbours avoided
them, 'some crossing themselves'. The prosecution of a prominent Haverfordwest
Quaker was indeed contemplated in 1668 after Hugh Lloyd had become 'distracted',
claiming that the Quakers had enchanted him, naming some of them. Lloyd was
restrained and confined to a chamber but managed to throw stones at solicitous
Quaker women who came to visit him, crying out that they were 'inchanted
Devills'. Later Hugh Lloyd became 'very unruly and rageing' and then died 'contrary to the expectacion of experience & practice of the condition of madd men.'
The death was regarded as suspicious, and it was not long before over thirty Quakers
were taken at an 'unlawful meeting' under 'pretence of religious woo[rshi]pp' and
committed to gaol.[69]

Some seventeenth-century dissenting congregations and their ministers may have
acquired sinister reputations because they were closed societies. But public preachers who went into the field to reform the religious habits of the people might also be
regarded as enchanters. Public conversion could be perceived as a form of enchantment akin to bewitchment to love. When the Puritan Walter Cradoc preached in
Cardiganshire in 1653 or 1654, a 'bitter rhyme' was composed against him which suggested that he was the 'Devil's messenger and a deceiving enchanter' ('Cenhadwr Diawl,
swynhudol ddyn').[70] The reputation for sorcery pursued Walter Cradoc to the grave.
After his burial in 1659, on the eve of the Restoration, the rumour spread that Cradoc
like Faust had been carried off body and soul by the devil. Eventually his brethren were
forced to perform a grisly exhumation to lay the rumour that they had put stones in
Cradoc's coffin to conceal this satanic abduction. It was reported that as the coffin was
reached, a bystander called out, 'Now for stones or bones!'[71]

5

CONJURERS AND THEIR MAGIC

There were numerous paradoxes connected with the belief in witchcraft and magic in the eighteenth century. The abolition of the witchcraft statutes in 1736, and the impossibility of bringing prosecutions against suspected witches, marks an obvious break in the legal significance of witchcraft. Yet repeal of the witch-craft statutes did not reflect a general scepticism about the existence of witches and wizards. Indeed, some aspects of popular belief in witchcraft and magic were to become more florid. In particular, conjurers dominated popular interest in magic and healing in the eighteenth and early nineteenth centuries. Of the sev-eral terms used to refer to cunning-folk (*dyn hysbys, dewin, rheibiwr*, etc.) the word 'conjurer' (*consuriwr, conjerwr, cynjer*, etc.), used in the Welsh Bible, was widely applied to those with the highest reputation for occult knowledge. In Welsh, as in English, the term did not acquire the dominant sense of a 'stage magician' until the later nineteenth century. Before then, the primary meaning of conjuring was the invoking and control of spirits.[1]

Charmers and soothsayers in the seventeenth-century tradition became less important as conjurers grew in reputation. Conjurers combined the roles of sooth-sayer and charmer and much else besides. Conjurers were healers, fortune-tellers, and detectives who located lost goods and identified thieves. Above all, they could summon and control spirits. Some had reputations as ghost-layers, and many were regarded as the doughty antagonists of witches. Most conjurers had a wide range of specialisms. One may instance a Llanidloes conjurer who was consulted in all cases of 'cursed fields', bewitched animals, unaccountable dairying prob-lems, 'backward lovers, and bewitched women, etc.'[2] The casual 'etcetera' could encompass many other arcane activities from raising winds to selling cock-fight-ing charms.

The rewards for a conjurer could be great, but a conjurer's reputation depended on public assessments of his competence and performance. Trickery and sleight of hand were inseparable from the art of the conjurer. Nevertheless, some conjurers (to judge from their manuscript books) seem to have had a professional, even academic interest in their craft. The sincerity of a conjurer is difficult to assess, especially in retrospect, but (as Mauss pointed out) the crucial social fact was that public opinion gave the magician his authority.[3]

Conjurers and Fortune-tellers

It is very probable that the repeal of witchcraft and conjuration as a felony encouraged conjurers to be more open about their activities, allowing them in the eighteenth century to develop extensive practices and more elaborate procedures. While most charmers and healers, who might specialise in particular ailments, were rarely known beyond their immediate localities, some conjurers achieved regional reputations that extended over many districts. Griffith Ellis of Caernarfonshire, John Roberts '*Mochyn-y-nant*' of Ruabon, and Siôn Gyfarwydd of Llanbrynmair were known far and wide throughout north Wales in the later eighteenth and early nineteenth centuries. A dynasty of conjurers based in Llangurig had extensive success reaching beyond Montgomeryshire into the surrounding counties. The Harries family of Cwrtycadno in Carmarthenshire were pre-eminent in west and south Wales for three generations. Conjurers made appearances as characters in ballads and interludes, and some became chapbook celebrities. Lives and 'mysterious transactions' of John Roberts 'Mochyn-y-nant' and Dick Spot were published at the turn of the nineteenth century. Successful conjurers were able to live very comfortably from their unorthodox business and might achieve an odd respectability. Most notably, Dick Spot, the Welsh Border conjurer, had a coach and liveried servants, and left some of his wealth for charitable purposes.[4]

Professional conjurers like Dick Spot (as we are told) distanced themselves from the numerous 'twelve-penny' fortune-tellers and other low-status occult practitioners. The fortune-teller was not learned, often itinerant, and more likely to be apprehended as a vagrant than the settled conjurer or cunning-man. In particular, there was discrimination against gypsy fortune-tellers. Rev. John Walters's *English–Welsh Dictionary* (1794) prejudicially described a gypsy as 'a vagabond of tawny complexion', too often found in town and country, drawing money from many a simpleton for telling their fortunes, while she, the wanderer, could not foresee that the stocks awaited her. It was expected that gypsies should be 'tawny' or yellow-skinned, but then as now there were worries about the authenticity of gypsies. A Denbighshire cleric condemned mock gypsies 'that now [about 1730] deceive the vulgar with their lard and walnut leaf faces', who pretended to tell fortunes while not knowing their own, begging money from those 'to whom they promise great riches'. But these distinctions were academic when it came to life on the road. All gypsies, whether 'true' or 'mock', were liable to experience discrimination. In 1765 at Hanmer, Flintshire, Abraham Wood, his wife Sarah, and their three children, were apprehended as 'wandering as Egyptians, pretending to tell fortunes and lying in barns.' This incident is particularly interesting because Abram Wood is regarded as the founder of the principal gypsy lineage in north Wales, and it is revealing that he gave his legal place of settlement as Llanspyddid (Breconshire) in south Wales. In the eighteenth century gypsies were associated with south Wales, and Aunty Sal from the South ('Anti Sal o'r Sowth') appears as a character in an interlude by Twm o'r Nant published in 1786. Sal is a gypsy fortune-teller, the cousin of Abram Wood, and the descendant of witches in the female line. She uses her books to tell the fortune of a suspicious miser, Rondol. He is won over, pays Sal five shillings, and praises her as a crafty, knowing person, declaring that the famous fortune-tellers of the town were useless creatures when compared to the gypsy fortune-tellers from the south.[5]

Most towns had their fortune-tellers, generally women, who did brisk business on market-days. Shâni Llanddona visited Caernarfon from Anglesey once a week 'and people used to flock to have their fortunes told'. Shâni rented a large kitchen, 'and while she was telling one visitor his or her destiny in one half of the room, the other half would be crowded by others waiting their turn, screened from the view of the prophetess by bedclothes hung across the room.' A succession of exotically-named fortune-tellers was associated with Georgian Denbigh: Sioned 'Gorn', Sudna or Sydney, and Bela (Arabella) Fawr. Bela (to her subsequent annoyance) was surreptitiously sketched by Edward Pugh (Fig. 2), and he was impressed by her respectable appearance and obvious prosperity, and the sound advice she gave in an overheard consultation. Magistrates and clerics regarded the consulting fortune-teller as 'too common' in Wales as well as in England, though contrary both to the law of God and the law of the land. Telling fortunes from the patterns of tea-leaves or coffee grounds in a cup, which might form significant letters, was especially condemned as a 'foolish and ridiculous' method particularly associated with 'weak women'. Fortune-tellers of varying status, often women, were sometimes prosecuted at the quarter-sessions. They included Sioned, wife of Evan Hughes, shoemaker, a woman of 'bad character', charged with telling fortunes by cutting cards and reading tea leaves at Mold in 1761.[6]

Literacy was certainly a key attribute that set apart new-style conjurers from fortune-tellers and old-fashioned charmers. Some conjurers, like Siôn Gyfarwydd who was also a bookbinder, lived surrounded by books, and others had specialist libraries. Cunning-folk of any competence were expected to have extraordinary books containing arcane knowledge. In an eighteenth-century ballad about Alis y Ddewines, an Anglesey charmer and soothsayer, two countrymen discuss the source of her knowledge. The sceptical enquirer (*goganwr*, literally 'mocker') asks from what sort of books did Alice derive her knowledge; were there any to be bought in town or fair? The enthusiast (*canmolwr*, literally 'one who praises') replies that her knowledge was not to be had in any book that was for sale; she had gained her understanding of charming (*swyngyfaredd*) from a sincere woman, one Elsbeth of Felin Hirdre-faig, an old charmer. The enquirer was not impressed. Similarly the reputation of William Pranch, a reputed wizard in the Vale of Glamorgan, whose 'advice was much run too, for to heal cattle etc.', probably suffered because 'he knewed not a word on book' but had 'learned some verse of one Cate Mathew, late of Tregurnog, of sorcery, and that was all his skill'. A conjurer had to be able to read. Robin, son of Abram Wood the Welsh gypsy patriarch, according to an evocation of life in early-nineteenth-century Denbighshire, 'would have been a wizard if he had been clever enough, but he wasn't. He had Cornelius Agrippa's book and one or two others, but he could not read them.' The books passed to a conjurer who could make better use of them.[7]

Conjurers and Reputation

There were many 'reputed' conjurers in the eighteenth century but not all those with the reputation of keeping spirits and practising magic, perhaps a minority, were actually professional cunning-men. There were a few dilettante gentlemen-conjurers, possibly influenced by the Hell Fire and similar clubs, whose activities disturbed their localities; people sometimes attributed hauntings to their experiments. The learned and ingenious might acquire an unsought reputation for conjuration. William Thomas's 'diary', essentially a collection of moralising obituaries of his neighbours, shows that there were several (perhaps a dozen) reputed conjurers in the south-east corner of the Vale of Glamorgan in the mid- and late-eighteenth century. William Thomas 'Ysgolhaig' himself, a bookish, inquisitive, and knowledgeable schoolmaster and clerk, records with chagrin that 'Old Judith' and Martha Water spread the rumour ('gave these years past the report out') that he was a wizard.[8] Because of the association between books and conjuring, those in literate occupations were more likely to be regarded as conjurers than other folk. Reputed conjurers therefore included excisemen such as 'old Henor' (fl. 1740) who, it was said, magically punished one John Howells for mutilating his horse and saddle, making him 'for 24 hours walk about the house with no rest'. George Morgans (1713–83) of Fonmon, also an exciseman, afterwards a 'great measurer' and agent, was another reputed conjurer. Rev. Samuel Richard (1674–1740), who kept a school at Bonvilston, was 'very learned in the Latin and Greek tongues' and 'a reputed conjurer', and 'very much dreaded by the vulgar'. Reputed conjurers were not simply literate but often ingenious. James the Wheeler of Llanharri (c. 1709–69) was 'a reputed conjurer and one that made several legerdemain tricks and was much reputed and dreaded by the vulgar'. One Richard William, a carpenter and shopkeeper, was 'a reputed magician' because he 'by mechanick' raised the great bell of Llantrisant. Lewis William Walter (fl. 1700) of Merthyr Tudful was 'a man of uncommon elevation of mind in the scientifick way, and of great skill in medicine' – but also 'proficient in the black art'.[9] Some practising conjurers were authentically ingenious. Dick Spot was credited with devising a wooden clock that was displayed at a Shrewsbury inn.[10]

Occasionally a completely new conjurer burst upon the social scene like a flare, brilliantly illuminating local mysteries, only to be abruptly extinguished.

This was true of William Griffith (or Edward) who died in Cardiff gaol in April 1768, where he had been committed for 'pretending to conjure'. William Griffith was from Carmarthen by birth and (according to William Thomas, the diarist) reputedly 'one of the sons of the last Meddvai'. The Meddygon Myddfai were legendary Carmarthenshire physicians whose special expertise had been granted them by their fairy mother, and they had set down their medical treatments in certain famous books; their fame had clearly reached Glamorgan. William Thomas, the local chronicler, evidently talked to the conjurer about his life history and subsequently memorialised him in some detail. William Griffith apparently initially resisted his family medical calling, claiming that he had been a cannon-founder and 'founded the first cannon, as he reported, in Carmarthen town'. Afterwards, he became a wool-merchant, and only latterly 'a physician walking about'. Griffith was an unlicensed wandering physician, and was eventually committed to Cowbridge bridewell 'for his rude discourses' by a licensed doctor, Dr Bennet, 'and others of his faculty'. The list of prisoners in the house of correction shows that Griffith was committed 'for pretending to conjure one piece of gold' and extorting the sum of two shillings. He was sent to Cardiff gaol to await trial at the quarter-sessions. Griffith turned his pre-trial incarceration to great advantage, making the prison his consulting room where he 'gave himself wholly to physick'. According to his memorialist, he had a 'very bold phraseable tongue' but was 'wary in his lies'. Great 'numbers of people [were] resorting to him daily, especially on market days, as to a mountebank ... for his advice and physicks.' Griffith seemed to have considerable expertise as a healer, but he was also regarded as a great conjurer. People were keen to consult him over the most 'trifling' losses, and he would instantly announce 'what a one the thief was'. William Griffith was evidently a sensation. 'He gathered very much money in [a] few weeks', and would have accumulated more had he not died in gaol unable to cure his own agual fever.[11]

Many conjurers were adept astrologers, taking advantage of a flood of astrological publications and almanacs. Others practiced as urine doctors, specialising in a technique that had largely been abandoned by the mainstream medical profession but was still held in popular repute. Given the explicit association between conjuring and the devil, some cunning-men were reluctant to advertise themselves openly as conjurers but circumspectly claimed to be astrologers or doctors when it suited them. Robert Darcy, a Wrexham cunning-man (so described in contemporary documents) who told fortunes and restored stolen goods, informed a client in 1740 that 'he was noe Conjurer' but could 'tell by the Planets' the identity of a thief. Similarly, Thomas Niclas of Conwy grandly called himself 'cheife fortoun teller yet no necromancer' in his early-eighteenth-century 'true book of fate' ('*y gwir lyfr tesni*'), adding that he intended no harm to anyone, 'but disayres all to be neighbourly least [and here was the veiled threat characteristic of the omniscient 'knowing man'] his dice be thrown which by the vertue of the book will open up all.'[12]

The rewards for the conjurer were potentially considerable, but they had to nego-tiate real occupational hazards. The conjurer when away on business risked arrest as an itinerant fortune-teller or quack-doctor. Jealous doctors, or so it was rumoured, had popular mountebank-conjurers committed to gaol. A greater risk was that a disappointed customer might indict a conjurer for deception, or for obtaining money under false pretences. After 1737 (under the Act 9 Geo. II c. 5) the statutory punishment for pretending to use any kind of 'witchcraft, sorcery, inchantment or conjuration' was imprisonment for up to a year with the ordeal of the pillory every quarter. Prosecutions against cunning-folk were not particularly common in Wales (nor were they in eighteenth-century England), but nevertheless cases against con-jurers came before the assizes, quarter- and petty sessions.

The 1740 bill of indictment against Robert Darcy, styled tailor of Wrexham, alleged that 'not being minded to get his living by honest labour' he had defrauded one Edward Phillips of sixpence 'by false and deceitful arts' pretending to discover where stolen and lost goods may be found. The indictment against Daniel James of Llanafan-fawr, Breconshire, recited that he intended to defraud Griffith Daniel of five shilling by pretending to discover by conjuration who had bewitched his milk. The Flintshire conjurer John Edwards of Rhosesmor, better known as Siôn y Rhos, was accused of gaining £5 by deception from Sarah Reece of Gwersyllt in 1828 by using witchcraft and playing-cards to predict events.[13] Imprisonment might continue until the person convicted was able to find sureties for his or her good behaviour. Occasionally a convicted conjurer was released from incarceration after making a public confession of fraudulent practice. In 1807 John Jones was induced to make a recantation, witnessed on 10 November at Cardiff Gaol, which was printed in *The Cambrian*, a newspaper which circulated where he had plied his trade. Jones confessed that under the pretence of knowledge in occult sciences he had acquired 'an extensive reputation as a conjurer', pretending through magic arts to be able to restore stolen goods to their proper owners, with other acts of conjuration. Jones acknowledged his total ignorance of and disbelief in the magic arts, promised never again to be guilty of similar offences, and hoped that his recantation would be a check to anyone inclined to the vile art of deceiving the unwary and pocketing their money.[14]

The conjurer's credibility was not always easy to maintain, especially in his own locality. Every consultation was a test of competence, and those who made mistakes (as was inevitable) could be held up to ridicule. Mochyn-y-nant's elab-orate but futile efforts to locate a missing sheep intended to provide dinners at Nercwys Wakes were satirised in a ballad. A magic paper induced a dream in which the sheep's owner saw the thief, whom the conjurer promised to mark on the nose; the owner was also to bury a charm that would afflict the thief with ter-rible uneasiness. Later the sheep was found to have died in the owner's own barn. The poet's concluding advice (apparently published in the conjurer's life-time) was, 'Don't go to consult this 'Pig' any more': '*Nid awn at un Mochyn i ymofyn ddim mwy*'.[15] Folk-stories suggest that there was a deep vein of scepticism about the

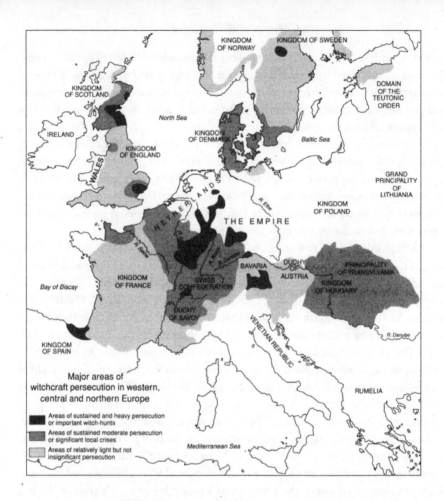

Major areas of
witchcraft persecution in western,
central and northern Europe

■ Areas of sustained and heavy persecution
or important witch-hunts

■ Areas of sustained moderate persecution
or significant local crises

□ Areas of relatively light but not
insignificant persecution

1 Wales and witch-hunting:
a map by Robin Briggs
showing the geography of
European witch-hunting.

2 The counties and circuits of
the Court of Great Sessions.

Decade	Chester Circuit	North Wales	Brecknock Circuit	Carmarthen Circuit	Totals
1550	0	0	0	0	0
1560	0	0	1	0	1
1570	2	0	0	0	2
1580	1	0	0	0	1
1590	2	0	1	0	3
1600	2	0	0	1	3
1610	0	0	1	2	3
1620	0	3	0	1	4
1630	1	0	3	0	4
1640	0	0	0	0	0
1650	2	1	2	5	10
1660	0	0	0	1	1
1670	1	0	0	0	1
1680	1	0	0	1	2
1690	0	0	3	3	6
1700	0	0	0	0	0
1710	0	0	0	0	0
1720	0	0	0	0	0
Totals	12	4	11	14	41

Key:
Chester Circuit: Flintshire, Montgomeryshire, Denbighshire.
North Wales Circuit: Anglesey, Caernarvonshire, Merioneth [few files preserved]
Brecknock Circuit: Brecknock, Radnorshire, Glamorgan
Carmarthen Circuit: Carmarthenshire, Cardiganshire, Pembrokeshire.

3 Witchcraft prosecutions in Wales: table showing persons indicted for witchcraft on the four circuits of the Court of Great Sessions.

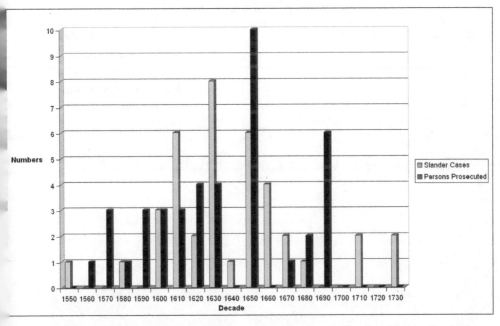

4 Witchcraft accusations and prosecutions: prosecutions for witchcraft and actions for slander at the Court of Great Sessions.

Term	Approximate translation	Source of power/technique	Tudyr's remarks
Dewin	Prophet		
Brudiwr	Soothsayer	Divine inspiration.	Highly revered by the best gentry and freeholders of the country. Good men who magnify God's greatness.
Daroganwr	Interpreter of prophecy		
Planedydd	Astrologer	Divine inspiration together with craft knowledge and reading books.	
Consuriwr	Wise-man	Perform their crafts through knowledge and reading books.	We do not hear so much about them. It is not now necessary to go to them for information or to ask about lost things. The *swynwyr* can do this.
Hudol	Enchanter		
Swynwr/ Swynwraig	Charmer	Prayer, knowledge of herbs and charms.	We cannot be without them. They do good to man and beast.
Rheibiwr/ Rheib(i)es	Wizard/Witch	Sacrifice.	Ravage people. Sacrifice to the devil for earthly gain. *Rheibwyr* have taught some how to sacrifice in some way, as *swynwyr* taught others to pray.

5 Welsh occult categories *c.* 1595 based on Robert Holland's *Dau Gymro yn Taring*.

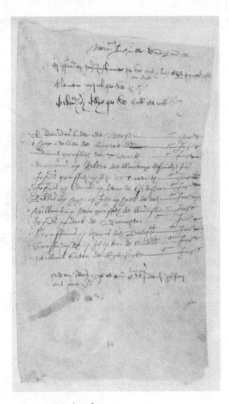

Above left 6 Title-page of Henry Holland's *A Treatise against Witchcraft*.

Above right 7 Trial-jury panel endorsed with Gwen ferch Ellis's plea, the verdict, and the judgment of hanging.

8 Indictment against Gwen ferch Ellis for witchcraft.

Above left 9 Instigation by the devil: a woodcut depicting the devil riding with a horse-thief, 1795.

Above right 10 Shân Bwt, the reputed Llanddona witch, drawn by Edward Pugh, for *Cambria Depicta* (London, 1816).

Above left 11 Bela Fawr, a well-known Denbigh fortune-teller, surreptitiously sketched by Edward Pugh for *Cambria Depicta* (London, 1816).

Above right 12 John Harries, Cwrtycadno. Photograph said to be of John Harries (junior).

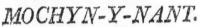

13 The Welsh conjurer. The woodcut illustrating *The Conjurer of Ruabon: being the Life and Mysterious Transactions of John Roberts, Known by the Name of Mochyn-y-nant....lately deceased* (W. Baugh, Ellesmere, n.d.).

14 Capel Llanelian: the Methodist chapel that faced Ffynnon Elian.

15 Cursing-pot with a slate inscribed 'Nanny Roberts' found in 1871 at Penrhos Bradwyn Farm, Holyhead, Anglesey.

Above 16 Cursing tablet with wax figure and initials from Ffynnon Eilian, Llaneilian, Anglesey.

Right 17 A late tract against superstition. Title-page of John Jones, *Llef yn erbyn Ofergoeledd* (1901).

Below 18 A nineteenth-century conjurer's charm.

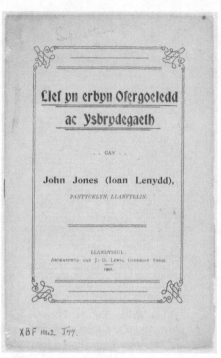

Llef yn erbyn Ofergoeledd
ac Ysbrydegaeth

. . GAN . .

John Jones (Ioan Lenydd),

PANTYCELYN, LLANFYLLIN.

LLANDYSSUL:
ARGRAFFWYD GAN J. D. LEWIS, GOMERIAN PRESS.
1901.

NLW MS 9140

competence of some conjurers. Indeed, they were sometimes deliberately tricked into situations that exposed their lack of prescience. The fame of William Pryse of Llangurig extended well beyond Montgomeryshire, but his local credibility never recovered after his watch was stolen and the conjurer was unable to locate it or identify the thief.[16] There was often scepticism about the powers of individual conjurers, especially from those who had known them since childhood and related to them as neighbours pursuing their ordinary, everyday occupations and concerns. But even if individual conjurers were regarded as charlatans this did not shake the belief that somewhere – perhaps many miles away – there was a conjurer with genuine powers. It was characteristic that those who consulted conjurers would often travel considerable distances while (presumably) ignoring other magical specialists nearer home. Rather like a religious pilgrimage to effect a cure, the journey to consult a conjurer was an inseparable part of the consultation process expressing a combination of faith and resolve – and sometimes desperation – on the part of the client.

Ars Magna: Conjuration

The conjurer's competences were measured against the powers attributed to certain legendary conjurers. Archetypal conjurers included a number of historical or pseudo-historical figures whose powers and abilities had become legendary and provided a kind of template for the activities of their eighteenth-century successors. The process of fabulation and its chronology is shrouded in mystery. The reputation of Siôn Cent or John o' Kent, said to have been a cleric or poet or both, was certainly well established by the end of the sixteenth century when Anthony Munday wrote his play 'John a Kent and John a Cumber', one of the characters claiming that 'Master John a Kent never goes abroad without a bushel of devilles about him'. John o' Kent's exploits were widely celebrated in south Wales and the March (especially about Grosmont and Kentchurch) and numerous landscape features were named after him which recalled his exploits.[17] Edmund Jones preserved several tales current in eighteenth-century Cardiganshire about Syr Dafydd (Davy) Llwyd, clergyman and physician, who learnt the magic art 'privately' in Oxford during 'the profane time' of Charles II and had died within living memory. One Mr Lewis who supplied the narratives had known Syr Dafydd's maidservant 'and the house he lived in'. In Gwynedd legendary conjurers included Dafydd Ddu and Robin Ddu Ddewin, both poets and scholars; in Merioneth, Huw Llwyd, scholar, bard and physician, and Dr John Davies of Mallwyd, parson, scholar and builder. The exploits of Dafydd (Ddu) Hiraddug were recounted in Flintshire. In Radnorshire and Montgomeryshire, 'Davies Sirevan' (or 'Davies Rivon') was as famous as his counterpart Dafydd Siôn Ifan in west Wales.[18]

The names of legendary conjurers varied from region to region, but the tales related of their exploits, especially their relationship with and eventual cheating of the devil, were essentially the same. A characteristic story told how the conjurer made a pact with the devil in return for his magical powers, agreeing that his soul should be forfeit when he died, whether he was buried inside or outside a church. This stipulation seemed impossible to circumvent, but nevertheless the conjurer outwitted the devil by instructing that when he died his body should be interred within a church wall so that it lay neither inside nor outside the church. This story was regarded as dramatically confirmed in 1718 when an intra-mural burial was discovered in Grosmont parish church. Carefully immured was 'a corps shrouded in leather & a pewter chalice lay on the breast', and it was 'conjectured that this was the body of the John of Kent soe much talked of in those parts'.[19]

Tales about conjurers dealing with but outwitting the devil were a type of trickster tale that celebrated human guile and intelligence. They also described a range of powers which conjurers of the highest reputation were expected to possess. Those who cultivated a reputation as a conjurer found that life was influenced by the story-teller. The conjurer was increasingly a showman and, like the quack-doctor and mountebank, involved in a theatricality that was driven partly by the expectations of his clientele, affecting his dwelling, professional costume, and, above all, the consultation with a client. The approach to a Pembrokeshire conjurer's secluded dwelling was signalled by protective pentangles cut into the bark of the surrounding trees.[20] The crude but informative woodcut that introduces the chapbook on Mochyn-y-nant depicts the celebrated Ruabon conjurer in his professional costume, wearing a full-length magician's gown with a scholar's cap, and possibly holding a urine flask (Fig. 13).[21] This was not necessarily artistic licence; some cunning-folk, men and women, certainly wore special professional robes, as did gentleman-conjurers when dabbling in the Black Art.[22] Hen Jem, a celebrated cunning-woman (*dynes hysbys*), caused a sensation when she appeared at the Breconshire petty sessions wearing her professional robes of purple silk.[23] The costume of a Montgomeryshire conjurer from the Llanrhaeadr-ym-Mochnant district, rather unflatteringly known as '*bwm-baili'r cythraul*' ('the devil's bum-bailiff'), was recalled in particular detail. He specialised in treating mental illness, and 'was much resorted to by the friends of parties mentally deranged, many of whom he cured'. When performing the conjurer's art, he put on 'a most grotesque dress' topped by 'a cap of sheepskin with a high crown, bearing a plume of pigeons' feathers'. His coat was of unusual pattern 'with broad hems and covered with talismanic characters'. His props included a wand with a bone handle and eel-skin thong, which he used to draw a magic circle. Outside the circle 'at a proper distance' stood those who had come to consult him and witness the 'mystic sentences and performances' made within the circle.[24]

The great magic book was another of the conjurer's indispensable props, and adventures connected with magic books were an important theme in tales about legendary conjurers. Syr Dafydd Llwyd once left his magic book at home and instructed his boy to fetch it, commanding him not to open it. Of course, the curious boy could not resist opening the book and an evil spirit emerged who immediately called for work. The boy had sufficient presence of mind to instruct the spirit to perform an endless task, casting stones out of a river (*'Tafl gerrig o'r afon!'*) and then throwing them back again, until his master returned and commanded the 'familiar spirit' back into the book.[25] A conjurer was expected to own impressive-looking volumes. When John Evans set up as the 'priest' of St Elian's well he was advised by another conjurer, Dr Bynian (or Benyon), that he needed to spread abroad that he could make devils do his bidding. Evans procured from Dic Aberdaron, a wandering scholar, a copy of the Apocrypha in Chaldaic, and with this impressive but unintelligible volume, reputedly a 'book for bewitching and summoning devils' (*'llyfr witchio a chodi cythreuliaid'*), Jac Ffynon Elian pretended to make magic and conjure.[26]

The ritual of perusing the 'black book' became an essential part of the theatre of consultation. After an initial consultation, the conjurer would withdraw into an inner sanctum to consult his books, sometimes just within view of the client. When Thomas De Quincey consulted the celebrated Mochyn-y-nant ('Mochinahante'), the conjurer retired to draw up his horoscope, but returned with a black book under his arm which he said was a manuscript of 'unspeakable antiquity' (but seems to have been a black-letter folio) from which he made various unlikely predictions, keeping it at arm's length from De Quincey.[27] When Daniel James, a Breconshire conjurer, was consulted about a case of suspected witchcraft, he tried by various means 'to find out the witch', 'having generally a book before him'. The conjurer's investigations were inconclusive, but he may have been using his second-best book. At any rate, the conjurer announced that 'there was a[nother] conjuring book of his at Glynllech [presumably a farm of that name] which he would give 5 guineas to have restored to him'. The most famous conjuring book in Wales was the chained and padlocked magic book of Cwrtycadno. The appearance of this volume was a piece of pure theatre. The large book secured with three locks was placed on the table during consultations but remained locked; it was rumoured that the conjurer's devils resided within it. The magician's library at Cwrtycadno was particularly wide ranging, and must have been accumulated over several generations. It survived long enough to be picked over by antiquarians and folklorists at the end of the nineteenth century but by then the great chained book had disappeared.[28]

Conjurers compiled their own manuscript books of recipes, charms and incantations, and a few have survived. Some were in the nature of commonplace books, like Cadwallader Davies's *Piser Sioned* ('Janet's Pitcher'), a compendium of magico-medical and astrological memoranda accumulated over more than a decade between 1733 and 1745.[29] The most interesting of these manuscripts is the secret book (*'llyfr cyfrin'*) of an unnamed Denbighshire wise-man. This stubby volume has been described by Kate Bosse Griffiths: it has 200 pages but was small enough to fit into the pocket of a great coat. The contents were written in Welsh and English and included several conjuring formulae to summon the spirits called fairies (*tylwyth teg*); a formula to invocate and converse with the spirits of the dead; methods of telling fortunes through astrology; and various charms in Welsh and English, one with the note that these 'words being spoke with grate revarens and faith has don wondars'. There are copious notes on geomancy derived from printed authorities (including William Lilly) and manuscript sources. An antiquarian interest in the conjurer's craft is shown by the copy of 'a legendary charm used in former days in gathering herbs' taken from 'an old black letter missal in possession of the Mercury'. Named authorities included Dick Spot or Dic Smot, the eminent conjurer based in Oswestry who drew customers from many parts of England as well as Wales.[30]

The title 'conjurer' implied a reputation for conjuration, that is the magical technique of invoking and controlling spirits. This was the *ars magna* of the conjurer. Some conjurers were believed to keep devils, which permanently resided in their magic books. At times, conjurors summoned and controlled spirits from the safety of the magic circle. Clients did not usually witness conjuration, but occasionally conjurers had to make public demonstrations of their ability to command devils and other spirits, particularly when asked to lay ghosts.

Ghost-laying was perhaps the most theatrical of all magical tasks that the conjurer was called upon to perform. It was an activity in which their semi-mythical predecessors were famously adept, consigning the unruly ghosts of gentry villains like Sir John Wynn of Gwydir or Vaughan of Hergest to watery imprisonment.[31] Narratives of hauntings were common in Wales, and ghosts were usually dismissed by the discovery of lost or hidden goods – an activity at which conjurers excelled. Some spirits were more persistent than others, and their lively activities were not unlike those attributed to modern poltergeists. In 1758 a family was driven from a farmhouse at Llanllechid, Caernarfonshire, by a spirit which flung river stones ('of different sizes up to 27 pound weight') in and about the house. There were 'similar troubles but more violent' at a Montgomeryshire farm on the Wynnstay estate. Other celebrated hauntings occurred in south and central Wales in the second half of the eighteenth century at Hafod (Ceredigion) and Trwyn Farmhouse (Mynyddislwyn, Monmouthshire), and elsewhere. It was apparently difficult to get rid of these maliciously boisterous ghosts once ensconced in a house, and it was sometimes believed that the spirits had been brought there maliciously by 'enchantment' (as at Bodeugan, near St Asaph) or accidentally by a novice conjurer trying out magic spells (as at Trwyn). The beleaguered tenants of Bodeugan were encouraged locally to 'try to discover the Conjerers [responsible, so as] to punish them', asking their landlord to join with them in prosecuting the guilty party. They had heard that Dr Bennion of Oswestry, 'a very prophane character for the Black Art', had boasted when drunk of 'some horrid arts he had done'.[32]

These local causes célèbres were probably related to a more general panic about ghosts in the second half of the eighteenth century which was fostered by pamphlets, ballads, plays, and prints.[33] Interest and anxiety about a haunting was sometimes amplified into a public spectacle. Volunteers armed with guns kept watch and occasionally tried to shoot an apparition; clergymen and conjurers were consulted about exorcisms and would try to rise to the occasion. Several clergymen who came to subdue the Llanllechid spirit with prayers were driven back to Bangor by the stone-throwing ghost. Exorcism was a long and exhausting business during which the conjurer (or clergyman) gradually obtained control over the spirit. The conjurer eventually commanded the spirit to assume various guises, and in the form of a fly was finally captured and imprisoned in a bottle, goose-quill, or snuff-box. The imprisoned spirit was then consigned to the bottom of the Red Sea, or at least placed in a local lake beneath a stone. There was a considerable body of folklore about this with 'hardly a pool in a river, or lake in which Spirits have not, according to popular opinion been laid'. Famously, Dic Smot imprisoned a spirit called 'Ysbryd Cynon' within a quill which was entombed beneath Carreg yr Ysbryd ('stone of the spirit') in Llanwddyn, though Dic did not foresee that the stone would eventually be disturbed when Lake Vyrnwy was constructed.[34] When conjurers carried out these dramatic exorcisms, as it seems they did, one can understand that the effectiveness of the ritual lay in the way the anxieties of the situation were first externalized in the form of the imprisoned fly and then assuaged by consigning the object to aquatic oblivion.

Conjurers and Crime

Conjurers in the eighteenth century were probably most frequently consulted to locate lost or stolen goods and to identify thieves. Their techniques would generally have been familiar to their seventeenth-century predecessors, although the magic book had assumed greater significance as an indispensable prop. Some cunning-men, like Robert Darcy, relied on simple divinatory techniques. Darcy asked clients to shuffle a pack of cards three times before spreading them on a table where he began interpreting ('spying into') them. This may have been regarded as an inferior technique, and Darcy did not satisfy a client in 1740, who later prosecuted a bill of indictment against him, unsuccessfully as it turned out. There seems to have been more confidence in the venerable but simplified technique of crystal-gazing, which was used by several conjurers to identify numerous thieves and the occasional murderer. The technique involved a dialogue between conjurer and the client, who peered into the mysterious crystal or glass and gradually discerned images or forms. The use of the mediating 'scryer' had been dispensed with, and the eighteenth-century conjurer encouraged his clients to look directly into the crystal.[35]

Such was the faith in crystal-gazing that the mere threat to involve a conjurer would have a dramatic effect on a criminal suspect and might even prompt a confession. In 1824 after John Jones was apprehended for suspected patricide, the constable, the suspect's brothers and friends announced that they intended to take the prisoner to another part of Flintshire to consult John Edwards 'who has the character of being a conjurer'. They had decided against disinterring the body and allowing the suspect to touch it, a traditional ordeal for a suspected murderer whose touch – if guilty – would make the corpse bleed. Instead, they would know the truth about the horrible crime because the conjurer 'could show the guilty party in a glass'. The suspect was less keen on the idea, protesting rather lamely that it would cost them money. Jones was left in no doubt that 'if he was guilty he had better confess for that the murder would out, and it would be better for him and easier on his trial.' It was not long before Jones confessed to the murder.[36] Information allegedly obtained by means of the conjurer's crystal was sometimes offered to magistrates. In 1764 David Lloyd of Cadoxton-Neath, a shoemaker, announced to an examining justice of the peace that he knew 'as well as ye almighty God' who had murdered Benjamin Price. He had consulted a 'cunning man' and had seen the murder in his glass in remarkable and troubling detail. Lloyd claimed that (even though the room had been filled with afternoon sunlight) the glass showed two brothers, whom he recognized, one kicking the victim's head and the other seizing him by the throat. The witness named the cunning-man as William Prosser, describing him unflatteringly but presumably accurately as a one-eyed doctor who specialised as a clap-surgeon.[37]

Theft and losses provided routine work for the conjurer. Up and down Wales conjurers were visited when goods were lost or stolen, and many tales, some with tragi-comic elements, clustered around this type of situation. Usually the victim of a theft consulted a conjurer, but sometimes the suspect consulted the conjurer to clear his or her name or divert suspicion to another. This was easily achieved since it was the client who interpreted the images in the conjurer's glass and could announce the identity of another suspect. On New Year's Eve 1758 Anne David went with a friend to Llandyfaelog to consult Thomas Morgan, a Breconshire conjurer, after the theft of money from one William Walter. On arrival Anne went 'in private' to consult the cunning-man and gave him five shillings. Afterwards, Anne described how Morgan 'had shewed her ... in a glass' the person who had stolen William Walter's money. The details of this crystal revelation were remarkably specific. Anne could see William Walter's dresser, the drawer in which he kept his money, and then the thief with pipe in mouth, whom she identified as John Jones the tanner, drunkenly counting the gold taken from a purse. In this case the conjurer, apparently concerned for his reputation, took it upon himself to interview the suspects. He saw Anne privately and 'Charged her to speak the Truth, for that he had heard no Truth from her as yet'. Anne confessed that she herself had stolen the gold coins, lamenting, 'Wo is me that I have been so unhappy as to meddle with them.' Subsequently Anne David was prosecuted for the theft and the conjurer himself was obliged to appear at the Breconshire Great Sessions to give evidence.[38]

When a suspect could not be readily identified, as must often have happened, conjurers offered (for a fee, of course) to afflict the unknown thief with a debilitating ailment. Robert Darcy, the Wrexham cunning-man, told a client at an initial six-penny consultation that if he could not identify the thief of some missing yarn he would make him 'uneasy in his mind and trouble him for three moons afterwards'.[39] A thief so punished would realise that his affliction was caused by magic, and return the stolen goods so that the punishment could be lifted. Entertaining stories circulated about the unforeseen consequences of afflicting thieves with magical maladies. A farmer who insisted that a conjurer should punish a persistent vegetable thief returned home only to find that his best pig was running mad.[40] Conjurers sometimes offered to 'mark' a thief or witch. The facial mark was simultaneously a punishment, a warning to other thieves, and an expression of the conjurer's power. A vile facial sore that afflicted a suspected witch in Machynlleth was supposed to have been a mark inflicted by a local conjurer, whose reputation was correspondingly enhanced.[41] It was believed that the most powerful conjurers could make a horn grow out of the culprit's forehead, a phenomenon that was the subject of some medical curiosity.[42] This feat was attributed to the legendary conjurer Huw Llwyd of Cynfal and also to Dr Harries, Cwrtycadno. The mere threat of the conjurer's mark was sometimes enough to make thieves confess or decamp. When in 1788 John Price, a Radnorshire farmer, discovered that savings of £7.3s.6d. was missing from a box in his bed-chamber, he announced his intention of going to a conjurer, saying that 'he would find out who had stolen his money and that he would mark them'. Shortly afterwards one of his servant-maids, who had recently indulged herself by buying a tea-kettle and some bedding, hurriedly left his service.[43]

The presence of a conjurer in a community may have acted as a deterrent to thieves and cheats, or so the chapbook account of Mochyn-y-nant suggests. It claimed that the Ruabon conjuror 'frequently caused those to deal honestly, who, but for the reported power of such people, would act in open defiance of all Laws, both human and divine, and plunder their Neighbours with Impunity.'[44] Nevertheless, it was part of the ever-present ambiguity of cunning-men that the same person might combine the helpful services of a conjurer with the harmful activities of a wizard. Conjurers might help catch thieves but they might also assist others to steal. When Henry Thomas, a Carmarthenshire shoemaker's apprentice, joined a gang of horse-thieves in the Merthyr area about 1805 he was impressed by the ease with which they caught ponies on the Black Mountain. He was told by the horse-thieves that 'they had power from the Devil in writing upon paper which they had had from conjurors', unfortunately unnamed, which was to remain in force for three years. The new gang member was given this powerful 'writing' and told that if he kept it safely no one could detain him. Henry Thomas was eventually apprehended and (no doubt believing he would soon be free) artlessly told the examining magistrate about the conjurer's paper, explaining that when he had the charm the ponies were 'so tame that I could catch them when I pleased' but when he was without the 'writing' he could not catch the ponies any easier than anyone else.[45]

Conjurers and Healers

Conjurers were often physicians and healers and were sometimes called 'doctor' as a courtesy: Dr Bennion in north Wales, and in south Wales, Dr Harries of Cwrtycadno, Carmarthenshire, and his namesake, Dr Harries of Dinas, Pembrokeshire. The doctor-conjurer had to compete with numerous charmers, herb-doctors, and bone-setters about whom very little is usually known. Fortunately the diary of William Thomas provides us with a view of the ubiquitous but elusive local charmers and healers. In the south-east corner of the Vale of Glamorgan in the latter part of the eighteenth century the diarist noted half-a-dozen specialist healers. Some were herb-doctors who specialised in particular ailments; others were charmers who used special formulae, or healers who had 'secret' cures.[46] Charmers who specialised in curing shingles, styes, and warts were known in many parts of Wales. Those who charmed away shingles and herpes (*yr eryr*) had a special claim to fame in that it was believed that their ability was inherited from ancestors who had consumed eagles' flesh after which (according to a folk etymology) the disease was named.[47]

In addition to these specialist healers one must mention the custodians of objects with special healing virtues. These unique objects included the famous Nanteos Cup, said to have been made from the True Cross, kept at Nanteos mansion, Cardiganshire, and the skull of St Teilo kept at Ffynnon Deilo, Carmarthenshire. Despite the claims of great antiquity made for them, these relics seem to have acquired their reputations relatively late.[48] Some special curing objects, notably hydrophobia stones and snake- or adder-stones, were in fairly wide circulation and can be documented from the later seventeenth century. Several healing stones ('*llaethfaen*': 'milk-stone') were in the keeping of respectable families in different parts of south Wales; others were hawked around the countryside. Iolo Morganwg encountered a healer in north Pembrokeshire who carried a healing stone (here called '*llysfaen*') scraped for a powder sold at about five shillings an ounce as a cure for rabies. The vendor claimed that the stone was only to be found on the mountains after a thunderstorm, and that not every eye could see it. When Iolo pointed out that the stone was nothing but a piece of Glamorgan alabaster, a little crowd confounded him by saying that they had seen the powder cure hydrophobia in man and dogs.[49]

Unlike most folk-healers who tended to specialise in particular ailments, conjurers were generalists who were particularly skilled in diagnosis, and sooner or later difficult cases were brought to them. Their strength was an insight into the origin of different ailments, including supernatural causes. Their diagnostic techniques, as would be expected, included astrology, but it is particularly interesting that many eighteenth-century conjurers were 'water-doctors', appropriating the technique of uroscopy, the examination of urine for diagnosing diseases, which had been gradually abandoned by mainstream medical practitioners. 'By the close of the seventeenth century', Roy Porter observes, 'urine-gazing as a self-sufficient medical art …was becoming stigmatised as a special trade-mark of quackery'. Welsh conjurers were among the 'various unorthodox healers [who] kept up the art in country areas through the eighteenth century' and – it may be added – well into the nineteenth century.[50]

There is ample evidence for the continuing popularity of water-doctors in the latter part of the eighteenth century. Thomas James (d. 1781), who kept an alehouse by Trevethin church, was regarded as 'a great urinal doctor and reputed conjurer' and 'much people resorted to him'.[51] The Trevethin area of Monmouthshire seems to have been famous for its water-doctors. William Thomas notes the death of William Read of Trevethin, a water-doctor. According to the diarist, he had been taught by his uncle, John William Bevan of Pontypool, 'that famous urinal doctor', but 'had more judgement as reported than his teacher'. He was 'a man of the greatest judgement concerning man and to cast urine in our parts', and patients came to him daily from England and Wales. He would honestly tell them their infirmities and give them medicine and advice at a reasonable rate.[52] It was not absolutely necessary for patients to present themselves to the urine doctor. A friend might bring a flask of urine from the patient's sick bed and expect the urine doctor to make a diagnosis. Rhisiart Cap Du, a celebrated Monmouthshire conjurer, not only diagnosed urine without seeing the patient but, it was said, sometimes predicted when it would be brought to him.[53]

Not all water-doctors were conjurers, of course, but many conjurers were water-doctors. Urine casting certainly appealed to the theatrical element in the conjurer's craft. When William Edward (or Griffith) the conjurer burst upon the Vale of Glamorgan in 1768 he was hailed as a great urine-doctor. His clients reported that he 'knew all that belongs to them without they express nothing'. All that was needed was a sample of urine 'which he throw'd for nothing', but his clients had to pay for 'sham drugs' after the diagnosis.[54] The urine was placed in flasks that were viewed in different lights, shaken ('thrown'), and sometimes boiled. The water-doctor made diagnoses that the licensed doctors would or could not make, including sickness from witchcraft. One of the Monmouthshire urine-doctors ('he of Pontypool') advised Thomas Philip of Caerau that 'he was witched', after Philip had unsuccessfully 'try'd the most of doctors and the Infirmary at Bristol' to cure his fits.[55]

Cunning-folk and healers used their techniques to diagnose complaints not recognized by orthodox medicine, particularly ailments attributed to witchcraft and spells, which went under various special names: '*liveranartegro*', '*clwyf yr edau wlân*', and '*ymaendwnen*'.[56] '*Liveranartegro*' was a common debilitating ailment in south Pembrokeshire, understood to be caused by the liver and heart growing together, and was attributed to witchcraft. The symptoms were great weakness, anaemia, difficulty in breathing, and acute pain in the left side. Orthodox physicians would try and treat patients afflicted with 'liveranartegro' as if they were suffering from consumption, but this seems to have been ineffective. A Saundersfoot doctor was driven to dismiss sufferers from this mysterious ailment, saying, 'Go to the charmer, I can do nothing for you.' The charmer's cure was elaborate. The patient attended the charmer three times on alternate days, one being a Sunday. The charmer filled a cup to the brim with oatmeal, covering it with a handkerchief so that none of the meal could escape. The charmer applied the cup nine times to the affected parts of the body reciting certain formulae. The cup was then uncovered and the contents examined. If the patient had '*liveranartegro*' the meal would have diminished in proportion to the severity of the condition. The meal remaining in the cup underwent a change, becoming 'crustaceous and marked on the surface with reticulated fissures'. The residue of the meal was closely scrutinized by the charmer who could 'read' the significance of its changed appearance.[57]

In west and mid-Wales wise-men and -women took a special interest in '*clefyd y galon*', literally heart disease, but more generally melancholy or depression, or a consumption due to love-sickness or witchcraft, especially associated with young women. It seems to have been similar to '*clwyf yr edau wlân*', literally 'the woollen-yarn disease', a consumption sometimes said to have been caused by witchcraft.[58] 'The woollen-yarn disease' was so called from the special technique used to diagnose and cure the ailment. The cure had historical roots in the late-medieval technique of 'girdle measuring', but there are no early documentary references to it in Wales.[59] It seems that the measuring technique was rediscovered and popularised by eighteenth-century cunning-folk, becoming something of a speciality in north Cardiganshire and Montgomeryshire. The wise-man or -woman using unscoured, white, woollen yarn measured the patient from the elbow to the tip of the middle finger, naming the sufferer and his or her exact age, and reciting a prayer. This was done three times, and the movements of the thread provided an indication of the nature of the disease and its expected course. If the thread lengthened the patient was not suffering from the 'yarn disease'; if the thread shortened the patient was afflicted with the sickness, which was sometimes said to be 'hot'. The thread was then put round the sufferer's neck (sometimes around the leg) in a little skein and left for three (or seven) nights and then buried in the name of the Trinity. It was necessary to repeat the technique several times. The lengthening or contraction of the thread indicated the progress of the disease. If the wool lengthened the patient was recovering, if the yarn shortened to above the middle finger the patient was sure to die. There were many variations in the technique. Sometimes a 'messenger' was employed on behalf of the sufferer, and the wise-woman or wise-man measured herself while reciting the name and age of the afflicted person, ascertaining whether the sufferer believed in the cure. Sometimes a special medicine, which included meadow saffron, was given to the afflicted person and was taken hot with beer or gin at specified intervals. A special onus was placed was placed on the 'faith' of the patient in the cure. This protected the reputation of the charmer. Those who were not cured did not have faith in the treatment or had given the healer false information. It was sometimes said that some of the elderly didn't respond to the woollen-yarn treatment because they often gave unreliable information about their age. This was an understandable consequence of illiteracy; it was only in the nineteenth century that the date and sometimes the time of a birth was regularly recorded in a family Bible or other book.[60]

Conjurers and Witchcraft

Conjurers had special status not only because they could control spirits but also because they were the adversaries of witches. They could recognize the effects of witchcraft, identify the witch, and counteract the witch's curse. Some districts were particularly associated with witchcraft. In the eighteenth century Llangattock-Crickhowell had this reputation in south Wales. The witches of Llanddona were notorious in north-west Wales, and it was said their powers derived from a shipwrecked gypsy ancestor who had settled in the Anglesey parish. The gipsy's descendants were great fortune-tellers and included Shâni Llanddona (noted above) and the 'Little Llanddona Witch' ('*Witsh bach Llandonna*'), otherwise Shân Bwt, who was less than four feet tall and born with two thumbs on her left hand, whose portrait was drawn in the early nineteenth century (Fig. 10).[61]

A reputation for witchcraft was not infrequently inherited. An eighteenth-century diarist recorded the death of Ann Richmond of Cwm Cidy, Glamorgan, who died in 1763 aged well over 100, noting 'all folks about dread her – and believe she could witch', adding 'the same belief is of her son'. It was rumoured that before old Ann Richmond died the devil had appeared to her 'with a Bull's head and offered a year longer on earth if she at the end of the year would deliver her Body and all to he'. There were 'tales of hurt' that she and her son had done to cattle. The son, William Jenkins of Cwm Cidy (d. 1781) issued a writ when he was called a wizard, and in 1763 Dr Bates of Cowbridge determined a wager that Jenkins had teats. The family's reputation for witchcraft continued into the nineteenth century.[62]

Few Welsh communities seem to have been without a suspected witch in the eighteenth and early nineteenth centuries. A reputed Breconshire witch expected and received free food and pasture at farms in Ystradgynlais, but in 1832 met her match in the engineer constructing the Brecon Forest tramway. Rev. W. R. Jones was able to name five reputed witches in nineteenth-century Glynceiriog, the populous farming and quarrying valley in Denbighshire: Cadi Fawr, Catrin Jones, Mari'r Hen Siôp, Leisa Morus, and Gras Huws. In south Pembrokeshire the witches of Dale, Rosemarket, Carew Mountain, and other localities were household names. Most notoriously, Moll of Redberth made this disconcerting death-bed confession to her parson: 'For thirty-seven years I have been in possession of the power to bewitch. It pains me to think of it now – I have used this power scores of time to the injury of my fellow men.' Moll then told the parson how she acquired this power. On the occasion of her first communion she did not consume the wafer but brought it away from the church. On the road she met Satan in the guise of a dog and gave him the wafer. Satan in return gave Moll the power to bewitch.[63]

Reputed witches were generally elderly women in straightened circumstances, many of whom survived by begging in an interestingly oblique way, never actually asking directly for what they wanted. A revealing and amusing story from early-nineteenth-century Anglesey illustrates the cautious attitudes of the period. One day a strange woman poked her head round the kitchen door of a Llangaffo farmhouse and pointedly remarked on the fine quality of the salted hams hanging from the beams (*'Mae gennych gig da yma!'*). The farmer's wife hurried to cut off a piece of meat to offer the stranger. When she had gone a poor woman who worked in the kitchen was heard to remark, 'How wonderful it must be to be a witch!'[64]

Although some witches were known by name, more usually witches remained unknown unless they were identified by a conjuror or revealed their names when challenged by a good person. This was especially true of gypsies, who were most likely among wanderers to be suspected of witchcraft, and some people maintained a particular aversion towards them. An entertaining Monmouthshire narrative, placed by Edmund Jones at the end of the seventeenth century, related how the house of an 'honest substantial freeholder' in Bedwellty was often troubled at night by very mischievous witches who amused themselves by 'destroying the milk etc.' Hopkin David, a Quaker and turner, who was working at the house, hearing a disturbance one night came down to investigate and saw the witches 'in the shape of extraordinary looking cats'. Realising they were witches, he asked each of them 'Who art thou, and what is thy name?' They answered, *'Ellor Sir Gar'* (Carmarthenshire Eleanor), *'Mawd Anghyvion'* (Unrighteous Maud), and *'Izbel Anonest'* (Unjust Isabel). The witches had betrayed themselves and were in danger of punishment. The Quaker reproved and threatened them, and they did not trouble the house afterwards.[65]

Witches were often able to do their mischief by shape changing, metamorphosing into a hare, cat, or some other animal. The Welsh witch in animal guise sometimes challenged her human adversaries to track her down. A ubiquitous folktale described how a gentleman or substantial farmer was challenged by an elusive hare while out hunting. The hare would start up in front of the hounds but proved impossible to catch. Finally, the elusive hare was chased into a house where the astonished huntsmen found a witch within injured and panting from the long chase. This type of story often contained an element of ironic humour. In a tale set near Caernarfon, one Mary y Gors changed herself into a hare at the approach of a sporting gentleman with a gun and dog, saying to her granddaughter, *'Mi roi i rhai'n race rwan!'* ('I'll give these a race now!'), and ran in front of the dog. Both hound and witch had their supporters: *'Hwi y ci da!'* ('Come on, good dog!') urged the huntsman; the granddaughter cheered on the hare, inadvertently crying *'Hwi fy nain!'* ('Come on, my grandmother!') in her excitement.[66]

The subtext of these widely-distributed stories was that witches lived among ordinary folk but were not generally identified except in extraordinary circumstances. Informal action against suspected witches, including threats to 'scratch' witches or wizards, was occasionally reported, but these cases were rare.[67] The usual course of action in a case of suspected witchcraft was to consult a conjurer experienced in such matters. It seems that the conjurer would generally confirm the suspicions of a client and suggest a procedure that would counteract the witchcraft and draw the witch to the place that she had bewitched. Once the witch had revealed herself she was compelled to break the spell. Witchcraft cases seem often to have been long and difficult, requiring a number of consultations between client and conjurer, and might end inconclusively. If one conjurer failed (as well he might) then another might be consulted until the problem was resolved.

A Denbighshire conjurer's book records a successful instance of counteracting witchcraft in 1832. A memorandum describes how a farmer from Hope, Flintshire, 'complained much that his cattle and milk had been witched' and that 'some of cattle had lost their dids [= teats]'. This had continued for two or three months, the farmer's losses were great and 'all his cheese were spoilt'. The farmer's son had been seven times to see a certain 'wise man' known as Shôn y Rhose, but to no avail. Shôn y Rhose said that 'he could not do the work [within] three moons'. In desperation the farmer consulted a neighbouring gentleman farmer, who persuaded him to consult the Denbighshire conjurer. The conjurer promised to bring the farmer out of the 'ruinous concern' without delay. The conjurer notes with some satisfaction, 'Accordingly I did through God's assistance to the great astonishment and satisfaction of the farmer and his family. For they told me that the first cheese that was made after was richer and better than could be expected.'[68]

The Denbighshire conjurer does not describe his successful technique. However, a detailed account survives of the procedure used by a Breconshire conjurer to counteract witchcraft, although in this instance the conjurer was unsuccessful. In summer 1788 the milk of the cows at Cwm-nant, Ystradfellte, had a strange appearance and the farmer 'believed it was affected by witchcraft'. The farmer's son (who was also his farm-servant) was sent to consult the conjurer at Llanafan-fawr, at the other end of the county. Daniel James, the conjurer, confirmed that the extraordinary appearance of the milk was due to witchcraft, but reassuringly said 'he would prevent it'. The following morning the conjurer 'looked into a book' and instructed the farmer's son 'to take cows piss & some hair off their tails & to boil the same with salt & while he was doing it to permit no person to remain in the house but himself. Then he was to bury it by a stile near a particular woman's house.' Before departure the conjurer gave his client 'a paper to put over the door of the dairy'. This consultation, which cost five shillings, proved unsuccessful and the client visited the conjurer for a second time. The conjurer again promised 'to set the milk to rights', saying 'he should see who did the mischief to it'. The conjurer looked into his book, and this time 'described the person of a woman whom he said was the witch'. The client was instructed to prepare the same charm, but with the addition of two horseshoes 'having three nails in each of them'. The conjurer was paid a further 2s.6d.

This second attempt to lift the witchcraft also failed and the conjurer was consulted for a third time. It was obviously a difficult case, and the conjurer said 'he must be on the spot before he could effect the cure'. The date for the conjurer's visit was arranged, and the client was to inform his neighbours of the conjurer's visit and that he was available to 'tell fortunes and recover lost and stolen goods'. The conjurer came to Cwm-nant about Allhallowtide, that part of the ritual year associated with the appearance of spirits and witches, and stayed for four days 'pretending' by various means 'to find out the witch', *generally* 'having generally a book before him'. Finally the conjurer announced he would cause the farmer to see the witch. The conjurer insisted on borrowing the farmer's watch before theatrically shutting himself up in a room while ordering the farmer's family to another part of the house, saying they would see the woman, meaning the witch, entering the house. This should have been a dramatic conclusion to the case but the witch failed to appear on cue. The farmer's wife was distinctly unimpressed, and matters must have gone from bad to worse because the dissatisfied clients subsequently indicted the conjurer at the quarter-sessions for fraud.[69]

The technique of the Llanafan-fawr conjurer was an exercise in sympathetic magic. Taking hair and urine from a bewitched animal and boiling the bewitched substances would agitate the witch, and the addition of salt and iron horse-shoes (each with an odd number of nails) would be hateful to her. The idea was both to counteract the witchcraft and to identify the witch by compelling her to appear. The elaborate charade that the conjurer acted out seems to have gone badly wrong. It is interesting that the conjurer needed a watch; presumably the procedure depended on astrological timings. Montgomeryshire conjurers sometimes attributed the failure of a ritual to an imprecise time given by the client who had to read a clock. The method used by the Montgomeryshire conjurers to counteract witchcraft (as reported in the early twentieth century) was broadly similar. The animal was rubbed with a special written charm. Some of its hair was placed between two flat-irons placed on top of the range. The witch was afflicted with toothache and drawn to the farmhouse. With the appearance of the witch, she would be persuaded to lift her curse and the spell would be broken.

There was an important distinction between witch detection and witchcraft prevention. Detecting a witch and compelling her to appear was (as we have seen) a difficult and sometimes lengthy procedure that might leave the client unconvinced. Preventing witchcraft was a routine procedure involving written charms that most literate conjurers would have been proficient at producing. The Llanafan conjurer gave his client a charm which was to be placed above the dairy doorway. Numerous charms of this type have survived in Wales and examples are preserved in libraries and museums, as well as retained in private hands following chance discoveries during the renovation of buildings.[70]

The charms appear more archaic and mysterious than they actually are. The earliest probably belong to the eighteenth century, but many have a nineteenth- or even early-twentieth-century context.[71] The charms are written in ink on a strip of paper generally measuring about 18.5cm x 12cm. The charm was usually rolled up, sometimes gummed, and put in a bottle which was then sealed and placed over a doorway or buried under the floor. These charms, with some slight variations, follow the same formula. They are written in a mixture of English and dog-Latin with hardly a break between the words. The excessively cursive script is initially a barrier to intelligibility but the charms generally fall into three parts. There was first a prayer seeking the protection of a named client and his cattle from all evil men and women, spirits, wizards, and hardness of heart. Then the names of God, the magi, and the evangelists were invoked, each name generally followed by a cross, with the invocation generally concluding with the names of the archangels. At the foot of the charm there were often two magical signs, a diminishing abracadabra (left) and a circular magical sign (right), with astronomical or planetary signs between, sometimes concluding 'By Jah, Jah, Jah'. The magical circle has caused some palaeographical puzzlement. The British Museum offered the opinion in the 1930s that the circle was a seal 'clearly akin to that used by the Popes from the time of the Middle Ages in their bulls'. The device was however a magic seal and (as has been noted recently) derives from a protective charm illustrated in Scot's *Discoverie of Witchcraft*, captioned 'Who so beareth this sign about him, let him fear no foe, but fear God'. An edition of Scot's *Discoverie* was presumably among the Montgomeryshire conjurer's books, as it certainly was in the library at Cwrtycadno.[72]

The specific function of a charm was set out in an unpunctuated opening petition: 'relieve Thomas Ellis Pen y garnedd the cows calves milk butter catll of all ages and his wife and all of the children [and] to relieve [them] from all witchcraft and all evil diseases'; 'relieve Richard Davies and Gwarnas his mare that is bad now from all witchcraft and all evil diseases'; 'preserve me Edward Jones my horses cows calves pigs sheep and every living creatures that I possess from the power of all evil men women spinsters [= spirits] or wizards or hardness of heart'; 'deliver Elizabeth Loyd from all witchcraft and from all evil sprites by the same power as he did cause the blind to see the lame to walke the dum to talke'; 'deliver Thomas Thomas & his family & every living creature under his possession on his farm big & small from witchcraft & from all evil diseases whatsoever'; 'preserve Morgan Richards his cows milk and cream to churn and have good butter from witchcraft'.[73]

The use of these charms was widespread. Many seem to have been produced in Montgomeryshire over several generations, becoming a speciality of conjurers in the Llangurig district. The distinctive form of the anti-witchcraft charm seems to have achieved a settled form in the later eighteenth century and may have been devised by Edward Savage (1759–1849) and perfected by his grandson, John Morgan, but there were many imitators.[74] The charms are said to have cost five shillings each in the nineteenth century, the conjurer taking about half an hour to prepare it. A charm retained its virtue for no longer than twelve months, and some farmers seem to have bought a new charm every year – a useful regular income for the conjurer.[75] The survival of so many charms is a physical reminder of the constant demand for the services of the conjurer in eighteenth- and nineteenth-century Wales, and of the deep-seated anxieties about witchcraft in the Welsh countryside.

Harries of Cwrtycadno

The best-known lineage of Welsh conjurers was settled at Cwrtycadno in Carmarthenshire. The Harris family exemplified the professionalism of the conjurer and his ability to survive – indeed prosper – in the first half of the nineteenth century. The founder of the family business seems to have been Harry John or Harri Siôn (called Henry Jones on his tombstone), who died in 1805 aged sixty-six, and was remembered as a herb-doctor and astrologer. His son, John Harry, otherwise Dr John Harries (1785–1839), described as a 'surgeon' on his tombstone, became a conjurer of regional if not national reputation. His sons, Henry (d. 1849) and John (d. 1863) Harries, were also doctors and astrologers. The family were able, literate, and scientific. They were also firmly rooted in their community. As was customary among artisans and farmers (the classes who were the bulk of Harries's patients), a bidding letter solicited contributions after the marriage of Henry and his wife Hannah which were to be 'cheerfully repaid whenever called upon on a similar occasion'. There are several early photographs of members of the Harries family; these are unusual survivals given a local prejudice against portrait photography (Fig. 12). A late-Victorian historian maintained that the old people of the Caeo district 'had the most curious fancies about pictures, and a very general dislike to have their photographs taken. Doctor Harries knew this well, and no doubt he was able to play on their ignorance and superstition'.[76]

Dr John Harries built up the family business. He was 'an Astrologer and a Wizard, and these qualifications he made great use of in dispensing medicine to a large practice.' Harries was described as an educated man, with neat and polished handwriting and diction, and had evidently worked at some time in a hospital. The Harries family business was at its height in the 1820s–40s but continued into the 1860s. The principal specialisms were healing, discovering lost goods, and astrological advice. A local clergyman has left a sympathetic account of the method of consulting John Harries. According to Rev. Cunllo Davies 'the sick and the sorrowful' came to consult Dr Harries from all parts of Wales, and from the testimony of the oldest people Davies concluded that he was 'eminently successful in his cures'. According to Cunllo Davies, he was 'more successful in curing pulmonary diseases than dislocations, tumours, and cancer'. He specialized in pain relief (not always the priority of the licensed practitioner), and was so successful in 'charming away' pain that many believed he was in league with the devil. Consultations took place in an improvised surgery at Pant-coy. The anxious patient ('whose imagination is full of strange stories') was relieved to find the doctor although a man of 'rough exterior' has 'geniality of countenance of the most winning kind'. However on the table there was the paraphernalia of the conjurer, including 'some dozens of odd volumes'. Some books were open and the patient could see 'peculiar hieroglyphics and tables'. A few books were 'tied with shoe string, others are clasped with heavy brass, and one is actually padlocked'. A quiet talk disclosed valuable information about the patient's ailment, 'then the doctor consulted his tomes, brewed a concoction of herbs, and assured the patient that he would be cured through his knowledge of astrology'. According to Cunllo Davies, Harries's materia medica consisted almost entirely of herbs. Later Henry Harries developed a large herbal surgery at Glan-rhyd, keeping dried herbs in special earthenware containers ('healing jars').[77]

The Harrieses kept business accounts like other rural craftsmen and professional men. The surviving pages of Harries's day-book and bill-book show that he treated patients more or less daily. The records are far from complete, but it appears that the numbers of patients who visited Harries steadily increased during the year, peaking in the summer, and declining as winter approached and travel became more difficult. At his busiest in 1815, Harries saw some sixty patients in each of the summer months but by the winter fewer than twenty patients consulted him each month. Although Harries favoured herbal remedies, his prescriptions did include some patent medicines. The patients were charged relatively small sums for these medicines. A page from Harries's ledger shows that patients commonly had cumulative bills amounting to 7s.6d. or 15s., but sometimes bills were allowed to mount up to considerable sums. John Morgan's account for 1824–1830, which included the treatment of several relatives, finally totalled £9.12s.0d. In cases such as this, Harries would present a disconcerting printed bill to his client that concluded ominously, 'Unless the above Amount is paid to me ... adverse means will be resorted to, for the recovery.'[78]

Harries seems often to have treated difficult cases including those regarded as hopeless or incurable by licensed doctors. In particular, Harries dealt with the mentally ill. Lunatics were brought to him from distant parts, and it is said 'he had a wonderful power over them'. According to Cunllo Davies, 'Hundreds that would be lodged in lunatic asylums to-day were sent home completely cured.' Harries's method of treatment included 'the water treatment', as well as the 'herb treatment' and the 'bleeding treatment'. In the 'water treatment' the patient was taken to the brink of a pool on the river Cothi, probably at Pwll Uffern or 'hell's mouth', where Harries would fire an old pistol. The frightened patient would fall into the pool and emerge shocked but cured. In performing these treatments, Harris relied on young men from the Caeo village to restrain and support patients. These villagers regarded Harries as a hero.[79]

A large part of the Harries's work involved preparing horoscopes. Henry Harries was educated at a local commercial school ('Mr G. C. Birds' Commercial Academy') and was said to have been apprenticed to the celebrated astrologer 'Raphael' in London for several years. The truth was rather different. Raphael was the pseudonym used by a succession of editors of a popular astrological almanac. The young Henry Harries wrote to 'Raphael' in 1840 offering to 'prostrate' himself at the 'venerable feet' of the great astrologer, begging the great man to teach him how to make spirits appear.[80] About this time, father and son jointly issued an advertising card headed 'Nativities Calculated'. The astrological activities of the Harrieses were satirized in *Yr Haul*, an Anglican journal edited by David Owen ('Brutus'), who relished attacking religious quackery, but of course this may have served only to publicize the Harries family business to a wider audience.[81] Henry Harries's advertisement of *c.* 1840, which had so outraged Brutus set out what was offered. Nativities were calculated. The general transactions of the 'native' (an astrological term) through life were deduced from the influence of the sun and moon, with the planetary orbs, at the time of birth. Information was available on honour, riches, journeys (where best to travel to or reside in), friends and enemies, trade or profession (which best to follow), whether fortunate in speculations (the lottery and dealing in foreign markets), of marriage (if to marry and the nature of one's spouse), of children (whether fortunate or not). Henry Harries's astrological training was superior to that of the majority of fortune-tellers and, of course, advertising was an innovation. The card concluded with the caution that letters would be returned unless pre-paid. Letters probably poured into Cwrtycadno over the next twenty years, and two have survived. The writer of one, Thomas Thomas of Pen-lôn, asks if a certain person is to be his wedded wife – 'I shal leve it to you to judge', he tells Harries, and asks for the figure (or horoscope) to be sent by the bearer. William Lloyd of Ciliau (Cillia) writes on behalf of his sisters, one of whom has a pain in her breast. He gives their dates and times of birth.[82]

Like many conjurers, the Harrieses used horoscopes to try and locate lost or stolen goods. A draft horoscope dated 29 March 1856 is annotated 'Llwyntirnir, sheep lost'. Another drawn up in 1849 for Mr William Powell, Battle Fawr, Breconshire (to be left at the Swan Inn) concerned the time 'when the two heifers was lost'.[83] The Harrieses' recovery service was superior to that offered by most cunning men, and both John and Henry Harries were credited with having located missing persons. Dr Harries's reputation was greatly enhanced, and the event celebrated in song, when he apparently successfully deduced where a young woman had been murdered and buried by her lover. The murderer was found and confessed to his crime, but Harries, on account of his knowledge of the burial, was charged with being an accessory. Harries was later discharged by the magistrates, apparently after discomforting them by saying that if they would tell him the hour they were born, he would tell them when they would die.[83] Harries was remembered for his successes, but there were of course failures.

About 1820 a disappointed client in Merthyr brought an action against Harries for failing to locate his lost or stolen goods.[84]

Harries's successful career presented a challenge to the educational and religious establishment. Attacks from the religious establishment were to be expected, but they came also from the press. Harries was a controversial figure because he disturbed notions of national progress. On Henry Harries's death in 1849 *The Welshman* noted that hundreds of persons of both sexes used to go from the counties of Hereford, Radnor, and Monmouth, to seek medical advice, and knowledge of the future, from the Harrieses. It was rumoured that Henry Harries would be succeeded by a relation (presumably his brother John) 'who had been in training with him for some time'. The newspaper urged its readers to 'do as much as they can to deter the misinformed who may be inclined to go to such people' who practised 'conjuring and quackery'.[85]

Harries exemplified the contradictions of the conjurer. He was able to operate quite successfully in the space – albeit a contracting space – left by licensed physicians who were sometimes incompetent, brutal, and cruel. Much of his work was astrological but he certainly traded on his reputation as a conjurer. As with other conjurers, Harries's reputation was ambiguous: it was thought he could harm as well as help. An extraordinary case in the probate court in Cardiff in 1904 involved the contested will of a testator who had considered himself bewitched by Harries.[86] Perhaps Harries even believed that he was a conjurer. Among miscellaneous notes salvaged from his library is a transcript of the *Fourth Book of Agrippa* with instructions on conjuring. According to local witnesses, at least once a year he would spend a day clearing a circle in a wood and reading long portions from the volume usually kept padlocked. He was accompanied by three or four companions (those who usually helped him with patients), and although he never explained the purpose of the ritual, 'the whole country would call it the day "he sold himself to the Devil"'.[87] Harries apparently predicted that he would not die an ordinary death but would be 'translated like Elijah the Tisbite'.[88] In the event, Harries died on a stormy night while trying to extinguish a fire in the thatched roof of his house. At Harries's funeral it was said that as he was being carried to the graveyard, the bearers felt the coffin grow lighter as the devil took possession of him. The image was traditional, but it may now have been a metaphor for the lifting of a burden from the past. By the mid- and later part of the nineteenth century witches, conjurers and the like were increasingly thought of as part of an Old Wales (*Cymru Fu*) located temporally and mentally in the past. For later nineteenth-century historians and religious writers nothing more illustrated the ignorance and credulity of the earlier part of the century than the widespread belief in witches, fortune-tellers, and conjurers.

Transformation: Cursing Wells

Surviving conjurers' charms – and they are numerous – are tangible expressions of the perception held by many men and women that they lived in a threatening social world surrounded by actual or potential enemies whose envy and malice could harm them and their property. The petitions (as described in the previous chapter) in these charms were unambiguous: relieve A from all witchcraft and evil diseases; preserve B and every living creature that he possesses from the powers of all evil men, women, spirits, or hardness of heart, and so on. Conjurers flourished in a social world where personal misfortunes could be attributed to the malice of others. There was also reciprocal willingness on the part of those who believed they were the victims of envy and malice to punish those who had injured them – if they could. The desire for revenge, to get one's own back, and indeed to punish excessively, were actually traits commonly attributed to witches, though people failed to acknowledge them in themselves. The notion of witchcraft involved the idea of successful cursing without justification, but what if this powerful type of cursing became available to everyone? In a social world where it was commonly perceived that one might accumulate numerous unforgiving enemies, this was a terrifying prospect. The possibility was transformed into terrifying practice in the late eighteenth and early nineteenth centuries when it was believed that a new power to curse without restraint had become available to everyone. This was potentially a world where the constraints of social solidarity no longer fettered the selfish or vengeful individual – in other words, the state of anomie.

Witchcraft beliefs are conventionally understood to have been gradually abandoned in eighteenth-century Europe. Perversely, in later eighteenth-century Wales witchcraft beliefs, far from declining, became darker in nature and underwent a transformation. By the first half of the nineteenth century it was said, despairingly, 'the curses come at us from everywhere surrounding our heads like black clouds, pouring drops of destruction in showers upon our heads to destroy us and our possessions'.[1] A novel form of cursing had arrived which was available to anyone and everyone. It made people defenceless as victims but at the same time empowered them as aggressors. This new method of cursing depended on the special properties attributed to certain wells and was called *offrymu*. The verb is usually translated as 'to offer' or 'to sacrifice', and both elements were present in the imposition of the curse. An offering was made at certain wells with the intention of consigning an enemy to misfortune. The enemy's initials were generally inscribed on a piece of lead or slate and placed in the well. Cursing wells were an innovation in late-eighteenth-century Wales but the practice of making 'cursing tablets' reaches back to antiquity. While there is no suggestion of continuity from the Roman period, there are certainly some interesting parallels, especially in the way appeals to divinity to punish wrongdoers were made at certain wells and springs regarded as the thresholds to supra-human powers.[2]

The emergence of cursing wells in early-modern Wales has to be understood within the context of a flourishing well-cult. There were numerous wells and springs dedicated to saints in the eighteenth-century countryside, each believed to have its own special virtue. This was an extraordinary and perplexing phenomenon in a Protestant country, as some pained clerics pointed out. Some important wells had been destroyed at the Reformation, particularly those associated with pilgrimages, but many healing wells of purely local significance survived, and indeed may have multiplied. In the early eighteenth century (as a Denbighshire parson remarked) there was hardly a parish in Wales without a well locally famous for the curing of some distemper or another, even though the educated dismissed them as superstitious or fraudulent, or both. Miraculous wells seemed to bring out the worst in even the most indulgent antiquaries. According to Edward Lhuyd, 'prejudice and bigotry' maintained the reputations of miraculous wells which were first founded on 'superstition and ignorance'.[3] It was generally the custom to offer a silver groat, or some other coin, when seeking the saint's blessing at a well, and this offering was placed in a special box for the use of the poor or given to the guardian of the well. The afflicted person would drink or sprinkle the water saying a customary invocation. Saints' wells offered hope to the afflicted but the peculiarities of many wells show that they also appealed to the imagination.[4]

There was a secular dynamic to the well-cult. Pride in the extraordinary properties of local wells was inseparable from the parish patriotism of the early modern period, as parishes competitively sought to be as good if not better than their neighbours. Wells, like festivals, were part of the common imaginative and cultural terrain on which parishes elaborated their differences in the eighteenth century.[5] New curative wells were discovered in the eighteenth century, the properties attributed to old wells were sometimes enhanced, and some parishes went to considerable efforts to construct new well-houses and bathing places. And so it was with Ffynnon Elian, the pre-eminent cursing well, which only acquired its powerful reputation during the eighteenth century.

Ffynnon Elian: Description and Chronology

The notoriety of Ffynnon Elian eventually led to its complete destruction, but it is fortunate that several detailed descriptions of the well have survived. It was located a quarter of a mile from the parish church of Llanelian in a grove on the east side of the road leading to Llandrillo-yn-Rhos. Despite its proximity to St Elian's church, the well was actually just within the parish of Llandrillo. Given the special liminal properties attributed to the well, it was appropriate that it was sited on or near several boundaries: between private and common land, between the parishes of Llanelian and Llandrillo-yn-Rhos, and between the counties of Denbighshire and Caernarfonshire.[6] The siting of the well had distinct strategic advantages for the keepers of the well, who could evade the unwanted attentions of bailiff or constable simply by stepping across the county boundary.[7] The saint's well was part of a holding called Cefn Elian (latterly Cefnyffynnon), a farm of some sixty acres. At the beginning of the nineteenth century the farm was owned by a clergyman, the Rev. Royle, and was sold by his executors to the Gwrych Estate in 1841. The sales particulars noted that the farm included the 'far-famed' Ffynnon Elian, 'a feature of interest to the curious by the many traditions and reputed mysteries connected with it'.[8] It was alleged that the well had brought a substantial additional income to the owner of the farm. The tenants certainly derived an extra income from acting as custodians of the well, and their rent may have been correspondingly high. The keeper of the well maintained in 1818 that as the land was so poor they had very little means to pay the rent apart from the profits arising from the well, which, it was rumoured, amounted to an astonishing £300 a year.[9]

In the later eighteenth century, probably about 1785, a detailed description of the well was made for Thomas Pennant, the antiquary and topographer.[10] A perimeter wall some six or seven feet high then protected Ffynnon Elian. The special status of the well was signalled by its complete enclosure – a stone stile provided the only entrance into an inner court measuring about sixteen square yards within which the well-chamber lay. This area functioned as an ambulatory during the rituals associated with the well. Ffynnon Elian lay in the middle of the enclosure within a low, vaulted well-chamber. At each corner of the well-chamber was placed 'a loose stone of an uncommon form almost in the shape of a bowl'. These unusual stones were called 'Bara Elian' or 'St Elian's bread', and were 'held sacred by the ignorant country people'. A little gate on the south side of the well-chamber, kept locked by the keeper of the well, provided the only access into the inner sanctum where the saint's spring issued from the ground. Only the custodians of the well seem to have had access to the well-chamber, and those seeking St Elian's favour stood on a special stone near the entrance to the chamber while the keeper of the well performed certain rituals within.

The chronology of the well, in so far as it can be worked out, is fascinating and unexpected. There were many saints' wells in late-medieval Wales and Ffynnon Elian may have been among them. But, if so, the absence of any pre-Reformation references to Ffynnon Elian suggests that it was not among the pre-eminent medieval wells. Ffynnon Elian became a prominent well at some point during the early-modern period. The well's enhanced reputation seems to have coincided with its 'translation' to a new location. The late-eighteenth-century parishioners of Llanelian were convinced that the original well (which lay within the yard of *Plas Elian*, a substantial house) had lost its reputation some 200 years before, i.e. about the time of the Reformation, and a new well had been established near Mynydd Elian in the neighbouring parish. This new Ffynnon Elian became a well-known curative well. The earliest reference to it is in Edward Lhuyd's parochial memoranda of *c.* 1700. Lhuyd noted that 'St Elian's Well is in the parish of Lhan Drilho; and papists and other old people would offer groats there; and to this day they offer either a groat or its value in bread. They are used to say, you must throw out all the water out of the well 3 times for my sick child, & then they offer ye groat.'[11] Lhuyd was evidently describing a well-established curative well with customary offerings and rituals. An eighteenth-century poetic reference suggests that the waters of the well were thought to have a general virtue:

> *Rhoi grôt wen o arian i offrymu'n Llanelian*
> *A diysbyddu y ffynnon rhag pob trallodion.*[12]

(Put a white groat of silver to offer in Llanelian [St Elian's Church]
And empty the well against all afflictions.)

It seems clear from this and other references that there was a close association between St Elian's church and the saint's well. Those seeking St Elian's favour went to the well and performed the appropriate rituals, and then proceeded to the church to pray and make an offering in St Elian's coffer; the accumulated offerings were regularly distributed to the poor. Those who had been cured of an ailment by the well's virtue sometimes returned to Llanelian to show themselves to the saint.

The Cursing Well

The sinister reputation of St Elian's well was acquired quite suddenly, and the momentum of its fame as a cursing well, from its apparent beginning in the latter part of the eighteenth century, was quite startling. As late as 1765 the parishioners of Llanelian, presumably anxious to capitalise on the popularity of 'their' saint's well, constructed within the parish an elaborate bathing place fed from a stream adjacent to the well and advertised its salubrious qualities in the Chester newspapers.[13] However, barely a decade later it was common knowledge that many resorted to St. Elian's well not for its healing qualities but 'to curse their neighbours or others who may have disobliged them, and to pray that sudden death or some dreadful calamity may not fail to overtake them.' The reputation of Ffynnon Elian as an effective cursing well was firmly established by 1780 when Thomas Pennant, the naturalist and topographical writer, complained that 'three years have not elapsed since I was threatened by a fellow (who imagined I had injured him) with the vengeance of St. Aelian, and a journey to his well to curse me with effect.'[14] Subsequently, there are numerous references to the properties of *Ffynnon Eilian* for both blessing and cursing, to the great numbers who came from all parts of Wales to make offerings at the well, and also to the notorious activities of successive self-appointed custodians of the well. By the 1790s there seems to have been a law and order problem as the well became a weapon in the hands of an impoverished peasantry who, under its protection, were able to obtain some of the necessities of life. A magistrate described how farmers in the Whitford area of Flintshire gave up the successful cultivation of turnips 'by reason of the depredations the poor make on the crops. They will steal the turneps before his face, laugh at him when he fumes at them; and ask him, how can he be in such a rage about a few turneps.' Farmers and 'coal-adventurers', he continued, 'suffer likewise in a great degree in their trade, yet hardly complain. Incredible as it may appear, numbers of them are in fear of being cursed at St Aelian's well, and suffer the due penalty for their superstition.' Popular songs may have helped spread the fame of the cursing well. A late-eighteenth-century ballad on the traditional theme of the miser and a spendthrift acquired a new twist as the pair became unlikely partners in a shared wish for the deaths of their extravagant and bad-tongued wives (whom they call witches) and contemplate a journey to 'Ffynnon Llaneilian' to curse them. It was a remarkable historical moment: the time had arrived for those who so desired to repay old scores and take revenge with impunity, and innumerable stories circulated of the tragedies and mysteries connected with the well.[15]

At some point in the latter part of the eighteenth century, probably about 1770, Ffynnon Elian acquired its reputation as a cursing well. Ironically, its new prominence was probably inadvertently assisted by the reforming activities of some of the principal parishioners of Llanelian who sought to rid the church of its popish associations. The church still retained a splendid rood-loft with painted panels depicting Elian and other saints and the weighing of souls. An ancient coffer called '*cyff Elian*' (Elian's chest) was used as a poor-box. Offerings collected in St Elian's coffer were regularly noted in the vestry book and ranged from 19s.8d. in 1695 to £2.9s.5½d. in 1710. These sums presumably represented the yearly or half-yearly accumulation of offerings made by supplicants at the well. In 1710 the coffer was ominously referred to as 'the superstitious box' in the churchwardens' accounts, and sometime after it was taken out of the church and burnt.[16] The rood-loft survived until 1733, when the churchwardens resolved to take it down and sell the timber for the benefit of the parish. The parson and parish gentry had tried to discourage the veneration of St Elian by destroying the saint's relics within the church, but the effect of this reforming energy was to make the saint's well the focus of an extra-mural cult. The saint's cult was now completely located outside the church, beyond the control of parson and churchwardens, and it was conceded that the superstition would probably remain there 'as long as there is an old woeman in the parish', unless 'the minister and neighbouring gentlemen [successfully] discourage it'.[17]

The perception that the well had acquired a newly enhanced reputation was expressed in a homely narrative that described a defining incident that had revealed that St Elian not only cured infirmities of body and mind, restored lost goods, but also – uniquely – punished evildoers. In the 1770s the tale was 'related & firmly believed by many who, in other respects, are deemed persons of sense and understanding'. The version preserved by Pennant was obtained from an unnamed gentleman who had heard it from the well-keeper himself. A woman living in Llandegla, having lost a coverlet, asked a neighbour to accompany her to Ffynnon Elian, hoping to regain her property and discover the identity of the person who had taken it. Her neighbour readily agreed and the 'gossips' trudged to Llanelian. Having offered up their prayers at the well, they repaired to the parish church of St Elian, and after putting some money in the saint's coffer, knelt before the altar and prayed that St Elian would discover the thief and restore the coverlet. After finishing her prayers, the woman who had lost the coverlet sauntered up and down the church waiting for her companion, who remained rigidly kneeling. Eventually she was impelled to ask her companion why she knelt for so long. The poor wretch confessed that she was the thief of the coverlet, and had found herself from some supernatural cause, as she supposed, utterly unable to move from the spot where she knelt. She was convinced that she must remain kneeling until the person she had wronged freely forgave her. 'The offended party instantly and generously forgave the poor penitent who in consequence thereof immediately recovered the use of her limbs.' Afterwards St Elian was widely celebrated as a righter of wrongs who punished evildoers.[18]

This was in fact a revival of an older tradition of cursing associated with the judgements of St Elian, although not apparently with Ffynnon Elian. This is revealed by the pleadings in a seventeenth-century slander case. In 1610 David and Catherine Jones justified calling Agnes, wife of David ap Roger, a witch. They pleaded that (among other things) Agnes had offered 'bended silver' before a certain image called 'Llanelyan Kymyan' with the intention that her curses should prevail against her enemies and their goods and cattle.[19] This case gives an extraordinary insight into the popular religion of post-Reformation Wales. Protestant reformers often referred to 'superstitious' practices in Wales, including 'offering unto saints', but more often than not specific details are lacking.

The name 'Llanelyan Kymyan' is obscure but presumably means something like 'protector of St Elian's parish'. The saint is termed Elian 'Geimiad' (Elian the champion or hero) in medieval sources, and has the resounding epithet Elian 'Gyfiawnwr', Elian the justifier or righter of wrongs, in a nineteenth-century charm.[20] A partial life of St Elian is incorporated in 'Elian's Charter', a document known only from post-Reformation copies that purports to record the grant of certain lands to Elian.[21] It describes the punishment of Caswallon and his household with blindness after they had taken the saint's cattle and other goods. Elian restored their sight only after Caswallon prayed for forgiveness and promised restitution. Caswallon solemnly agreed to grant Elian an estate whose bounds would be determined by the route taken by the saint's pet deer (hart) when pursued by Caswallon's greyhounds. The image of Elian at Llanelian seems to have been the painted panel in the rood-loft depicting a saint with an antlered deer.[22]

These connections with the late-medieval cult of Elian are of extraordinary interest and illustrate the historical depth of popular religion in early modern Wales. However, despite the medieval antecedents of the cult, it must be appreciated that the cursing well became the focus of the saint's cult only in the eighteenth century. The new well-cult amplified Elian's reputation as a righter of wrongs, suggesting that the saint's power could be successfully invoked simply by offering at the well. A validating myth arose about the well: it was said that Saint Elian had fallen ill at the spot and had prayed for a drink of water. He drew his sword, plunged it into the soil, and a copious spring burst forth whose waters cured Elian. In gratitude Elian prayed that whoever drank from the water and prayed 'in faith' would obtain what they desired.[23] 'In faith' did not necessarily mean that the prayer was justified, merely that those who offered their prayers had faith in Elian's power, just as conjurers and charmers insisted that the effectiveness of a charm depended on the 'faith' of those who sought it.

The Keepers of the Well

The keepers of the well who acted as its guardians, and sometimes exploited the gullibility of those who came to offer at the well, are of considerable interest as promoters of the cult. In the latter part of the eighteenth century the well-keeper lived in a cottage adjoining the well and paid a small rent to the farm tenant in consideration of the donations given him for keeping the well clean.[24] As emoluments from the well increased, the farm tenants became keepers of the well. The earliest named well-keeper, Mrs Margaret Holland, was apparently the (estranged) wife of a local clergyman. She certainly managed the well profitably and with skill, making annually 'a pretty round sum'. Mrs Holland (who died in 1812) seems to have devised the elaborate rituals and appropriate, even bureaucratic procedures for the imposition and retraction of curses which her successors followed.[25]

Those who wished to impose a curse applied to the keeper of the well who, on receiving payment of a substantial fee, was expected to enter the name of the victim in a register. The intended victim's name or initials were written on a piece of parchment which was rolled up within a thin piece of lead which was attached by a string to a small slate. Slate and lead were then placed in the well to the accompaniment of prayers and imprecations. The curser might drink from the well and cast some water over his head while framing the curse, which was believed to affect the victim's person or property in the manner the offerer desired, usually striking the victim's cattle, farm, or well-being. News of the cursing 'soon reached the ears of the object of revenge. If this object was a person of credulous disposition, the idea soon preyed upon the spirits, and, at length terminated fatally.' So corrosive was the fear of Ffynnon Elian in north Wales that many 'among the lower ranks' had been brought to an early grave, 'terrified to death under the continued apprehension of some awful calamity befalling them.'[26]

Those who thought they had been 'put in the well', as it was termed, would go to the keeper to 'be taken out of the well'. Those who enquired if they had been cursed were apparently always answered in the affirmative, and the appropriate initialled slate was invariably found. The keeper made the victim repeat certain psalms before going to the well. The victim walked three times around the well and repeated a portion of the scriptures. The keeper then emptied the well, retrieved the initialled cursing tablet and gave it to the victim. The relieved victim was dismissed but advised to read large portions of the Book of Job and the Psalms. The fee for denying a curse was apparently double that demanded for imposing a curse.[27]

The keepers of the well made sure that the well was kept clean and that the appropriate rituals were observed. Some of the well-keepers were regarded as diviners or conjurers in their own right, especially the last keeper, John Evans, who deliberately cultivated the reputation. Ffynnon Elian certainly provided work for a network of fortune-tellers and conjurers, both because the well provided an explanation for clients' misfortunes and because the diviner might be employed to assist in lifting a curse. Edward Pugh (d. 1813) described in *Cambria Depicta* how he overheard a conversation about Ffynnon Elian while waiting to consult Bela, the celebrated Denbigh fortune-teller. Taking a seat in the passage adjoining Bela's consulting room, he heard the fortune-teller 'deeply engaged in her calculations' on the fate of a client who had travelled from Barmouth, some sixty mile to the south-west. The client was suffering from a complaint 'similar to consumption', which was 'not understood by the faculty of the neighbourhood'; this presumably was a type of *clefyd y galon*. The sufferer believed the consumption was 'the effect of a curse, [made] on a visit to Llanelian well, by some secret enemy'. Bela confirmed the diagnosis but 'managed this man's case with a good deal of art, and, it may be added, with excellent advice', counselling frequent and fervent prayer.[28]

However, the surest way to lift a curse was to consult the well-keeper, or a conjurer, who was expected to take the victim's name out of the well. Evidence given at the prosecution of John Edwards of Northop revealed that the conjurer took small parties of dejected people, believing themselves cursed, to the well to have the curse lifted. In 1815 Edward Pierce of Llandyrnog consulted John Edwards because he understood that his name had been put into the well and that Edwards 'pulled people out of the well'. Pierce told Edwards that 'something was the matter with me: I saw everything going cross'. Edwards immediately observed that Pierce's name 'was put in Ffynnon Elian' and, receiving this confirmation, Pierce 'trembled'. It was absolutely essential, Edwards insisted, to make a journey to the well to lift the curse, but they would have to wait for the next full moon. On the appropriate night Pierce met Edwards at St Asaph and found himself in the company of two other men on the same business. The sombre pilgrims set off for St Elian's well at 7.30 in the evening arriving there a little after midnight. Before starting their journey, Edwards had demanded fifteen shillings from Pierce, which he said he would give to the woman of the well. After arriving at the well, the men waited while Edwards went to the 'woman of the well' to obtain the key to the well-chamber. John Edwards returned and entered the enclosure, calling his clients in turn to the well for a ritual that lasted some fifteen or twenty minutes. Pierce was the second to enter the enclosure and was instructed to stand to one side of the well-chamber and say the Lord's Prayer. Afterwards, Edwards emptied the well with a wooden cup, praying as he did so to the Father, Son, and Holy Ghost. As the well refilled, Edwards gave Pierce a cup of well water which he said he must sip, throwing the residue over his head. This was done three times. With the ritual completed, Edwards announced, 'Now we will look for your name!' Putting his hand near the spring he immediately retrieved an object which he gave to Pierce saying, 'Here is something'. Edwards invited Pierce to put his hand into the well but nothing else was found. Edwards assured Pierce that now the object had been found 'everything would be right and go on well with me, and that I should come on better than usual'. It was too dark to see properly at the well, but when Pierce returned home he examined the disconcerting objects recovered from the well. They were 'a piece of slate, a cork, and a piece of sheet lead rolled up and tied together with a wire.' He unrolled the lead and found inside a piece of parchment marked with his initials 'E.P.' and several crosses.[29]

Other accounts of the rituals at the well are similar. The ritual to lift a curse was best undertaken at the new moon, a time of change, and the ritual action was often repeated three times in the way characteristic of rites of passage. The client (or surrogate) generally went home with the cursing tablet and a bottle of well-water. It was fundamentally important to find the cursing tablet, firstly to confirm that a particular name had been put into the well and to allow the victim of the curse to destroy this physical expression of the intention to harm. Anxious visitors to the well sometimes – rather touchingly – expected to find an orderly register of names of all those offered at the well, rather like entries in a parish register. It was observed about 1810 that Mrs Holland had assumed the role of an 'officiating clergyman' and registered all curses in a book. If this register existed – as it may well have done – it disappeared with the death of Mrs Holland in 1812 and a change of tenants at Cefnyffynnon. An earnest Conway currier asked the (new) woman of the well in 1817 'if she had any Book containing the names of those persons put in the well', but the well-keeper disappointingly replied she had not.[30]

By then cursers were boldly accustomed 'to go to the Well & to drop into it pieces of paper, & of slate, upon which were inserted the initials of the names of persons who were offered to desecration in that Well.' The woman of the well did not always have direct knowledge of those cursers because 'there were so many coming to offer, and to throw without their Knowledge'. The cursing tablets were shoved through a gap between the door and the frame so that they fell into the well. The only sure way to establish if a person's name had been put into the well was to find the appropriate cursing tablet. The woman of the well took Richard Pugh, the currier, to the well. She took up from the well 'a variety of pieces of Lead, Slate, Sixpenny Pieces, upon which were engraved the Initials of the Names of persons who had been offered in the Well'. The woman of the well observed that she periodically removed the accumulation of cursing tablets from the well and kept them in the house along with older tablets dating from the time of the former tenant of the farm, Mrs Holland. The clients were taken to an upper room in the farmhouse where there were 'a very great number' of cursing tablets with 'some hundreds' kept in an old hat. The initials of the cursed with several crosses were inscribed on thin slates or pieces of lead measuring only about one inch square. Having found a cursing tablet with the right initials ('here is his name, probably it is ...') the woman of the well sent the client to the barn where her son-in-law 'wrote some Characters' upon a piece of paper, enquiring 'the cause of their application, & whether the Person ... was ill, or what was the Matter with him'.[31] It seems likely that this was a petitionary prayer which recited the cause and effect of the curse, prayed for it to be lifted, and probably called for the punishment of the curser.[32] The client returned to the house with the paper and gave it to the woman of the well who 'wrapped it up, and secured it by sewing with a Needle & Thread, so that no person could open it without destroying it'. The client was expected to keep the paper always at his breast 'looking on it as a thing of great value and believing in it without ever doubting'. The woman of the well demanded fourteen shillings for taking a name out of the well at the approach of the full moon but would accept twelve shillings from an old neighbour. There often seems to have been an element of haggling between keeper and client before the fee was agreed.

The keepers of the well offered visitors various other services. Pennant says that Ffynnon Elian was 'made the instrument of discovering thieves, and of recovering stolen goods'.[33] People also made offerings at the well to protect their cattle. The woman of the well seems to have included this service as a matter of course when lifting curses. A client described that at the end of the ritual he was ordered to throw an extra shilling into the well, which the woman took up. She emptied the well for a fourth time saying 'she did that on Account of his Cattle', adding that 'great Numbers of people came there to secure prosperity to their Cattle.' The woman of the well could read the well like an oracle from the appearance of the water. She observed that 'the water would sparkle very much' if the name enquired for had been put into the well; if it did not sparkle significantly she did not believe that a particular name had been put into the well. During the ritual to lift the curse, the woman of the well used the water in much the same way as a conjurer's crystal or glass. A client described that when

the woman first cleaned the well she said 'she saw the person who had offered
G.R.': 'There she is, there she is, she is a tall thin woman.' The client asked
'Where is she?' but by then the woman of the well said, 'she has now hid herself.'
At the second cleaning of the well she observed, 'here is a Woman who wished to
have him' and that 'she pressed him very much'. On the third cleaning of the well
the woman observed that 'this must be occasioned by some Quarrels with his old
Neighbours.' It was then recalled that the daughter of John Hughes Tan'rall[t] had
said G.R. 'would never enjoy any prosperity in the world'.[34]

Other Cursing Places

The services of the keepers of the well were not essential for the imposition or
retraction of a curse. Profiteering by the keepers of the well prompted Robert
Roberts, an Anglesey almanac-maker, to print instructions for the removal of
curses which might be observed at any well with the appropriate prayers and rituals.[35] As curses might be removed at any well, so curses could be made at any
well and indeed in other locations. Ritualized cursing seems to have spread from
Ffynnon Elian in Caernarfonshire to St Eilian's Well on Anglesey, and to other
wells. The occasional chance discovery of cursing pots and similar objects suggests that ritual cursing became a generalized activity in the nineteenth century
and was not necessarily confined to particular wells, although those dedicated
to Eilian remained pre-eminent.[36]

Ffynnon Eilian, Anglesey, was a well without a keeper, and 'witching pennies'
were regularly found there. The saint's well was 'situated in a barren part of the
parish, among wild and broken rocks' near the sea. Those seeking the well had
to scramble down a cliff to a secluded creek called Porth Eilian. About twenty
yards above high water a small spring issued through a fissure at the base of a
large cracked rock. This was *Ffynnon Eilian*, and a well enclosure about four-
yards square was defined by a low wall, possibly the remains of a well chapel
referred to in the seventeenth century. It was said that St Eilain had landed at
this creek, and finding no fresh water for his cattle had struck the rock with his
sword making a stream of water gush out from the rock, which afterwards was
known as *Ffynnon Eilian*.[37]

Ffynnon Eilian (Anglesey), like Ffynnon Elian (Caernarfonshire), had been primarily a curative well. Devotees would visit the well, especially on the saint's festival,
and after drinking some well water made their way to the parish church where they
would make an offering in the saint's chest (*cyff Eilian*). However at some point the
saint's well became notorious for cursing. The curser would make an offering at the
saint's well by placing a penny under a stone in the well. The pennies, significantly
named 'witching pennies', were regarded with particular horror by adults, who
would have nothing to do with them, although children sometimes collected them.
Witching pennies were not only placed in the well but in the sea below the well. It

was more difficult to place offerings in the sea, but they were regarded as particularly dangerous because they were so difficult to find. Curses placed in the sea had to be secured so that they would not drift too far from the waters of *Ffynnon Eilian*. An offering found by children in the sea just below the saint's well had been placed in a linen bag and tied to a piece of iron. The bag contained two witching pennies placed between cursing tablets inscribed with the names of John and Mary Pritchard. In addition, a large cork, like a bung, pierced by 'hundreds' of needles and sail nails was also secured to the piece of iron by a short string. Another cursing tablet found at Llaneilian (Anglesey) in the twentieth century had a wax effigy pinned to the centre of a slate between the scratched initials 'R F' of the victim. At the four corners of the slate were further initials, all ending in M, possibly the initials of the cursers who were consigning their victim to destruction (Fig. 16).[38]

We know that many hundreds – presumably thousands – of men and women visited St Elian's well with the intention of destroying others. Knowledge of the particular social situations, which led to cursing, is of course irrecoverable. Nevertheless, Robert Roberts, the Anglesey astrologer, who printed the procedures for lifting curses at any well, provides a general insight into the circumstances that led to cursing. He gives an interesting list of the most common personal wrongs that prompted visits to St Elian's well. The list is mostly concerned with dishonesty, slander, and betrayal. Cursing arose if a man behaved dishonestly, taking someone else's possessions by force or by cheating him, or stealing land from a rightful heir, or occasioning loss to someone through 'obscure malice'; by slandering a man by telling lies about him; by betraying people into the hands of their enemies; by luring women with fair words into adultery so that they come bringing their love behind them, and then abandoning them so that they turn to wicked ways.[39] There are innumerable grievances here. Some idea of the lost conversations with the keepers of the well can be gained from letters written by clients to Jac Ffynnon Elian, the last keeper of the well. One letter in Welsh written from Eglwyswrw parish, Pembrokeshire, complains that the writer is in much trouble (*Yr ydw fi mewn cryn helbyl yma ...*) because his landlady has obtained a judgment for £4 less sixpence against him in the Country Court and the writer, explaining that he has faithfully paid his rent, seeks Jac's help in getting the money back from his landlady. It was probably characteristic that a social inferior was seeking redress from a social superior. Another letter, dated 1842, written in English from Llannerch, Betws Cedewain, Montgomeryshire, vividly explains that the writer and his family are all in poor health and, moreover their 'horses has been very bad'. The writer seeks Jac's help so that they will all 'have a turn for the better'. The writer has 'enemies' and hopes that Jac 'will beat down our Foes under our Feet that they might not triumph over us.' The writer names his particular 'enemies': one Thomas Owen Sturkey of Highgate and the vicar of the parish. He adds the names of four magistrates in Berriew and then three others from whom 'we cannot have no peace'. Now into his stride, the writer names nine other enemies in Tregynon 'always keeping a noise or another', a further eleven or so in Newtown, and remembers moreover 'there is no peace to be had' from others in Betws and Manafan and elsewhere. The writer asks Jac to consign these names into the well: 'for goodness sake put these names Safe, we Cannot have no peace of them Skulkin about us always.'[40] The paranoia expressed in this letter was probably as much social as psychological. Like the 'incendiary' letters of the period, this letter conveys real anger and bitterness deriving from the class-based perception that the world was readily divided into friend and foe.

Prosecution

The momentum of the cursing well episode from its sudden beginnings in the second half of the eighteenth century to its demise in the mid-nineteenth century was remarkable. The authorities were at first slow to respond to this potentially alarming situation. There was a clear partition of belief along class lines. The reaction of the respectable, at first puzzled, became increasingly hostile. Genteel curiosity at the well was not encouraged. A traveller recorded the affront when his questions about the ceremonies at the well were not politely answered. He 'received the most vague, shifting, artful answers' from a woman at the well who was preparing it for use, and she hurried away 'not pleased with my interrogations'. Mounting pressure was placed on the magistrates to find a solution to the problem of the well, which was undoubtedly causing some social dislocation. Magistrates were urged to make an example of the keeper of the well, and the clergy were asked to preach against the well. 'Is it not the indispensable duty of the clergy to preach it out of countenance and use?' asked Edward Pugh. Those associated with the well were warned in print that they participated in the crime of murder. An unknown number of deaths, especially among 'the lower ranks', were attributed to the terror of the curse. 'A Lover of his Country', in a letter to the press, claimed that the profits arising from the 'infernal commerce' of the well amounted to £300 annually and denounced the landlord ('dead to the honour that characterises a gentleman') who received additional rent from the 'horrid traffic' on his land.[41]

Prosecution was not a straightforward matter however. The well was on private property, and the offerings at the well were in the nature of private transactions between the parties concerned. The location of the well in the township of Eirias (Caernarfonshire rather than Denbighshire) posed jurisdictional difficulties. The problem had frequently been canvassed at the Denbighshire quarter-sessions but even the efforts of Sir Watkin Williams Wynn, the greatest power in the land, proved ineffectual, and all attempts 'to abolish this infamous trick upon human ignorance' had failed. Caernarfonshire magistrates had actually apprehended the 'woman of the well' more than once but, in the judgement of a lawyer, Edmund Hyde Hall, 'superstition [had] proved the superior of the Law', and there was no discernable impact on the well traffic.[42] Two Caernarfonshire justices took voluntary depositions from three persons who had visited the well to lift a curse in 1818. In the event the keeper of the well was not prosecuted, but the following year an exemplary prosecution was brought at the Flintshire Great Sessions against John Edwards, a conjurer, for obtaining money under false pretences for lifting a curse. Edwards was convicted of the fraud and sentenced to twelve months' imprisonment (escaping transportation), but his successful prosecution did not deter offerers at the well, as was presumably hoped, and the traffic in cursing seems to have continued unabated.[43]

There were attacks on the physical structure of the well, which stood within a walled enclosure 'embosomed' in a pleasant grove. By 1814 the enclosure walls had been thrown down and the sheltering trees felled. The well-chamber itself survived (or had been rebuilt), because ten years later a tourist recorded that he unsuccessfully attempted to prise open its little locked door ('Vulcan had set his seal upon it').[44] It was noted in 1826 that the magistrates of the district had forbidden use of the well and would punish those who went there. This must have been ineffectual because growing numbers of Nonconformists expressed mounting concern about the continuing popularity of the well. In 1828 *Goleuad Cymru* (Light of Wales), a Calvinistic Methodist journal, printed two uncompromising letters from prominent inhabitants of Llanelian condemning the well as a superstitious hoax, and pointing out that the site of the well had moved within the memory of the oldest inhabitants, and that some of the purported miracles were undoubtedly bogus.[45]

According to *Goleuad Cymru*, men and women from every corner of north Wales, as well as different parts of England, resorted to the well. The writers of the letter gave a solemn warning that in future they would take offerers at the well before the magistrates, and would shame them by naming them and their ignominious errands in the newspapers. It is not clear whether or not the magistrates would have intervened in this way. However, the following year the Methodist congregation as a body took matters into their own hands and tried to erase Ffynnon Elian utterly from the landscape, leaving not one stone upon another. As it happened the Methodist Chapel had been built within sight of the well, and Ffynnon Elian must have presented an unavoidable challenge to the reforming energies of the congregation (Fig. 14).

A triumphant letter to *Goleuad Cymru* headed '*Llwyr-ddiddymiad* Ffynnon Elian' – the annihilation of Ffynnon Elian – described the destruction of the structure in February 1829. The well had been completely demolished and a deep trench dug around the site. Stone from the demolished well lined a deep ditch which emptied the spring water into an adjacent stream. The Methodists looked forward to seeing a crop of potatoes flourishing on the spot. Those foolish enough to enquire for the well in Llanelian would now find nothing but derision, 'the parish children shouting "ha, ha" after them'![46]

Jac Ffynnon Elian

It might have been reasonably supposed that the reputation of Ffynnon Elian would have faded with the destruction of the well, but this was not to be the case. The destruction of Ffynnon Elian only served to enhance the reputation of another well in the garden of an adjoining cottage singularly named 'Meddiant' ('Possession' or 'Power'). John Evans, an enterprising tailor, managed to divert water from the old well into his own cottage garden, and business carried on much as usual, if not with more enthusiasm. John Evans's cottage had been built as a squatter's dwelling (*tŷ unnos*) on common land adjoining the well. He enclosed a garden with a bank and constructed several wells within the garden which had a pleasant cobbled walk. The tailor, otherwise called Jac Ffynnon Elian, became the best known of all the well-keepers and, by his own account, presided over Ffynnon Elian for some thirty years interrupted only by a period of imprisonment.[47] In 1831 Jac (John Evans of Llanelian, labourer) was indicted at the Denbighshire assizes on several counts of deception by unlawfully pretending to use sorcery, enchantment and conjuration. The indictment recited that on 1 September 1830 he had unlawfully obtained seven shillings from Elizabeth Davies by falsely pretending that her husband, Robert Davies, was afflicted with a certain sickness because his name had been put into Ffynnon Elian, and claiming that he could cure him by taking his name out of the well.[48]

The case was widely reported.[49] *The Times* professed itself amazed at the superstition of the Welsh peasantry in an age of progress, and gave a full account of the court proceedings. Elizabeth Davies said in evidence that her husband had been ill for many years and, thinking that he had been cursed in St Elian's Well, she had walked twenty-two miles to have his name taken out of the well. She gave a revealing account of her consultation with Jac. She had asked Jac if her husband's name was in the well. He replied that he did not know but would see, and sent a child to the well who returned with a dishful of pebbles and small slates marked with different sets of initials. Elizabeth's husband's initials were not among them so more cursing tablets were gathered from the well. They were strewn across a table and Elizabeth eventually found a stone marked with the appropriate initials 'R D' and three crosses. Jac said these must be her husband's initials, but Elizabeth wanting to be sure asked if her husband's name was 'in a book'. Jac replied that as he had not put the name in the well it was not in the book. There was only one way to be sure: 'the water would tell whether it was his name or not'. They went to the well and Jac took out some water and examined it saying, 'The water changes colour; it is your husband, sure enough.' Jac told Elizabeth that he would charge ten shillings (his lowest fee) for taking her husband's name out of the well. Elizabeth agreed to bring the money, and Jac allowed her to take away the initialled stone, instructing her not to show it to anyone before she reduced it to powder and consigned it to the fire with some salt. Elizabeth returned two months later with her brother-in-law. Jac said she must have a bottle of well-water costing nine shillings. Elizabeth bargained him down to seven shillings, which he said 'must be given to the well', though Jac afterwards pocketed the money. Jac then muttered something 'in Latin' which Elizabeth did not understand apart from the invocation of Elian's name. Jac advised that Elizabeth's husband was to take the well-water for three nights successively, and he was to say a portion of the thirty-eighth Psalm. Jac offered to put the person who had cursed her husband into the well, 'and bring upon him any disease' Elizabeth cared to name. It is not clear if Elizabeth took advantage of the offer, but it seems to have been a common desire to return a curse.

Jac's defence was of the 'more-fool-them' type. He maintained that 'he never sent for anyone to come to the well, nor did he say there was any efficacy in the water; but if a person believed that there was, and chose to give him some money, he took all that they had a mind to give.' The jury were unimpressed and returned a verdict of guilty. The judge, after reflecting on the ignorance and credulity of those who believed in the power of Ffynnon Elian, sentenced Jac to six months' imprisonment with hard labour.

On his release from prison Jac returned to his cottage and business seems to have carried on much as before. He was still the 'minister of the well' in 1846 when he was named in the tithe schedule as owner and occupier of 'Ffynnon Elian Cottage' with its little garden of two roods.⁵⁰ But towards the end of his life Jac became a reformed character. He wrote a penitent letter to the Baptist minister in Llanddulas, confessing to the fraud, wanting it publicly known that he had reformed and wished to have nothing more to do with Ffynnon Elian.⁵¹ With the sale of his cottage in January 1854, Jac formally broke his connection with the well.⁵² Not long before his death Jac travelled to Anglesey to see the Methodist minister and publisher, William Aubrey of Llannerch-y-medd. According to Aubrey, Jac wanted to show that he was fully converted by publishing a history of his life and times that would expose Ffynnon Elian as a superstitious hoax. Aubrey interviewed Jac, and Jac presented him with a small bundle of letters from his old customers. Jac died in 1858 but his 'confessions' were published posthumously, initially as a series of articles in a periodical, *Y Nofelydd*, and subsequently as a shilling booklet.⁵³

Jac's history of his life was a remarkably frank chronicle of deception and exploitation of gullibility somewhat in the style of the confession of a condemned felon. Jac relates that he was born in Llanllechid, Caernarfonshire, at a time when superstition flourished and the wakes (*gwylmabsant*) caused much trouble. As a boy of ten he became a farm-servant at a place called Nant-y-glyn but experienced much trouble there. Aged thirteen he was apprenticed to a tailor, 'D.D.' of Llandrillo, and going about the district with his master became acquainted with the superstitions and traditions of the people, including those relating to Ffynnon Elian.

Tailors were sometimes associated with magical powers, but Jac describes how his connection with Ffynnon Elian was something of an accident. One day Jac saw a man wandering about near his cottage and, suspecting he was looking for the well, accosted him. The stranger asked who had charge of the well. Jac answered that it was he, for he thought he might as well have the stranger's money as anyone else, because in reality no one could impose or retract a curse. The man paid what Jac demanded for his services, and went on his way perfectly satisfied with the bargain. This was the beginning of Jac's deceptions. Partly in sport and partly from love of money, Jac continued the fraud, and his fame spread quickly and people visited him from distant parts. Those with a professional interest in magic were anxious to see the new pretender to the magic arts. Dic Aberdaron, a wandering polyglot scholar, visited Jac and gave him a copy of the Apocrypha written in Chaldaic. With this impressive book Jac pretended to conjure and raise devils. Dr Bynian (Bennion) of Oswestry, a conjurer of considerable reputation, also paid a visit, and Jac requested from him a few lessons in the Black Art. Dr Bennion's astute advice was, 'Spread it abroad that you can raise the Devil, and the country will believe you and credit you with many miracles. All that you have to do afterwards is to be silent and you will be as good a raiser of devils as I am, and I as good as you.' Jac followed the conjurer-doctor's advice, and confessed that he was amazed and frightened by the consequences: 'the people in a very short time started talking about me, and they soon came to entrust everything to me, to be afraid of me, for they looked upon me as if I were God'.

One of the most interesting parts of *Llyfr Ffynon Elian* is the purported interview between the editor (William Aubrey) and Jac (John Evans) based on conversations had in the last years of Jac's life. The interview provides valuable information about the well and Jac's pragmatic attitude to it. Jac begins by saying that the well had been held in high regard for over 200 years and that he had officiated there for about 35 years, that is from about the time of the prosecution of John Edwards. The interview continues:

W.A. Have you seen many people coming there to the well?

J.E. Yes, hundreds in my time.

W.A. What sort of people would go there – the poor and ignorant, perhaps?

J.E. Not so, some of the best people in the land in terms of wealth and education.
I have seen some in carriages coming.

W.A. Did some come from countries other than Wales?

J.E. Yes they did, indeed, from Ireland and England.

...

W.A. From what parts of Wales did most come?

J.E. From Cardiganshire and Montgomeryshire, and districts further to the south.

W.A. What were the chief errands people commonly had?

J.E. Firstly, worldly success for themselves or disaster for others. Secondly, to hasten their own marriage or to hinder the marriages of others. Thirdly, to seek happiness for themselves in this world and the world to come, or to contrive failure for others. Fourthly, deliverance from some circumstance caused (they considered) because someone had put them in the well. It was this trouble which brought people here more that I can say.

W.A. Have you ever summoned devils?

J.E. Yes, several times according to the people's opinion, but according to my own testimony, I have never done so, nor has anyone else greater than myself.

W.A. Have you ever sacrificed people to the well?

J.E. Yes, several times, according to the thought of others; but according to my own thought, I have never done so, and I don't think anyone has ever done so.

W.A. Have you ever conversed with spirits?

J.E. Yes, a few times, to please the people; but in truth I didn't ever see anything of that sort, and I don't expect to see [any] until I go to the spirit world to live.

The cynical exploitation of gullibility described in Jac's biography provides a disturbing contrast to the anxieties and hopes of the many clients who came to Jac to offer at the well. However, before dismissing Jac as a complete charlatan, the complex relationship that existed between the magician and his clients has to be appreciated. Although the conjurer may think that he is in control of the situation that he exploits, he can in fact only play his role because he has the confidence of his clients. In a revealing passage Jac describes how he was empowered by his clients: 'and the people quickly spoke much about me, entrusted everything to me, and they scared me as they regarded me as the Lord'. The magician (as Mauss saw) is not a free agent (although he might think he is) but always dances to a tune called by his clients.[54] Jac (pretended) to raise devils, pull people out of the well, and sacrifice others because it was expected of him. There is inevitably a dialectic between the expectations of clients and the successful performance of a magician. It is difficult to believe that Jac over his thirty-year career was completely alienated from his clients and did not reflect on the effects of his 'magic', which by all accounts were remarkable, and he may sometimes have believed that he was indeed a magician. Jac's confession, made at the end of his life, is inevitably coloured by the circumstances of its production and cannot reflect the true complexity of his biography. Certainly, the popularity (or notoriety) of Ffynnon Elian depended on confidence in its high priest. Ffynnon Elian had been physically dismantled at least once but Jac revived it. Those who promoted Jac's confessions clearly saw that Ffynnon Elian could be discredited once and for all not by destroying the well but by destroying the reputation of its high priest.

People still came to offer at the well in the second half of the nineteenth century, but sometime after 1860 Jac's cottage was taken down and his well completely destroyed. The site of 'Meddiant' became overgrown, and still is today. Towards the end of the century curious antiquaries came to visit the spot, but it was not easy to gain information about the well, which had been obliterated from the landscape. It was the heyday of Nonconformity and a veil had been drawn over the whole nightmarish affair.

EPILOGUE: WITCHCRAFT, PRACTICAL RELIGION AND DISENCHANTMENT

Witchcraft

It is quite a long historical journey both temporally and conceptually from the prosecution in 1594 of Gwen ferch Ellis to the prosecution of Jac Ffynnon Elian in 1831. How does the chronology of Welsh witchcraft relate to the history of witchcraft beliefs elsewhere in Europe? In terms of witch-hunting, as this study has tried to show, Wales was undoubtedly an area of marginal importance: prosecutions began late and were relatively few in number. The inference from linguistic and literary sources that the notion of witchcraft was in some ways borrowed from England is consistent with the late development of witch-trials in Wales. The late prosecution of witches was characteristic of some of the geographically peripheral regions of Europe, but unlike parts of northern and eastern Europe Wales did not suffer delayed but severe witch-hunting in the seventeenth and eighteenth centuries. (Fig. 1) Since it is important to try and understand why some regions experienced a witch-hunt and others did not, it is worth posing the somewhat counter-factual question, why wasn't there a witch-hunt in Wales? The elements of belief were certainly in place by the end of the sixteenth century, as well as an efficient machinery for managing prosecutions, but, to borrow a metaphor in bad taste, the bonfire was not properly set alight.[1]

Witchcraft was a felony, and one has to understand the prosecution of witches within the broader context of prosecuted crime, especially in relation to the priorities of the state. It is particularly important to appreciate that there were always other victims of the judicial process who could be hunted as assiduously as suspected witches. The establishment of the Court of Great Sessions in Wales, a system of assize circuits, coincided with the first Act against witchcraft (1542) but it took over fifty years before a case of causing death or injury through witchcraft was prosecuted before the court. This was not because the Welsh assize courts were ineffective. On the contrary, the criminal side of the Great Sessions, which were held twice a year in every Welsh county, was generally extraordinarily busy with hundreds of suspected felons appearing before the courts annually. During the periods of significant and cruel witchcraft prosecutions in England and Scotland, and in parts of continental Europe, from 1560–1630, the gaols in Wales were filled with other types of suspected felons. Wales did not experience a witch-hunt but it did endure a prolonged 'thief-hunt' of quite extraordinary intensity. Prosecutions of suspected thieves increased with regularity through-out the second half of the sixteenth century, with the courts and gaols in some Welsh counties probably reaching saturation point at the beginning of the sev-enteenth century. The overwhelming emphasis on the prosecution of grand larceny (theft of goods to the value of 12 pence and above) in Elizabethan Wales tended to exclude most other felonies, apart from murder and treason, leaving little scope for the prosecution of suspected witches except in exceptional cir-cumstances. The thief-hunt reached its peak about 1600 at the same time that multiple prosecutions for witchcraft occurred elsewhere in the British Isles. Wales, with a population of a quarter of a million at the time of the Acts of Union, witnessed in the second half of the sixteenth century the prosecution of some 60,000 felony suspects (and the apprehension of many more), which had resulted in the cumulative execution of about 4,000 male thieves by the end of the century.[2] All communities in Elizabethan Wales would have experienced the taking of suspected thieves, and most would have known first-hand of the exe-cution of a felon. The relentless campaign against thieves in Wales was a direct consequence of late Tudor state-building policy, which sought to eliminate dis-order from the periphery of the realm. At times it seemed that the executions would never end. As the Queen's Surveyor grimly observed in about 1570, theft would never be 'extirped owte of Wales, by hanging, or slawghter of Men, as dayly experience dothe teache'.[3]

The relative absence of witchcraft prosecutions in early modern Wales reflected the priorities of the Court of Great Sessions in eradicating theft from Wales. The Welsh experience of judicial slaughter during the period of the witch-hunt must prompt reflections on the nature of the relationship between witch-hunting and state building. Revisionist analysis tends to associate witch-hunting in the periphery with the lack of control from the centre: where the state was weak local elites could initiate witch-hunts. Where witchcraft prosecutions were cen-trally managed, as in Scotland, the falling away of prosecutions as the periphery was reached can be understood as the progressive loss of prosecutorial energy over distance. The relative absence of prosecutions in parts of the Highlands and Islands has been interpreted as a consequence of 'distance from Edinburgh'.[4] The Tudor state's policy of consolidating its control over the periphery by eliminat-ing disorder in Wales is apparent from successive memoranda of the Council in the Marches which placed special emphasis on the role of the courts in eliminat-ing theft through the Great Sessions, and gave strong direction from the centre to judges and justices of the peace. The Court of Great Sessions was considered so successful in Wales that it was commended as a model for peripatetic courts in Ireland, which would push back the Pale. Moreover, the Council encouraged civility by periodically instructing local elites, as justices of the peace, to apprehend vagabonds and minstrels, suppress unlicensed alehouses, and control other disorders and misdemeanours. These policies entailed a considerable expenditure in administrative and prosecutorial energy, in which the involvement of elites was indispensable, and left little scope for the systematic prosecution of other felonies and misdemeanours. All societies need their enemies, and it is interesting to reflect that thieves were not unlike surrogate witches. In an oblique way thief-hunting in Wales was a way of eliminating adversaries who – like witches – could be regarded as both enemies of the state and, according to popular belief, enemies of God who, lacking in grace, had been tempted into crime by the devil.

Most research on European witchcraft has concentrated on the classic period of early modern witch-hunting when perhaps (estimates vary) some 40,000 suspected witches were executed. Witchcraft prosecutions were dramatic occasions of life or death and have understandably fascinated and preoccupied social historians. Much valuable attention has been paid to analysing the situations of conflict inseparable from witchcraft prosecutions, but preoccupation with the social structuring of accusations can lead to an analytical focus that makes it difficult to account for changes in belief both before and after the witch-trials of the sixteenth and seventeenth centuries. As a consequence, historians of early-modern witchcraft have not been particularly adept at acknowledging and discussing changes in witchcraft beliefs. However, some recent regional studies have made it easier to see long-term structures in witchcraft beliefs. Indeed, Burke has tentatively proposed a three-stage model of witchcraft beliefs (although not to be taken as 'representing any kind of norm'). This has never been elaborated, but he suggests that 'behind the diabolical witchcraft of the witch-hunters has been discovered a more traditional, neighbourly witchcraft. Behind this in turn we are seeing glimpses of a still more archaic, shamanistic witchcraft.' This latter category was the culture of magical specialists who mystically counteracted witchcraft, like the now-famous blessers ('*benandanti*') of Friuli.[5]

Given these changes in notions of witchcraft, the decline of witchcraft beliefs after the ending of prosecutions seems even more complicated. It is now well established that witchcraft trials declined in England and continental Europe not because of widespread scepticism but because of the problem of proof in the legal process.[6] However the analytical interest in 'traditional' witchcraft beliefs in the period after the ending of prosecutions is relatively recent and underdeveloped.[7] The assumption that witchcraft beliefs merely faded after the ending of prosecutions is demonstrably false. Indeed, Wales provides a particularly dramatic example of the transformation (rather than the 'survival') of belief after the ending of prosecutions.

It has been neatly suggested that in any study of witchcraft over the long term, 'the evidence from the European periphery is absolutely central.'[8] Burke's aperçu refers particularly to regions where the witch-hunt arrived late and evidence survives of the nature of beliefs before 'diabolisation'. Regions peripheral to the classic witch-hunting areas, but inevitably influenced by them, are important because they can reveal the dynamics of witchcraft beliefs structured by the borrowing, accommodation, and transformation of ideas. Welsh notions of witchcraft can be shown to have a certain internal dynamic with different phases expressed in different sets of social relations.

As I interpret it there were three main phases of belief, which can be summarized chronologically:

I. Sorcery (*'rhaib'*). Conceptualized as attacks on people and their cattle by unidentified and probably male witches and associated with the evil eye. Counteracted by religious specialists. Chronology: [?]–circa 1550.

II. Witchcraft (*'wits'* = witch). Elements of cultural transmission but accommodated in terms of the inversion of existing notions of blessing and cursing. Suspected witches were mostly women who had formally cursed neighbours, particularly men. Counteracted by a retraction or blessing. Chronology: circa 1550–1750+.

III. Sacrificing (*'offrymu'*). The ritualized cursing of enemies at wells and other places by men and women. Partition of belief along class lines; finally marginalized in the mid-nineteenth century. Chronology: circa 1750–1850.

How does one conceptualise the continuities and changes of belief over this longue durée? Witchcraft beliefs have to be contextualised within the discourses of a practical Christian religious culture, straddling the Reformation, which included numerous modes of communication between God, mankind and the Devil: prophecy, possession, and prayer – both for blessing and cursing. It is possible that in late-medieval Wales the dominance of theocentric modes of communication, especially prophecy, led to the marginal significance of sorcery. The dynamic or historicity of Welsh witchcraft lay in its progression, which was expressed by the dialectical tension between blessing and cursing. The borrowed notion of witchcraft was the inversion or antithesis of existing notions of blessing and cursing. The opposition between thesis and antithesis was resolved by the synthesis of the morally 'neutral' cursing wells. Looked at in another way, one can say that the various phases of witchcraft are different 'answers' to the perennial problem of the social location of evil.[9] As we know, witchcraft was linked with situations of tension and conflict that might have changing definitions. In late medieval Wales sorcery (*rhaib*) seems to have been conceptualized as located on the boundary of society among faceless, envious 'wolfish' men who threatened to destroy people and their cattle unless warded off by specialists and their charms. But in the early modern period, the borrowed notion of witchcraft was the evil attributed to neighbours living within the community. Finally, the witchcraft of the cursing wells acknowledged that all people may bear a grudge and seek revenge on their enemies, a novel recognition of the capacity for evil within everyone.

Practical Religion

An analytical emphasis on witchcraft prosecutions highlights systems of state control but at the same time inevitably abstracts witchcraft beliefs from their context within religious cultures in which the mundane and the fantastic coexisted. Witchcraft beliefs have to be contextualized within post-Reformation religious structures. There were of course as many Reformations in Europe as there were witch-hunts. The process of reform among the nations of Britain and Ireland, like witch-hunting, was not uniform but nuanced by complex regional structures. The very different course of reform in the west, in Wales and Ireland, both considered religiously conservative, was remarkable. In Ireland the Reformation was rejected; in Wales the Reformation was imposed relatively easily. A self-serving gentry elite, empowered and rewarded by the Act of Union, which had leadership in the country, was able to accomplish the formal changes required relatively quickly. There can be no doubt about the impact of reform, not least in terms of the abolition of the Mass and in the iconoclastic reordering of churches. However there is a striking tension in accounts of the Reformation in Wales. On the one hand, it was successfully achieved by the end of the Elizabethan period; on the other hand, the reformed church coexisted with a vigorous unreformed popular religion dominated by petitionary prayer (including the blessing and cursing inseparable from witchcraft beliefs), death rituals, and respect for the saints. The resilience of popular religion in Wales was astonishing. Elizabethan complaints about well-cults and devotion to saints were repeated more or less in the same terms in the mid-seventeenth century and again in the eighteenth century. By the early eighteenth century we are chronologically very far removed from the initial movement of reform, but a popular religious culture far from atrophying, though deprived of an institutional focus, had successfully reproduced itself over six or seven generations.[10]

How coherent was this popular religion? Much depends on the words used to describe it. If popular religion is labelled 'traditionalist' or 'survivalist' we immediately think of it as a religious culture whose relevance largely derives from the past. The popular religious culture of early-modern Wales was structured by practicality rather than inertia. Assent to the doctrines of the reformed church was mostly a matter for intellectuals; the participation of the people in new forms of worship was a consequence of the structures of authority that compelled formal conformity.[11] At an everyday level people's lives were structured by a religious culture which in terms of morality, eschatology, and accommodation to authority is best described as a 'practical' Christianity which had little direct connection with the 'doctrinal' Christianity of Anglican divines and radical Protestants.[12] This practical Christianity was (to borrow George Gifford's useful phrase)[13] 'a country divinity' concerned with the relations between mankind and God, and the nature of spiritual beings, but was in a formal sense neither Catholic nor Protestant, although it drew freely on the 'surplus meaning' of traditional Catholicism jettisoned by official Protestant forms of worship and booted out of the parish church.

This practical religious culture coexisted with the established church but did not really compete with it in the same social spaces. It was more practice than doctrine, almost exclusively oral with little expression in print, and physically more embedded in the landscape than contained within the walls of religious buildings. It is correspondingly difficult to isolate elements of belief except through their expression in action and experience. Practical religion in Wales was an extra-mural affair in a dramatically literal sense as so many churches became dilapidated after the Reformation. An Anglican divine, Erasmus Saunders, referred to the great physical 'Desolations of Religion' in Wales in the early eighteenth century: 'so many of our churches are in actual Ruins; so many more are ready to fall, and almost all are robb'd and pillag'd.' Parish churches never recovered their pre-Reformation status as the focus for popular religious devotion and craftsmanship, and iconoclasm robbed them of an important visual dimension.[14]. Parish churches were often in a state of desolation, sometimes truncated with the loss of chancel or tower, their roofs tottering, and 'their walls green, mouldy and nauseous, and very often without wash or plaister'. Some churches suffered almost total neglect, becoming 'the solitary habitations of owles and jackdaws' if not converted to agricultural buildings; many chapels of ease, particularly important in large upland parishes as the focus for formal worship, had become 'bury'd in their Ruins'.[15] So great were the physical desolations of religion that it seemed to Saunders that a visitor might think that the Turks or an 'Oliverian' army had passed through the Welsh countryside. He attributed the physical decay of churches largely to the appropriation of tithes by the gentry, resulting in a defeated and poverty-stricken clergy and the neglect of the fabric of the church. The rapacious and (just as bad) complacent elements within the gentry, by implication, were enemies of the Church.[16]

Although the physical setting of formal worship might be decayed, the religiosity of the people was unmistakable and surprised observers. The unselfconscious but demonstrative prayers and songs of the people impressed Erasmus Saunders. Special carols or divine songs (*halsingod*), an expression of the 'popular addiction' to poetry, were sung 'in their own houses, as well as upon some public occasions' including wakes and funerals. Saunders was particularly struck by the respect paid to the dead. In the mountainous parts (where he thought old customs and simplicity prevailed more) he observed that 'when people come to Church they go immediately to the Graves of their Friends, and kneeling offer up their addresses to God, but especially at the Feast of the Nativity of our Lord'. At Christmas they came to church about cock-crow bringing candles and torches with them to place about the graves of departed friends and kin. Saunders found these customs somewhat reminiscent of the piety of the Primitive Church but he also detected 'some Roman superstitions practic'd in the later Ages'.[17] The extra-mural cult of the saints was particularly odd in an officially Protestant country.

Erasmus Saunders found that truth and error, superstition and religion were 'so very odly mix'd', especially in terms of the people's prayers and respect for the saints. Making the sign of the cross was part of a larger body of signs, vocal prayers, and greetings which punctuated the routines of everyday life, and which all (except the ungodly and evil spirits) observed and reciprocated. On many occasions, Saunders observed, the people invoked the names 'not only the Deity, but the Holy Virgin, and other saints, for Mair-Wen, Iago, Teilaw-Mawr, Celer, Celynog, and others are often thus remember'd, as if they had hardly yet forgotten the use of praying to them.' Women in labour called on Mary as well as God to see them through their travail.[18] Most parishes claimed some special connection with a patron saint who had protected them in the past and who was commemorated in the folklore and topography of the parish. The popular, practical religion of early-modern Wales was partly grounded in a religious landscape that lay outside the (decaying) walls of the parish church.

The folklore of the saints clustered around local place-names emphasising the singularity of the parish and its privileged link with its patron saint. Rocks, springs, caves and other natural features dedicated to the saints abounded and were often fancifully named. It was not surprising that the last phase of ritualized cursing in Wales was expressed in this dominant saintly idiom. The consuming interest of the Welsh in the traditions and festivals of their saints is difficult to parallel elsewhere in early-modern Protestant Europe. It was clear to evangelical Protestants that the bulk of the Welsh people were more obliged to the religious observance of custom than to the benefit of the preaching and catechism of a regular ministry. 'And thus it is that the Christian Religion labours to keep ground here', was Erasmus Saunders' sombre conclusion.[19]

In eighteenth-century Wales there was certainly the perception among some Protestants that the Reformation had not yet been accomplished and that there was still much work to do to capture the hearts and minds of the people. The practical religion of the people was readily identifiable as superstitious by Anglicans and dissenters who had a more doctrinally-structured faith. A hostile Methodist commentator, Robert Jones of Rhos-lan, summarised it in this way. The simple religious beliefs held by the people were essentially a doctrine of good works and last things, pithily put in a rhyming popular saying: '*os da y gwnawn, da y cawn*', 'if we do good [on earth], we shall have better [to come]'. They believed that all the works of a lifetime were put in the balance on judgment day, and if God's works were the heavier then sweet heaven was the reward of those people, but if bad works were the weightier they must expect hell. The final judgement was hidden of course, but it was believed that the soul could be saved at the last moment, and there was a correspondingly strong belief (more 'than in the whole Bible') in the importance of the corpse-candle, and other portents which warned of death, and in observing certain rituals at the situation of death, especially the death-watch (*gwylnos*).[20]

Providentialism helped explained good and bad fortune: those who were good and charitable were sometimes rewarded on earth; those who did evil might be punished on earth. There was moreover a certain consequential fatalism within popular culture. The attitude was expressed in a contemporary song preserved by Humphrey Foulkes (d. 1737):

> *Rhaid i'r Haul y boreu godi,*
> *Rhaid i wellt y Ddaiar dyfy,*
> *Rhaid i ddwfr yr afon gerdded,*
> *A rhaid i bawb groesawi eu dynghed.*

This suggested that everyone should welcome their fate (*tynged*) which was as natural and inevitable as the sun rising in the morning, the grass growing on the earth, and water running in the river. As Foulkes observed ('I am very sorry to say it'), the song expressed 'the common opinion of the countrey'.[21]

Experience of the supernatural was part of practical religion. In early modern Wales, as in many parts of Europe, the extraordinary and the quotidian commonly intersected, bringing the fantastic and the supernatural into everyday concerns. It was common enough for people to claim they had encountered with supernatural beings – ghosts, fairies, or other spirits – or to have heard or seen presentiments of death. These experiences were not private matters but were known far and wide, as Edmund Jones's *Relation of Apparitions of Spirits* (1780) showed. However, the worlds of spirits and human beings should be kept apart. Those who saw spirits were often afterwards debilitated. A maidservant who helped the release of a ghost by finding a hidden object was afterwards 'sick for a yeare and afterwards could not look steadfastly in any man's face'. A young man who claimed he had been transported from south Wales to north America and back again by a spirit had the characteristics of those who were believed to have encountered spiritual beings: 'He could hardly speak, and his skin was somewhat like leather, and looks rather sickly.'[22]

The supernatural was encountered in many guises: sometimes in the form of creatures – bulls, dogs of many types, horses, strange birds, and other animals that 'piffed' like the turkey or 'jetted' like the weasel; sometimes heard as great noises (once memorably described as the noise that five or six coaches might make together); and sometimes seen as very bright lights that moved and changed in size, variously appearing as large as a church tower or as small as glow-worm. These were interpreted as evil spirits. Sometimes the devil himself, the constant tempter of mankind, was encountered. The devil was most frequently encountered as an unsought and silent companion on lonely journeys at night across the mountains. The devil often inadvertently revealed his identity, especially when not responding appropriately to the familiar and expected greetings. A Radnorshire man journeying by night courteously wished another traveller on the same path good night ('*nos dawch*') but became terrified when the stranger answered in a 'strange language' and afterwards, as often happened, he 'fell sick for some time'. Similarly, Hugh, a Merthyr Tudfil shoemaker, when walking home from Pontypool had a silent companion who did not bid him good night, as was the usual custom. Eventually, Hugh saw with fear and oppression of spirit that his companion had hoofs. A group of travellers returning on horseback from Llantrisant acquired an unwanted companion 'of a dark disagreeable aspect', who weaved between them without exchanging any greeting and went through a gate soundlessly. Only three of the four travellers saw this person, a circumstance which actually reinforced the supposition that he was an evil spirit: 'if it had been a man, every one of them would have seen him.'[23]

Fairies, ghosts, and other spirits were imaginative constructs. They were fantastical but not exactly fantasy. The witch-figure, ghosts, and fairies were symbolic constructions but they were representations of an accessible experience. Characteristically some experiences were objectified so that they appeared as external to the person. It is a mode of thought that has often been described by anthropologists.[24] This was certainly true of dreams, which might sometimes seem as external messages sent to the dreamer, or the action of the conscience, which was often understood as temptation by the devil. The witch-figure is readily understood as embodying the reversal of moral behaviour. Beliefs about ghosts and fairies are not analysed here, but they can be shown to be externalised representations of ideas about the self and of society. Practical religion was not a coherent and systematic body of doctrine. However through analysis we can make connections (not made by contemporaries) and see how, characteristically, beliefs were structured by a logic of opposition, inversions, and reversals. It was of course a logic that could be extended to transform everyday life, as the pre-political rituals of reversal of Rebecca and the *ceffyl pren* showed in the first half of the nineteenth century.[25]

Reforming Practical Religion

In 1721 Erasmus Saunders claimed that the Reformation had made little headway in Wales: the people had not unlearnt the errors of their ancestors 'because the Doctrines of the Reformation begun about two hundred Years ago in England, have not yet effectively reach'd us'. Nor was it likely that they would, Saunders concluded, 'without a fit and learned clergy.' One imagines that Saunders would have subscribed to the historians' notion of the 'long' Reformation still being played out in the later seventeenth or eighteenth century.[26] The reform of popular religion and custom, which was interlinked, arrived relatively late in Wales as compared with much of Europe.[27] The call for religious reform had been clearly made in print, particularly in the latter part of the seventeenth century, but it is probable that these polemics had little impact on popular religious culture.[28] As Robert Jones of Rhos-lan noted, in those dark days few people could read.

Although the reform of religion and custom is often associated with religious radicals, the role of Anglican parsons in attempting to reform custom and popular religion in the eighteenth century needs also to be appreciated. The attitudes of the educated Anglican divine were articulated by Humphrey Foulkes, a Denbighshire parson, whose dissertations on ancient religion, literature, laws and other matters (presented to his bishop in 1737) are a valuable commentary on popular beliefs and related to the concerns of Lhuyd and Aubrey.[29] When describing aspects of practical religion, like prayer or the death-watch (*gwylnos*), Foulkes adopted a historicist approach, for the most part regarding the customs and practices of popular religion as having a pagan origin with a Catholic superstructure. 'Slavery' under popery 'gave room for these weeds to grow so plentifully amongst us', asserted Foulkes; their survival after the Reformation was a consequence of inertia. Foulkes felt some embarrassment in exposing the 'foibles' of his countrymen, but found occasional comfort by citing similar customs from England and other nations. Foulkes proposed to 'chalk out some few superstitions' (he uses the word in a modern sense), hoping that in time they would be 'rooted out by the care and diligence of my brethren the clergy', by the magistrates putting the laws more vigorously into effect against them, and by educational progress. But banishing these superstitions was not easily accomplished. Parsons might try to discourage custom, sometimes opposing the more florid aspects of the saints' festivals, but often their authority was not particularly great beyond the walls of the parish church. Parsons made the greatest impact where their authority was unopposed. Throughout the eighteenth century a steady iconoclastic reordering of the parish church initiated by parsons and gentry families erased much remaining pre-Reformation woodwork and artefacts.[30]

Humphrey Foulkes and other clerical reformers were unrelentingly historicist, generally viewing custom as a dead weight inherited from the past without really understanding or conceding that custom might have contemporary relevance, especially as the cultural property of a particular class. Outside the walls of the churchyard, parsons encountered unexpected intransigence when trying to reform apparently small matters of custom and might provoke a local cause célèbre. Funeral customs were among the most sensitive issues, as the Rev. William Harris, parson of Caerau, Glamorgan, discovered when he tried without success to prohibit a 'silly' burial custom. Whenever a parishioner was carried for burial at Caerau, the bearers took the coffin off their shoulders at the churchyard gate and made it touch the ground before the parson received it. The custom seems to have infuriated and perplexed the parson. He interrogated his parishioners about the custom but 'could never hear any reason for it, but yt it was the practice of their forefathers'. The parson tried to forbid the custom but his authority did not reach beyond the churchyard. Nothing he could say to his parishioners would 'prevail with them to part with this silly custom'. Having encountered their intransigence, the parson concluded that his countrymen were 'perfect Rechabites' in such matters, and 'of all people in the island the most tenacious I believe of their antient customs and traditions'.[31] Later the parson was given to understand that a 'popish' statue had formerly stood at the spot where the coffin was made to touch the ground, and this historical explanation satisfied him as to the origin of the custom. What was at stake, however, was the proprietorial nature of custom – 'our' custom and 'our forefathers'' custom rather than 'your' custom.[32] Burial customs were among the most revealing aspects of practical religion because the observance of custom was clearly combined with accommodation to the requirements of the established church. Throughout much of Wales there were held burial customs of the type accurately described but erroneously interpreted by Aubrey as 'sin-eating'. The death-watch and symbolic distribution of food and drink were observed without the parson. The coffin was afterwards carried to the churchyard, stopping at accustomed 'resting places'. The parson then received the coffin at the churchyard and the burial service was carried out as directed by the rubric.

There was an element of cultural resistance about the attachment to custom, but reformers generally attributed intransigence over the reform of custom to the tyrannical hold of the past over the present. In theory at least it was possible to reform the customary elements of popular culture through education and preaching. It was more difficult to come to terms with the fantastic element in popular belief which made the people appear credulous and irrational. An early collector of folk-stories from tenantry in the Vale of Neath, Maria Jane Williams, the daughter of the squire of Aberpergwm, confided to her editor, 'I cannot help expressing my surprise at finding so many labouring under delusions which seem inexplicable. Many of my old friends are highly respectable in their line of life, farmers and farmers' wives, of strict veracity on all other topics save supernatural agencies; and they relate these stories with an earnestness and an air of truth that is perfectly confounding. Some have actually seen the fairies ...'[33] The fantastic element in popular belief was not simply a matter of repeating the narratives of the past, although this was important. The stock of tales about ghosts, fairies and other spirits was constantly replenished by new narratives (structured along familiar lines) concerning encounters with spirits in the present. The more florid narratives perplexed and infuriated some magistrates and other authority figures since they seemed not only contrary to common sense but blatant examples of deceit. In the mid-eighteenth century a young Breconshire man disappeared for three days and three nights and on his return claimed that he had been transported by a spirit from Ystradgynlais to Philadelphia on a mission that involved (characteristically) the retrieval of lost or hidden goods. The case aroused much interest in the district, of course, with speculation on the identity of the ghost, said to be one Elizabeth Gething who had gone to Pennsylvania eighty years before. However a local gentleman 'threatened to punish the harmless undesigning lad for telling lies.' 'Why is it', Edmund Jones asked in exasperation after reporting this case, 'that so many of the gentry affect to deny these important matters of fact?'[34]

For some fifty years Edmund Jones (1702–93) collected narratives ('relations') of apparitions and spirits in Wales in order to confound the sceptics, deists, and freethinkers who denied the existence of spirits, and were influential among the gentry and professional class. His published selection of narratives was designed to prevent the tendency to irreligion and atheism spreading throughout the kingdom. 'Our modern Deists are worse than the ancient Sadducees', wrote Jones in a rebuke to infidels and atheists. Jones was concerned that his numerous accounts of apparitions might make some English readers think that Wales was a hellish place, far worse than England. Jones acknowledged that spirits did appear in England, but there were some types of apparitions peculiar to Wales, including certain presentiments of death like the corpse-candle. In some respects Wales had a special knowledge of ghosts, fairies, and witches that it was important to pass on. Jones allowed himself to rebuke king and Parliament which had repealed the witchcraft acts in 1736: 'Had his Majesty King George II read the history of witchcraft, and known as much as we do in some parts of Wales, he would not have called upon his Parliament to determine that there are no such things as witches, and his Parliament would hardly have complimented him therein.'[35]

Edmund Jones emerges as an interesting champion of the authenticity of some spiritual aspects of popular belief. The genre in which he wrote, which had seventeenth-century origins, was more usually a collection of narratives derived from ministers and the godly. Jones's relations of apparitions were collected not only from fellow ministers but also recorded the experiences of farmers, labourers and craftsmen. Jones's relations of the appearance of spirits reveal the structuring of belief along class lines. In Wales 'where such things have often happened', Jones observed, 'we scarce meet with any who question the being and apparition of spirits', though he wistfully wished that the people 'stood more in awe of the world to come and made a greater preparation for eternity'. Jones considered that scepticism about apparitions was learnt 'especially from the gentry'. The gentry in Wales – as in England – 'affect to disbelieve, dispute against, and ridicule the account of apparitions and agencies of the spirits'. The growing class divide was apparent from the belief in death portents. In 1656 Richard Baxter had received detailed information about presentiments of death from a Cardiganshire squire and justice of the peace. The brightest portents were seen before the deaths of the gentry and freeholders. By 1780 corpse-candles were still seen in Wales 'by many honest, wise men', but these witnesses were by and large proletarian.[36]

Wales lacked a substantial middle class, and popular religion in Wales was structured along class lines dividing the relatively poor from the relatively affluent. The narratives or 'relations' of apparitions were collected from farmers and artisans who would not normally have had their experiences preserved except through the spoken word. Edmund Jones is often at pains to stress the veracity and good reputation of his informants. The workingman travelled the countryside and saw and heard many things that the gentry did not. The gentry had few encounters with spirits because they 'do not travel so much alone, and by night, as others do'. Was it reasonable, Jones asked, that gentlemen should speak against things they had no experience of? Should these few sceptics be believed against the many that had experienced such things and were also people of sense and probity? Given the division of belief along class lines, it is interesting that some relations of apparitions seem to have been told against the gentry. One may note a narrative concerning an unnamed Carmarthenshire tailor who was also a conjurer. A local squire, Mr Gwynne of Glanbrân, began to talk to the tailor about his conjuring 'rather in the way of blaming him'. The tailor was a little, 'mean-looking man', and the squire offensively wondered aloud 'how such a man as he had the courage to look upon the devil'. The tailor affirmed that he had the necessary resolve to face the devil, but the squire challenged him, 'Canst thou show him to me?' The tailor retorted that the squire would not be able to look upon him. The squire expostulated, 'What! Thou able to look upon him, and not I?' The tailor responded that if the squire thought he was able to look upon the devil, then he would make him appear. The tailor went to a nearby wood and conjured a spirit, but of course it was too terrible for the squire to gaze upon, and he implored the tailor to take it from his sight.[37]

Evangelical Protestants may have shared with the common people a view of the immediacy of the devil's presence, but in other respects they attacked the more marvellous aspects of popular belief. Robert Jones of Rhos-lan (1745–1829) in *Drych yr Amseroedd* ('Mirror of the Times', 1820) provided a classic description of popular religion and its transformation by the Methodist revival in north Wales.[38] A dialogue between an Enquirer and an Observer gave a description of the way of life in the dark times before the means of grace became plentiful. Observer describes how great ignorance formerly filled the land, Bibles were scarce and there were few other books. The prayers of the people were relics of popery and little more than charms; confidence was placed in 'the letter under the stone' and other written protective charms.[39] Observer describes the customs and superstitions then prevalent. Many believed that fortune-tellers could fortell their destiny or fate; there was great resort to the conjurer or charmer (*swynwr*) whenever man or beast was sick; many had great faith in almanacks and prophecies of Robin Ddu, and there was much interest in dreams and their interpretations. There was a consuming curiosity in omens: 'Scarcely a bird would fly, lamb appear, or snail crawl without some conjecture about what would come to pass.' Observer says that in short the people would scarcely do anything ('not even grow a finger-nail') without some superstition. In terms of custom there was strong belief in the corpse-candle and the death-watch, the Sabbath was often profaned by sports (*twmpath chwareu*) and ball-games, but the devil's chief feast was the *gwylmabsant* which combined the celebration of a patronal saint's festival with feasting, drinking, and fighting.[40]

Although many Methodists and dissenters had a strong sense of the external and immediate presence of the devil, this co-existed with a well-developed sense of the self and spiritual growth – a self-consciousness – that was alien to the importance of external spiritual agencies in popular culture. The theological preoccupation with salvation by personal experience led to an emphasis on the self. To be saved involved an awareness of having sinned, to repent, and to experience the forgiveness of God. This was the spiritual re-birth of regeneration. When Observer is describing popular religion (and good works), Enquirer professes himself amazed that there was no awareness of these theological preoccupations. For those – and there were many – who were concerned with regeneration and spiritual re-birth, the popular interest in spirits, omens, planetary influences, and the like was not only superstitious but irrelevant and fell away with the emphasis on self-knowledge and spiritual growth.

Robert Jones, writing a little before 1820, tends to use the past tense when refer-ring to popular beliefs; indeed Enquirer is curious about customs and beliefs which had apparently been current among the previous generation. In *Drych yr Amseroedd* contrasting images of darkness and light are constantly employed to describe past and present Wales. The light of the gospel was dispelling a darkness that could almost be felt and covered the land like a mist. It is difficult to assess the impact of the revival in putting down custom and superstition, especially as denominational histories and ministerial biographies tended to exaggerate the reforming success of exhorters and ministers. Some customs, e.g. the parish wake (*gwylmabsant*), had a dynamic that was closely related to other social factors, and suppression was undoubtedly assisted by changes in social organization.[41]

Assessing the vitality of beliefs in fairies and ghosts and other spirits is even more difficult. William Howells of Carmarthen, an early collector of folk tradi-tions, acknowledged that the traditions he described were fading in the 1830s: 'It is now extremely difficult to extract from any of the peasants such a thing as a ghost or a fairy tale.'[42] There was a sense in the early nineteenth century that ghosts and fairies were in retreat, but perhaps they had been for some time. As long ago as 1780 Edmund Jones had noted that the fairies had last appeared in Aberystruth parish about 1746. They had since appeared in other places, of course, but the plentiful appearances in the past were often contrasted with the infrequency of appearances in the present. In the 1820s a Vale of Neath nonagenarian, John Jones, better known as Cobbler Jig, maintained that 'fairies were to be seen in the days of my youth by the thousand, and I have seen them myself a hundred times.'[43] In the early eighteenth century Humphrey Foulkes drew attention to the vulgar error 'that the former days of our ancestors were better than these'.[44] Much of the evi-dence about the decline of custom and folklore is impressionistic and anecdotal, and related to a heroicized past when festivals were better celebrated and ghosts and spirits bolder and more importunate.

A more sensitive index of changing mores was the process of reform of custom intended to appropriate the situation of death from popular culture. There was no doubt that the death-watch (*gwylnos*) was a target for reform by Nonconformists, especially because (as Robert Jones put it) 'greater trust was placed in the corpse-bird (*aderyn y cyrff*, a presentiment of death) and the death-watch than in the whole Bible'. The reform of burial customs was an index of the success of Nonconformity, although the process had been begun in the eighteenth century by Anglican parsons. By the early nineteenth century in some parts of Gwynedd, once a stronghold of the *gwylnos*, the custom had been transformed into a sedate prayer meeting. Indeed, by the early nineteenth century the greater part of the 'fooleries and pastimes' of the people of Caernarfonshire lay 'buried in the grave dug for them partly perhaps by the growing intelligence of the people, but certainly with a more immediate effect by the sour spirit of Methodism.'[45] There were many locally-fought battles over custom, but some had special significance like the campaign against Ffynnon Elian. Capel Llanelian (the Methodist chapel) and Ffynnon Elian more or less faced each other on opposite sides of the road, symbolizing the opposed reformed and unreformed ways of life (Fig. 14). The physical destruction of the well in 1828 showed the increasing self-confidence of the local Methodists, but the revival of the well by Jac Ffynnon Elian demonstrated the continuing resilience of popular culture in the 1820s and '30s.[46]

Superstition was attacked by the new *eisteddfodic* culture, another expression of progressive and patriotic elements in Wales. The second Powysion *eisteddfod* held at Welshpool in 1824 attracted numerous entries for poems on the theme of the foolishness of witchcraft and all other superstition: '*Cân ar ffolineb swyn-gyfaredd a phob ofergoelion eraill*'. The intention of setting this subject, it was explicitly stated, was 'to extricate deluded people of weak or untutored intellect from the shackles of prejudice and the gloom of mental darkness'. The seven published poems were unrelentingly hostile to popular culture. The editor, a literary parson, considered that these compositions would be more useful in enlightening the darkness of the ignorant than the publication of the best sermons written on the subject.[47] Ffynnon Elian and its keeper were attacked of course, but there were many other practitioners of magic. A stanza entertainingly strung together the names of a clutch of disreputable diviners (*dewiniad*) who specialized in telling fortunes and finding lost goods in north-east Wales. Clearly, there was still much work to be done by the reformers.[48]

The diviner and conjurer still exercised a hold over the imaginations of both radical religious and unreformed conservative elements in Welsh culture. In some respects the conjurer and the minister appeared to represent opposed tendencies in Welsh society. The conjurer and the exhorter were the twin poles of rural society, one representing old Wales, error, superstition, and darkness, the other representing new Wales, light, truth, and religion. It was not unknown for these tensions to be present within the same family. Dr Pugh of Pennal, Merioneth, a wise-man (*dyn hysbys*) of considerable reputation was the half-brother of a Methodist exhorter, William Hugh (1749–1829) of Llechwedd, Llanfihangel-y-Pennant.[49] The continued presence of the conjurer in the mid-nineteenth century was regarded as a grotesque and embarrassing fetter from the past, and was attacked by progressives of different type. In north Wales in 1841 Griffith Ellis of Waunfawr, Caernarfonshire, was rebuked as a 'miserable wretch following the satanic calling of a cunning-man' in the Welsh version of a bilingual tract on the progress of the Welsh nation.[50] In south Wales Harries of Cwrtycadno was satirized in the periodical religious press and in the regional newspapers. However, the mid-nineteenth-century conversion and recantation of Jac Ffynnon Elian represented an important, even a decisive break with the past.

Disenchantment: Raised and Silenced Voices

The 1840s was a critical decade for the definition of a new Nonconformist Welshness, especially in the aftermath of the 'Blue Books' controversy (1847), which resulted in an alliance of Welsh Nonconformity hypersensitive to allegations of backwardness and immorality in Wales.[51] It was perhaps unfortunate that a copy of Edmund Jones's *Relation of Apparitions* fell into the hands of J. C. Symons, a censorious Anglican barrister, one of the Commissioners appointed to enquire into the state of education in Wales. 'I have before me', Symons wrote bleakly in his Report, 'a little book ...written by a clergyman named Jones ...in which he relates above forty or fifty cases of apparitions as having occurred and being attested by creditable persons in several parishes in my district.' It reinforced Symons's conclusion that 'The wide belief in ghosts and the almost incredible amount of superstition afford perhaps of all others the strongest proofs of the depth of ignorance which prevails throughout my district.' Moreover, 'Belief in charms, supernatural appearances, and even in witchcraft, sturdily survives all the civilisation and light which has long ago banished these remnants of the dark ages elsewhere. Little or none of such light has as yet penetrated the dense darkness which, harboured by their language, and undisturbed by availing efforts of enlightenment, enshrouds the minds of the people.'[52] The wounding and patronising language of the Blue Books was bitterly resented, but the contrast between light and darkness, civilization and ignorance, was no more than some Nonconformists had employed to describe Old Wales before the religious revival.[53] As Robert Jones Rhos-lan had put it, before the religious revival an almost palpable darkness had enveloped the land, akin to the darkness that had enshrouded Ancient Egypt. That was in the first decades of the nineteenth century. It was a blow for a later generation to encounter the official perception encapsulated in a shockingly short sentence that in Wales 'Superstition prevails'.[54]

The 1840s were an extraordinary period in terms of social and economic changes. Industrialization co-existed with a rural crisis and families were often split between two radically different social worlds. Nevertheless, urban migrants (who might return to their rural homes) brought with them the culture of the countryside, which might include the belief in magic. Symons, in a paragraph on prevalent superstitions, noted a recent collection among Gwent workmen to send a carpenter fifty miles to Lampeter to consult a 'wise man' so that he might recover his lost tools.[55] The oddity of the conjunction of the old rural and new urban ways of life in early Victorian Wales has often been commented on, but we must also appreciate the complexity of rural society in the period. Robert

Roberts ('*Y Sgolor Mawr*') beautifully conveys the nuances of rural society in his fictionalized autobiography. He presents a picture of life on a family farm in upland Denbighshire in autumn 1840. The senior generation of the farm are church people. The great-grandmother, aged ninety, is representative of a past generation. 'She is superstitious of course, like her generation. She has implicit faith in the fairies, of which interesting beings she has many a story, equally firm faith in omens, of which she knows an incredible number.' As regards religion, 'She is a heathen in religious matters or at least our Methodist friends so regard her, she has never been at a chapel and cares nothing for sermons or prayer meetings. She calls herself a churchwoman.' On the other hand, the farmer and his wife (her grand-daughter and her husband) are chapel people and welcome the Sunday School to Hafod, which is attended by most in the valley. The farm-servants are interestingly diverse: the 'hwsmon' or bailiff is 'a grave, taciturn man, a "professor" of religion and a great judge of sermons as well as of sheep and cattle'; the younger farm-servant 'does not go to chapel much and never cares to discuss religious topics'. He is 'fonder of profane songs than hymns, knows a good many stories of fairies, *Tylwyth Teg*, Abram Wood, and the Gypsies'. Lastly Old Cadwaladr, the odd-job man, is a churchman after his own fashion, that is 'he hated Methodism because there was no fun in it. He liked the wakes and faction fights which the Methodists had abolished, and he hated the Methodists with a double hatred for so doing.'[56]

Robert Roberts is drawing a picture of a socially complex society nuanced by age, status, and religious loyalties. By the mid-nineteenth century an older generation that had known Welsh society before the Revival was passing away and with them went a stock of narratives about customs and belief. The younger generations were by no means homogenous and there were respectable and rough elements within it. Chapel society and chapel civility began to dominate Welsh society from the mid-nineteenth century, emphasizing the values of hard work, temperance, thrift, education, and religious knowledge. For a brief period Nonconformity unified rural and urban society, as the architectural heritage of chapels still shows, but its domination was never complete. There were many who stood outside the church or chapel, but they were in effect a minority and socially diverse. To some extent chapel society defined itself against the world outside the chapel and possibly amplified some of the negative aspects seen there, including superstition. In the nooks and crannies of the social structure there was still a lingering belief in witchcraft, the power of the conjurer, and the marvellous might unexpectedly reappear like a blow from the past.[57]

Any residual taste among the educated and respectable for the marvellous was effectively destroyed by the controversy over the Welsh fasting girl in the late 1860s. Sarah Jacob, the daughter of a Carmarthenshire tenant-farmer and chapel member, claimed that God had favoured her with life without bodily sustenance, and took to her bed dressed more or less fantastically as a bride of Christ. The miracle of the fasting girl – which had many historical antecedents – was publicised by the local doctor, minister, and parson, and taken up by the Welsh and London press but with predictable results. A leader in *The Lancet* maintained that the claims made for Sarah were attributable to 'the credulity of Welsh persons'. The marvel of the fasting girl uncomfortably resolved itself into issues of Welsh versus English, and science versus superstition. Those 'jealous for the honour of their country, and the good name of Welsh men and women' (as a prominent Welsh journalist, 'Y Gohebydd', put it) proposed a scientific test of Sarah's fast. A team of nurses from Guy's Hospital were set to watch the girl strictly, and tragically but inevitably she faded and died from lack of sustenance. The parents were indicted and convicted of manslaughter, but the case had really been brought (according to the defence counsel) 'to free the ignorant Welsh mind from the trammels of superstition and darkness' by showing the deluded believers in the Welsh fasting miracle that the poor girl had died from starvation.[58]

There was little place for marvels in respectable Welsh society after this, and there were renewed attacks on superstition and marvellous cures, some quite narrowly focussed. A remarkable example of local eisteddfodic condemnation of superstition is provided by the competition held at Talerddig (a railway settlement serving the Llanbrynmair district of Montgomeryshire) for the best poems satirizing the cure of the 'woollen-yarn disease' or '*clwyf yr edau wlân*'. The three best poems were published at the request of the meeting in 1876.[59] It will be remembered (above, chap. 5) that the woollen-yarn disease was thought of as a kind of consumption often caused by witchcraft whose cure was beyond the expertise of conventional physicians, who generally refused to recognize it as an 'authentic' ailment. The disease represented both an unorthodox appeal to the supernatural and a backward traditionalism, a kind of anti-modernity that ran counter to the idea of progressive improvements in medicine and science. The contributors were quite clear that:

> *Myn'd heibio wnaeth hen ofergoelion*
> *Pan wawriodd dygeidiaeth i'n gwlad,*
> *A chleddir y son am ysbrydion*
> *Yn ngoleu gwareiddiad heb wâd.*

(The old superstitions went / When the dawn of knowledge broke in our country [i.e. the Revival] /And the talk of ghosts was buried / Undeniably in the light of civilization.)

Here again old and new, darkness and light, superstition and religion are sharply opposed in binary fashion. The poets maintained that the belief in the woollen-yarn cure should be outlawed, or (more poetically) buried in a bog like Cors Fochno or some other dark place out of the light of the sun where the diviner (male or female) would never see it.

According to the satirists of the woollen-yarn disease, '*Mae dosbarth o bobl yn credu / Yn hen ofergoelion y byd*': 'There is a class of people who believe / In the old superstitions of the world'. Who were these people? The answer is by no means straightforward. Chapel civility (Prys Morgan's helpful phrase) demanded sobriety and religious knowledge, including freedom from superstition. Those outside the chapel may have had some of these vices, but within the chapel there were backsliders, and it was important to maintain discipline by policing the attitudes of chapel members. Accordingly, there were pamphlets that reinforced warnings from the pulpit against drunkenness, luxurious living, and concupiscence of all kind – but also superstition. It was from the world of the chapel and the *eisteddfod* that the last published attack on witchcraft beliefs came. The tract was a condemnation of popular belief in witchcraft and (in a long tradition) the magical specialists (conjurers) who preyed on the superstitions of ordinary folk. It was a 'Voice raised against Superstition': *Llef yn erbyn Ofergoelion*, and its author, John Jones (Ioan Lenydd) of Llanfyllin, Montgomeryshire, was a Nonconformist and *eisteddfodwr*. His pamphlet published at the very turn of the twentieth century (1901) was certainly the last printed attack on 'traditional' witchcraft beliefs in the British Isles, and possibly in Europe (Fig. 17).[60]

The pamphlet takes the didactic form of a *dadl* or dramatic dialogue of the type which was performed in the chapel at Sunday school quarterly meetings.[60] Two respectable women (their social status is important since people of their background were the mainstay of the chapel) meet and exchange greetings and news. Anne, a farmer's wife, tells Gwen that her family has been in great trouble: they had been bewitched without knowing anything about it. They were well enough now, but Anne urges Gwen not to tell anyone about it; there was clearly a sense of shame in acknowledging that one had been bewitched. Before the event there had been several ill omens, and the family was afraid that some great trouble would befall them. After these omens, Jane the old witch (*Shâni yr hen reibes*) – (don't ever repeat this, Anne asks again) – came to the house asking for some butter. There was none to be had in the house, and Anne could tell from Shâni's bitter expression that she was angry. Various disasters followed, and in her distracted state Anne was ready to go to the conjurer, if necessary crawling on her hands and knees although it wasn't seemly ('manners') for a respectable woman to consult a conjurer. In the event Anne's husband ('the Boss') consulted the conjurer, looked into a glass and saw the image of old Shâni, purchased a written charm, and after this the family had peace of mind – until Gwen challenged Anne's composure.

Ioan Lenydd called his tract 'a voice against superstition'. The image of a dominant voice raised against superstition is a powerful one. In his dialogue the voices of superstition and godly reason are both raised. At one point Anne says to Gwen, 'I have heard much noise about the length of a woman's tongue, but your tongue is the length of two or three common women's tongues.' Gwen's voice against superstition is insistent, and in the end the voice of reason reduces the superstitious voice to silence; a case of one discourse overwhelming another. Finally Gwen and Anne sing a hymn together which looks forward to the end of superstition: 'We will oppose together today evils of every sort; / strength to learn a new creed – a creed consonant with the Word of God; / Let the time come / when conjuring will have completely disappeared.'

The abandonment of superstition was about assuming an identity. Assuming a respectable chapel identity entailed dissociation from the superstitions and customs of old Wales. There was always an unregenerate world outside the chapel which was characterized by a different way of life (*buchedd*), which included adherence to various superstitions.[61] A Nonconformist writer on superstitions in Wales was able to identify four classes of superstition in 1867: soothsaying (including consulting wise-men), witchcraft (including Ffynnon Elian), omens (mostly death portents), and apparitions. Those who believed they had seen ghosts or death-portents were generally nervous or weak-minded. Particular scorn was reserved for those, including old women, who repeated tales about witchcraft and soothsaying (knowing they were untrue) which continued to make people afraid. However, the writer was confident that superstitions would scatter with the increase of knowledge, both scientific and religious. The weapons against superstition in Wales were three: the press, Sunday school, and pulpit.[62] Chapel civility was indeed a hegemony maintained by this triarchy. Ministers and deacons policed the morality of their congregations, and sanctions ranged from shaming (naming) to expulsion (suspension and excommunication). In Ioan Lenydd's Sunday school debate the ministers are portrayed as very 'hot' in their opinions as to what is right or wrong. Consulting a conjurer or resorting to the woollen-yarn cure had become clandestine, shameful, and marginal activities hidden from minister and congregation.[63]

The rationalism of the nineteenth century has been exaggerated, not least by historians of witchcraft. One must note Devlin's cautionary discussion of the superstitious culture in nineteenth-century France, the mother country of modern liberal rationality. Devlin identifies a mass sub-culture in nineteenth-century France 'characterised on an intellectual level by irrationality and confusion, and at the emotional level by fear and instinct.'[64] Nineteenth-century rationalists considered that education and scientific understanding would eradicate a superstitious culture. The idea that secular education gradually overcame superstition in Europe is superficially convincing, but it was not a uniform process. We must certainly imagine other processes at work, especially in the religious culture of nineteenth-century Wales. In Wales there was not so much the rational explanation of superstition and folklore as the re-definition and rejection of their narratives as an inappropriate form of discourse. The voices encountered in the upland farmhouse in the 1840s, so brilliantly described by Robert Roberts, talked about ghosts, fairies, and witches but gradually fell silent, sometimes because of death and sometimes because authority figures (farmer, deacon, minister) did not want to hear them. There was a conscious effort to destroy knowledge about superstitious customs. This was clearly expressed by the eisteddfodic satirists of the woollen-yarn cure. The prize-winner hoped that every tale about the woollen-yarn cure would be consigned completely to oblivion, so that no-one would be there to transmit the knowledge to the future generations of the world.[65]

There was a deliberate resolve by many religious people – and the majority of Welsh people were chapel members by 1850 – in nineteenth-century Wales not to pass on their folk traditions. Patriotic antiquaries who began collecting folklore (to demonstrate the antiquity of Welsh traditions) in the later nineteenth century some-times recorded that they had the utmost difficulty in obtaining information. When Rev. Elias Owen visited the site of Ffynnon Elian in 1889 a neighbouring cottager maintained a rigid silence when questioned about the well, but showing consider-able emotion volunteered the information that although Jac had been 'dipped by the Baptists in a hole at the bottom of his garden' he was now 'burning in hell'. Sir John Rhŷs, the eminent Celticist, regretted that as a village schoolmaster in the 1860s he had not made more enquiries about folk beliefs, but he acknowledged that his education 'such as it was' had discouraged all interest in anything that 'savoured of heathen lore and superstition'. He 'grew up without having acquired the habit of observing anything, except the Sabbath.' Sometimes a conscious resolution was made not to pass on old traditions even – perhaps, especially – within the family. Thomas Gwynn Jones (1871–1941) an academic and folklorist reflected that 'My own father used to tell me stories and sing songs for us when we were very young, but later, having come under the influence of the religious activities of the time, he gave up the practice, considering it to be sinful. When later I became interested in Folklore and prayed him to repeat for me some of his former stories and songs, he refused to comply. Thus, throughout the district, a mass of such material was for ever lost.'[66] There is no single explanation for the decline of witchcraft and allied beliefs in Europe. However in nineteenth-century Wales there was a delib-erate religious resolve to disenchant the world by refusing to pass on the narratives which reproduced knowledge of witches, wizards, and spirits. This rejection was an acknowledgement of the power and continuity of the spoken word. As one of the most memorable and (of course) anonymous old stanzas (*hen penillion*) of early-mod-ern Wales expressed it:

> *Yr hên wr llwyd o'r gornel*
> *Gan ei dad a glywodd chwedel,*
> *A chan ei dad fe glywodd yntau,*
> *Ac ar ei ôl mi gofiais innau.*

> (The grey old man in the corner
> From his father heard a story,
> Which from his father he had heard,
> And after him I have remembered [it].)[67]

ACKNOWLEDGEMENTS

The text of this book was written more quickly than I would have preferred, but it
has been in the making for a long time. My first encounter with witches was in the
pages of bed-time stories which my mother excelled at reading. Close scrutiny of
Arthur Rackham's illustrations gave me a childhood dream that has stayed with me
ever since in which I saw a witch flying over our garden silhouetted against a full
moon. I still remember the feeling of rather detached but horrified amazement felt
in my dream as I realized that not only were witches real but they could be seen even
from our home. The figure of the witch that invaded my childhood was in due course
intellectualised and historicized by reading Keith Thomas, whose attitude to the
discipline of historical writing I greatly admire. Religion and the Decline of Magic,
his inspirational book, was published and discussed when I had the good fortune to
be taught anthropology in Durham and then at Oxford by Lucy Mair, Philip Mayer,
Wendy James, Godfrey Lienhardt, Edwin Ardener, and others who had themselves
written on witchcraft. Indeed, as a prospective anthropology student I was asked
by Philip Mayer to discuss a woodcut of witches by Dürer which hung distract-
ingly on the wall behind his desk. In one way or another I have been trying to think
anthropologically about witches ever since. Research on early-modern witchcraft
accusations and prosecutions demands sustained archival work, and I was able to
explore the records of the Court of Great Sessions as a University of Wales Fellow,
and here I pay tribute to the memory of Jaap van Velsen, who welcomed me into
his short-lived Department of Sociology and Social Anthropology at Aberystwyth.
Afterwards I pursued a different career with the Royal Commission on the Ancient
and Historical Monuments of Wales. Michael Roberts and Gareth Williams encouraged me to pick up the threads again of my research with invitations to publish on
witchcraft. This book certainly couldn't have been written without access to a great
library. Over the years I have spent more time than perhaps I should have done in
the National Library of Wales at Aberystwyth, and I must pay tribute to its professional and friendly staff. I must specifically mention Glyn Parry, who has reordered

the archive of the Court of Great Sessions. A calendar of witchcraft cases from the Great Sessions records, which proved too long for this book, is to be published elsewhere. Battling with difficult sources is a humbling experience which makes one realize one's limitations. My engagement with recalcitrant sources, especially the older Welsh-language documents, has been eased by many experts, often accosted in the streets of Aberystwyth with particular queries. I should like to thank particularly Dafydd Bowen, Iestyn Daniel, Pat Donovan, Dylan Foster Evans, Michael Freeman, Daniel Huws, Huw Ceiriog Jones, Gerald Morgan, Charles Parry, Huw Walters, among other scholars. Mary Burdett-Jones has helped me especially and read the text in draft. Geraint Jenkins has involved me with the work of The Centre for Advanced Welsh and Celtic Studies, an engagement with current historical and literary scholarship that I value greatly and hope is reflected in this book. My family has indulged my bookishness over the years, and I offer this book to them; without their indulgence it couldn't have been written.

Richard Suggett
Aberystwyth
March 2006

NOTES & REFERENCES

Abbreviations:

AC: *Archaeologia Cambrensis*
BBCS: *Bulletin of the Board of Celtic Studies*
Bodl: Bodleian Library, Oxford
Cardiff: Cardiff Public Library
DWB: *The Dictionary of Welsh Biography down to 1940* (London, 1959)
FHSP: *Flintshire Historical Society Publications*
GPC: *Geiriadur Prifysgol Cymru: University of Wales Dictionary of the Welsh
Language* (Cardiff, 1950–2002)
JEH: *Journal of Ecclesiastical History*
NLW: National Library of Wales, Aberystwyth
ODNB: *Oxford Dictionary of National Biography* (Oxford, 2004)
P&P: *Past & Present*
PRO: Public Record Office, London (The National Archives, since 2003)
THSC: *Transactions of the Honourable Society of Cymmrodorion*

Chapter 1

1   The literature on early-modern witchcraft is now vast and of variable interest, but
    the studies noted below have extensive bibliographies. Particularly relevant recent
    studies with a comparative or sociological focus include: Bengt Ankarloo and Gustav
    Henningsen (eds.), *Early Modern European Witchcraft: Centres and Peripheries* (Oxford,
    1993); Jonathan Barry, Marianne Hester, and Gareth Roberts (eds.), *Witchcraft in Early
    Modern Europe* (Cambridge, 1996); Robin Briggs, *Witches and Neighbours: the Social and
    Cultural Context of European Witchcraft* (London, 1996); Wolfgang Behringer, *Witchcraft
    Persecutions in Bavaria* (Cambridge, 1997). Ronald Hutton reviews a difficult relation-
    ship in 'Anthropological and historical approaches to witchcraft: potential for a new

collaboration?', *The Historical Journal* 47 (2004), 413-34. Wolfgang Behringer's *Witches and Witch-Hunts* (Cambridge, 2004) grasps the nettle and attempts a comparative history, global in scope with a chronology.

2   A.D.J. Macfarlane, *Witchcraft in Tudor and Stuart England* (London, 1970); Marianne Hester, 'Patriarchal reconstruction and witch hunting' in Barry et al. (eds), *Witchcraft in Early Modern Europe*, 288-306; Christina Larner, *Witchcraft and Religion* (Oxford, 1984).

3   Christopher Hill, 'Puritans and "the dark corners of the land"', in *Change and Continuity in Seventeenth-century England* (London, 1974), ch. 1, with quotations from 19-20, 26, 28-9; John Lewis, *Contemplations upon these Times. Or, The Parliament Explained to Wales* (1646; Cardiff, 1907), 30; Glanmor Williams, *Wales and the Reformation* (Cardiff, 1997), chaps 11-12. See generally Stuart Clark's discussion of 'superstition' as a key contemporary concept in the history of early-modern culture in *Thinking with Demons: the Idea of Witchcraft in Early Modern Europe* (Oxford, 1997), ch. 32.

4   Discussion of *The Birth of Merlin* and Shakespeare's *Henry IV, Part I*, in K.M. Briggs, *Pale Hecate's Team* (London, 1962), ch. 8, esp. 112-18; *The Chronicle of Iohn Hardynge in Metre* (1543), ch. 202, cited by G.L. Kittredge, *Witchcraft in Old and New England* (Cambridge, Mass., 1929), 156. Cf. generally, Helen Fulton, 'Owain Glyn Dŵr and the uses of prophecy', *Studia Celtica* xxxix (2005), 105-21.

5   *John Capgrave's Abbreuiacion of Cronicles*, ed. Peter J. Lucas (Early English Text Society No. 285, Oxford, 1983), 219; Christina Hole, *A Mirror of Witchcraft* (London, 1957), 129.

6   *The Last of the Astrologers. Mr. William Lilly's History of his Life and Times from the year 1602 to 1681*, ed. Katharine M. Briggs (Mistletoe Books No. I, London, 1974), 21-3; Arise Evans, *An Eccho to the Voice from Heaven* (London, 1650), 31-5; Arise Evans, *The Voice of King Charls the Father* (London, 1655), 39-40; Hill, 'Arise Evans: Welshman in London', in *Change and Continuity in Seventeenth-Century England*, ch. 2 (quotation from 62).

7   Kittredge, *Witchcraft in Old and New England*, 37, 122 and *passim*; Keith Thomas, *Religion and the Decline of Magic* (London, 1971), 178-9; D.G. Hey, *An English Rural Community: Myddle under the Tudors and Stuarts* (Leicester, 1974), 187. Two versions of *The History of the Lancashire Witches* are recorded in the *Eighteenth-century STC*, both tentatively dated *c.* 1785.

8   Briggs, *Pale Hecate's Team*, 112. On the significance of the modern witch story, see Lyndal Roper, *Witch Craze: Terror and Fantasy in Baroque Germany* (New Haven & London, 2004), 247-56. Depictions of witches varied throughout Europe. German illustrations of the witch in Hansel and Gretel generally show her with a headscarf rather than a tall hat.

9   *A miraculous...discourse of a woman...in the midst of whose fore-head...there groweth out a crooked horne* (London, 1588), noted by Alexandra Walsham, *Providence in Early Modern England* (Oxford, 1999), 201-2, 223; *Wonderful News from Wales: Or, a True Narrative of an old Woman living near Llansilin in Denbighshire* (London, 1677) reprinted in *The Harleian Miscellany*, vol. VI (1745), 65-8. The horned woman, Margaret Owen, having been examined by Montgomeryshire justices of the peace, and subsequently at the Council in the Marches, was sent to London for further investigation by the Privy Council. The pamphlet implies that Margaret had been punished by God for fornication but it was

often believed that conjurers could 'mark' people with a horn-like growth; cf. chap. 5 below.

10   'The History of Jack and the Giants' (Shrewsbury, n.d.) reprinted in Iona & Peter Opie, *The Classic Fairy Tales* (Oxford, 1974), 51-65.

11   Richard Gough, *The History of Myddle*, ed. David Hey (Harmondsworth, 1981), 107. See chaps 4 & 5 below.

12   H.R. Trevor-Roper, *The European Witch-Craze of the 16th and 17th Centuries* (Harmondsworth, 1969), 28-9.

13   John Aubrey, *Three Prose Works*, ed. John Buchanan-Brown (Fontwell, 1972), 132. See generally, Michael Hunter, *John Aubrey and the Realm of Learning* (London, 1975), 162-78, esp. 165, n.11.

14   David Williams, *The History of Monmouthshire* (London, 1796), 99-101.

15   Malcolm Chapman, *The Gaelic Vision in Scottish Culture* (London, 1978), ch. 5; idem, *The Celts: the Construction of a Myth* (London, 1992), *passim*, esp. 114-16 (religion), 287 (cult of the severed head); Ronald Hutton, *The Triumph of the Moon: a History of Modern Pagan Witchcraft* (Oxford, 1999), 303-5, discusses a claim made in 1996 that 'the Old Religion' survived in twentieth-century Anglesey. Cf. also Patrick Sims-Williams, 'The visionary Celt: the construction of an ethnic preconception', *Cambridge Medieval Celtic Studies* 11 (1986), 71-96.

16   C. L'Estrange Ewen, *Witchcraft and Demonianism* (London, 1933), 422; J. Gwynn Williams, 'Witchcraft in seventeenth-century Flintshire', Parts 1 and 2, *FHSP* 26 (1973-4), 16-37, 27 (1975-6), 5-35.

17   Brian P. Levack, 'The decline and end of witchcraft prosecutions' in *Witchcraft and Magic in Europe, Volume 5: the Eighteenth and Nineteenth Centuries*, series ed. Bengt Ankarloo and Stuart Clark (London, 1999), 77-8.

18   On the records of the Welsh assize courts, see G. Parry, *A Guide to the Records of Great Sessions in Wales* (Aberystwyth, 1995), which supersedes PRO, *List and Indexes*, no. 40 (London, 1914).

19   Thomas, *Religion and the Decline of Magic*, 449.

20   See generally, Richard Suggett, 'Slander in early-modern Wales', *BBCS* xxxix (1992), 119-53.

21   Cf. Giles Jacob's *A New Law-Dictionary* (London, 1729), entry 'Action on the Case for Words': 'To say that he is a witch, and did bewitch such a person, etc.' is actionable, 'but not to call a person witch, without more words'.

22   James Sharpe, *Instruments of Darkness: Witchcraft in England, 1550–1750* (London, 1996), ch. 4.

23   For Robert Holland's biography, see *DWB*, 363; *ODNB*, vol. 27, 689-90, and chap. 2.

24   Robert Holland, *The Holie Historie of Ovr Lord and Saviovr* (London, 1594), dedication.

25   The first edition of *Dau Gymro* is known only from a manuscript version 'Ymddiddan rhwng Tudur a Gronw' (A Conversation between Tudur and Gronw) printed in *Rhyddiaith Gymraeg II...1547–1618*, ed. Thomas Jones (Cardiff, 1956), 161-73, which is cited here. R.G. Gruffydd, 'Religious Prose in Welsh from the Beginning of the Reign of Elizabeth to the Restoration' (D.Phil. thesis, Oxford, 1952–3), discusses the literary con-

text and merits of *Dau Gymro*. Stuart Clark and P.T.J. Morgan, 'Religion and magic in Elizabethan Wales', *JEH* 27 (1976), 31-46, discuss the historical context.

26 Presumably a reference to William Salesbury, *Oll Synnwyr pen Kembero ygyd* (London, 1547), with the proverb at sig. B.iiiv. Cf. Clark and Morgan, 'Religion and magic in Elizabethan Wales', 35, n.2.

27 'Ysgotland' or 'Alban' were the more usual names for Scotland. It is not impossible that Holland's 'Albania' was a wryly oblique reference to his domicile in south Pembrokeshire and Alban Stepney's influence there. Alban Stepney, MP and registrar of St David's, owned the manor of Prendergast where Holland was rector. Holland became associated with the literary circle of Stepney's brother-in-law, George Owen of Henllys. In his will (1611), Stepney remembered eight godsons all named Alban, including George Owen's eldest son. With the popularity of the name Alban among the gentry, Pembrokeshire became a veritable 'Albania'. For further details of these associations, see B.G. Charles, *George Owen of Henllys: a Welsh Elizabethan* (Aberystwyth, 1973), esp. 51-2, 115-17; Francis Green, 'Stepneys of Prendergast', *West Wales Historical Records* 7 (1917-18), 118-24.

28 Clark & Morgan, 'Religion and magic in Elizabethan Wales', 39, note Rhys Prichard's allusion to these customs in *Canwyll y Cymru*, but Prichard seems to have borrowed from Holland.

29 The sub-title of 'Tudur a Gronw' suggests that it may have been intended as the first in a series of dialogues: 'Dychreyad y Llyfr yr Ymddiddannon', i.e. 'The beginning of the book of discourses'. *Rhyddiaith Gymraeg II*, ed. Jones, p. 161.

30 The different editions are discussed by John Ballinger, 'Vicar Pritchard. A study in Welsh bibliography', *Y Cymmrodor* XIII (1900), 1-75.

31 Henry Holland, *A Treatise against Witchcraft* (Cambridge, 1590); George Gifford, *A Dialogue Concerning Witches and Witchcraftes* (London, 1593), *Newes from Scotland* (1591; Edinburgh, 1966); esp. 16-7.

32 It is possible that Holland, like some of his Cambridge contemporaries, would have taken an active interest in the sensational case of the witch of Warboys as well as in prosecutions at the assizes and Ely consistory court.

33 But cf. several references in George Gifford's *Dialogue*, esp. sig. B1v, to 'neighbours [who] wishe me to burn something alive, as a henne or a hogge'. Cf also the reference c. 1621 to those 'wise men and wizards' who teach the common people such 'wicked fopperies' as 'to burn young calves alive', Edward Fairfax, 'A Discourse of Witchcraft', *Miscellanies of the Philobiblon Society* V (1858-9), *passim*. See also Clark & Morgan, 'Religion and magic in Elizabethan Wales', 36.

34 My debt to *GPC* will be apparent.

35 *GPC, s.v.* 'dewin'.

36 Edmund Gibson (ed.), *Camden's Britannia* (London, 1695), col. 647, a tradition somewhat sceptically noted by Edward Lhuyd; NLW MS 1663, ff. 23ᵛ· 64ᵛ.

37 Thomas, *Religion and the Decline of Magic*, 398; Richard Suggett, 'Vagabonds and minstrels in sixteenth-century Wales', in Adam Fox and Daniel Woolf (eds), *The Spoken Word: Oral Culture in Britain, 1500–1850* (Manchester, 2002), 146-53; NLW MS 9051E, item 12.

38 Glanmor Williams, 'Prophecy, poetry, and politics in medieval and Tudor Wales',
    in *British Government and Administration. Studies Presented to S. B. Chrimes*, ed. H.
    Hearder & H.R. Loyn (Cardiff, 1974), 104-16; idem, *Religion, Language and Nationality
    in Wales: Historical Essays* (Cardiff, 1979), 71-80; Griffith Aled Williams, 'The bardic
    road to Bosworth: a Welsh view of Henry Tudor', *THC* 1985, 9-26, for the *mab dar-
    ogan*. Manuscript collections of prophecy are noted by Margaret Enid Griffiths, *Early
    Vaticination in Welsh with English Parallels* (Cardiff, 1937), 219-20. Graham C. G. Thomas
    notes some astrological and related manuscripts in 'From Manuscript to Print—I.
    Manuscript' in *A Guide to Welsh Literature, c. 1530–1700*, ed. R. Geraint Gruffydd (Cardiff,
    1997), 245, 247.

39 Suggett, 'Vagabonds and minstrels in sixteenth-century Wales', 147-53, for some exam-
    ples.

40 See generally, Ceri W. Lewis, 'The decline of professional poetry' in Gruffydd (ed.), *A
    Guide to Welsh Literature, c. 1530–1700*, 29-74; *The New Companion to the Literature of Wales*,
    ed. Meic Stephens (Cardiff, 1998).

41 See the *Oxford English Dictionary*, s.v. 'conjurer' for the range of meaning of the English
    word, and for the Welsh term, *GPC*, s.vv. 'consuriwr' and related forms. *Notes & Queries*
    X (ser. I., 1854), 243, 472, has a useful note on 'conjurer'. See also chap. 5 below.

42 In the English Wycliffe version the spirit invoker is called 'a devel clepere', in later ver-
    sions an enchanter, exorcist, or conjurer. Salesbury favoured the term *consurwyr* in his
    translation of the Acts of the Apostles where the English New Testament translators had
    used 'exorcists'. The translators of the 1588 and 1620 Welsh Bibles followed Salesbury in
    using *consuriwr*, and related forms, most strikingly in the 1620 chapter summary of Acts
    xix, where it is stated: *Y consurwyr Iuddewaid yn cael eu curo gan y cythraul. Llosgi y llyfrau
    consurio*. This more or less conformed to the Authorized Version's new summary, 'The
    Iewish exorcists are beaten by the deuill. Coniuring books are burnt.' See especially Acts
    xix in *The English Hexapla…of the New Testament Scriptures* (London, 1841); *Testament
    Newydd ein Arglwydd Iesu Christ* (London, 1567); *Y Beibl Cyssegr-lan* (London, 1588); Y
    Bibl Cyssegr-lan (London, 1620).

43 Thomas, *Religion and the Decline of Magic*, 68.

44 *GPC*, s.v. 'rhaib' and related forms; J. Morris-Jones, *A Welsh Grammar, Historical and
    Comparative* (Oxford, 1913), 90.

45 R.B. Roberts, 'Rhai swynion Cymraeg', *BBC S* 21 (1965), 210-11, citing NLW Peniarth MS
    205, p. 7, for the charm against the evil eye. Unfortunately the MS text is faded.

46 *Testament Newydd ein Arglwydd Iesu Christ* (1567), Gal., iii, 1. 'Ribodd' is misprinted
    'vibodd'. Salesbury elsewhere defines 'llygadtyny' as to 'forspeake', that is to bewitch
    or curse, with the emphasis on the tongue rather than the eye: William Salesbury, *A
    Dictionary in Englyshe and Welshe* (London, 1547), sig. L.iii^v. The word was rarely used in
    early-modern slander actions; only two instances have been noted.

47 Roberts, 'Rhai swynion Cymraeg', 210-11 (texts from NLW Wrexham MS 2 and
    Peniarth MS 53); NLW, Trovarth & Coed Coch Deeds 30, with a partial transcript in
    *Catalogue of Manuscripts, Charms, Remedies, and Various Objects Illustrating the History
    of Medicine in Wales* (Aberystwyth, 1928), 25-6. The beneficiary of the charm was still

alive in 1558 (NLW, Trovarth & Coed Coch Deeds 71, 126-7, 131). E.A. Lewis, 'A Reformation episode in Radnorshire', *Trans. Radnorshire Historical Soc.* 9 (1939), 19-22; Glanmor Williams, *The Welsh Church from Conquest to Reformation* (Cardiff, 1962), 332-3. See further, chap. 4.

48   Cf. J.K. Campbell, *Honour, Family and Patronage* (Oxford, 1964), 337-40; Brian Spooner, 'The evil eye in the Middle East', in *Witchcraft Confessions and Accusations*, ed. Mary Douglas (A.S.A. Monographs 9, London, 1970), 311-9; Godfrey Lienhardt, 'Some notions of witchcraft among the Dinka, *Africa* XXI (1951), 309-10. Lienhardt cites Bacon (Essay IX, *Of Envy*): 'There have been none of the affections which have been noted to fascinate or bewitch but love and envy; they both have vehement wishes . . . and they come easily into the eye . . .'

49   *Gwaith Tudur Aled*, ed. T. Gwynn Jones (2 vols, Cardiff, 1926), I, 198 (ll. 57-8), 318-9 (ll. 53-4); *Gwaith Gruffudd Hiraethog*, ed. D.J. Bowen (Cardiff, 1990), 376, ll. 13-20. I am most grateful to Mary Burdett-Jones and Dylan Foster Evans for discussing the texts in notes 49-50 with me and for suggesting translations.

50   *Gwaith Tudur Aled*, ed. Jones, I, 318-9 (ll. 52, 61-2); *Gwaith Lewys Môn*, ed. Eurys I. Rowlands (Cardiff, 1975), 24 (ll. 9-10), 145 (l. 52), 272 (l. 4).

51   Roberts, 'Rhai swynion Cymraeg', 210-11; *Gwaith Gruffudd Hiraethog*, ed. Bowen, 376. Cf. also the charm cited in chap. 2.

52   C. Trice Martin, 'Clerical life in the fifteenth century, as illustrated by proceedings of the Court of Chancery', *Archaeologia* LX (1907), 375. Tanglwst was initially attached on suspicion of heresy. Cf. Thomas, *Religion and the Decline of Magic*, 467.

53   NLW, Great Sessions 25/9/m.7.

54   Examples of entertainers called 'hudol' in Suggett, 'Vagabonds and minstrels in six-teenth-century Wales',144. A fifteenth-century poet applied the term *hudol* to describe the elusive Robin Hood: 'hudol oedd Robin Hwd lan' (kind Robin Hood was a magician), T. Gwynn Jones, 'Cultural bases: a study of the Tudor period in Wales', *Y Cymmrodor* XXXI (1921), 182-3.

55   William Salesbury, *A Dictionary in Englyshe and Welshe* (London, 1547), sigs. C.ii^v, R.iiiv. This entry is also a calque on the entry for witch in John Palsgrave's *Lesclarcissement de la langue francoyse* (1530): 'witche a woman vandoyse sorciere'. On Salesbury, see generally, R. Brinley Jones, *William Salesbury* (Cardiff, 1994), especially p. 16 for Salesbury's view of deceitful women humorously expressed in his definition of an onion!

56   John Rhŷs has useful remarks on some of these terms in 'The Nine Witches of Gloucester' in H. Balfour et al. (eds), *Anthropological Essays Presented to Edward Burnet Tylor* (Oxford, 1907), 285-93. *Gwrach* is discussed in chap. 3.

57   *Testament Newydd ein Arglwydd Iesu Christ* (1567); *Y Beibl Cyssegr-lan* (1588); *Y Bibl Cyssegr-lan* (London, 1620).

58   Note the following examples: witch: *hudoles* (f.) (Exod.xxii.8); witchcraft: *dewiniaeth* (I Sam.xv.23), *chyfareddion* (2 Chron.xxxiii.6), *swyngyfaredd* (Gal.v.20); witchcrafts: *hudola-eth* (2 Kings.ix.22), *swynion* (Mic.v.12; Nah.iii.4).

59   Cf. Chap. 3.

60   'Breuddwyd Rhisiart Fychan' (Richard Fychan's Dream), *Canu Rhydd Cynnar*, ed. T.H.

Parry-Williams (Cardiff, 1932), 423-36, lines 233-40. A reference in the poem to the commissioners for musters suggests a late-Elizabethan date when military service for Ireland became particularly unpopular in Wales. Cf. J.J.N. McGurk, 'A survey of the demands on the Welsh shires for the Irish war 1594–1602', *THSC* 1983, 56-67.

Chapter 2

1 Trial documents in NLW, Great Sessions 4/9/4. Nia Watkin Powell first drew my attention to this case.

2 I am grateful to Mary Burdett-Jones and Daniel Huws for their advice in translating this charm. For the Welsh text, see Richard Suggett, 'Y ddewines o Gymraes gyntaf i'w dienyddio', *Cof Cenedl* 19 (2004), 69-96.

3 On the 'three Marys', see Marina Warner, *Alone of All her Sex: the Myth and Cult of the Virgin Mary* (London, 1976), Appendix 2.

4 On the werewolf, see generally, Carlo Ginzburg, *Ecstasies: Deciphering the Witches' Sabbath* (New York, 1991); John Carey, 'Werewolves in medieval Ireland', *Cambrian Medieval Celtic Studies* 44 (2002), 37-72.

5 See generally, A. D. Carr, 'Gloddaith and the Mostyns, 1540–1642', *Trans. Caernarvonshire Historical Society* 41 (1980), 33-57.

6 'Araith Gruffydd ap Ifan i Ruffydd ap Robin ap Rhys', *Rhyddiaith Gymraeg I*, ed. T.H. Parry-Williams (Cardiff, 1954), 62-4 (MS dated 1561–2).

7 NLW, Great Sessions 4/9/4/56v.

8 'Plant Huw Holant o Aber Konwy, esgwier': the genealogy of the Holland family registered with Lewys Dwnn in 1597 by Robert Holland, who signed the document: NLW, Peniarth MS 268, p. 135; Lewis Dwnn, *Heraldic Visitations of Wales*, ed. Samuel Rush Meyrick (2 vols, Llandovery, 1846), II, 118; Thomas Erskine Holland, *The Hollands of Conway. Five Hundred Years of Family History* (rev. edn., London, 1915); Cardiff MS 2.28, which notes that Jane Conway 'had ffyftene sonnes & daughters' of which 'xi lyved & weare almost all maried and had sonnes & daughters'.

9 John Venn & J.A. Venn, *Alumni Cantabrigienses, Part I, Volume II* (Cambridge, 1922), 394; Clive Holmes, 'Henry Holland', *ODNB*, vol. 27, 663; Leonard W. Cowie, 'Robert Holland', op. cit., 690. The connection between the Holland brothers is not recorded in the *ODNB*. W.P. Griffith, *Learning, Law and Religion in Wales, c. 1540–1642* (Cardiff, 1996), 248, notes that Robert Holland's ordination was deferred twice because of insufficiency in Latin.

10 I am most grateful to Peter Meadows, Keeper of Ely Diocesan Records (Department of Manuscripts, Cambridge University), for confirming that Robert Holland was licensed curate and schoolmaster of Dullingham on 19 August 1580 (Ely Diocesan Records, G2/18, f.162). On 6 April 1582, John Norridge was licensed as schoolmaster there; presumably Holland remained as curate only. There seems to be no documentary confirmation that Holland became curate of Weston Colville, as stated (but not referenced) in the *DWB* and repeated in the *ODNB*.

11   For the Cambridgeshire background, see Margaret Spufford, *Contrasting Communities: English Villagers in the Sixteenth and Seventeenth Centuries* (Cambridge, 1974). Spufford discusses Orwell (a Crown manor) and Dry Drayton. Gifford's connection with Dry Drayton is noted in the *ODNB*, vol. 22, 140.

12   Robert Holland married Jane, daughter of Robert Meyler of Haverfordwest, and had six sons, 'wherof fowre are alyve' (among them 'Deverox') noted George Owen *c.* 1595, Cardiff MS 2.28. Owen also notes (apparently unrecorded elsewhere) that Henry Holland married the daughter of 'one Stynedge' in Cambridge and had two sons and three daughters.

13   B.G. Charles, *Calendar of the Records of the Borough of Haverfordwest, 1539–1660* (Cardiff, 1967), 207. Holland received £1.12s.3d. from William Walter, a wealthy merchant, who had established a special fund for the Corporation's use during his mayoralty. J. Phillips, 'The oldest parish registers in Pembrokeshire', *AC* III (6th ser., 1903), 298-300, shows that Holland acted as clerk, making entries in the parish registers of St Mary's.

14   Robert Holland, *The Holie Historie of Ovr Lord and Saviour* (London, 1594), sig. Aii^{r-v}. Holland may have been disappointed not to succeed William Tilbrook, the long-serving vicar of Dullingham, 1566–89. Tilbrook had provoked some trouble in the parish (which might conceivably have affected his curate) by 'naming his unlearned brother as parish clerk and harbouring an immoral daughter', according to *A History of the County of Cambridge and the Isle of Ely, Volume VI*, ed. A.P.M. Wright (Victoria County History, London, 1978), 167. More conventionally, Holland also says that the race of his youth was inadvisedly run.

15   Stuart Clark & P.T.J. Morgan, 'Religion and magic in Elizabethan Wales: Robert Holland's dialogue on witchcraft', *JEH* 27 (1976), 33.

16   Henry Holland, *A Treatise against Witchcraft* (Cambridge, 1590), sig. B1. Holmes, 'Henry Holland', 663.

17   Holland, *Treatise against Witchcraft*, ch. 3. See generally, Stuart Clark, *Thinking with Demons: the Idea of Witchcraft in Early Modern Europe* (Oxford, 1997), part IV.

18   Holland, *The Holie Historie*, sig. Aii^v. It is impossible to be absolutely certain of the chronology, but Holland specifically refers to *The Holie Historie* as 'the first fruits of my labors' in his dedication dated Aug. 1594 (sig, AiiR). *Dau Gymro* must therefore have been published after *The Holie Historie*, and presumably after Gwen ferch Ellis's trial in October.

19   Holmes, 'Henry Holland', 663, with additional information in Paul S. Seaver, *The Puritan Lectureships* (Stanford, Cal., 1970), 193-4, and Margaret Pelling, *Medical Conflicts in Early Modern London* (Oxford, 2004), 158n, 323, for Holland's treatment of nephritis. Cf. Thomas, *Religion and the Decline of Magic*, 251, 256, 493, for Greenham's observations on witchcraft, and *The Works of . . . Richard Greenham*, ed. H. H[olland] (London, 1599), esp. 74.

20   W.Ll. Davies, 'Robert Holland and William Perkins', *Jnl. Welsh Bibliographical Society* II (1916–23), 273-4; R.G. Gruffydd, 'Religious Prose in Welsh from the Beginning of the Reign of Elizabeth to the Restoration' (D.Phil. thesis, Oxford, 1952–3). Gruffydd's judgement (110) is that Robert Holland was transformed in Pembrokeshire 'from a mediocre English poet into an author of Welsh books of considerable merit and importance . . . Like his brother he remained a Puritan but became (unlike him) a Welsh Puritan.'

21 King James I, *Basilikon Doron . . . Translated into the true British tongue* by Robert Holland (1604; repr. Cardiff, 1931), with quotations from 'The Epistle'. The reprint has a useful 'Bibliographical Note' by John Ballinger.

22 NLW, Great Sessions 4/779/5/16A (1612).

23 Indictments were endorsed with the names of prosecutors and witnesses. Women were prosecutors in only two witchcraft trials in Wales. Clive Holmes, 'Women: witnesses and witches', *P&P* 140 (1993), 45-78, notes the role of men in organizing prosecutions in England but is able to show that women's participation in witchcraft trials as witnesses increased during the seventeenth century.

24 NLW, Great Sessions 4/270/1/504-5; Great Sessions 16/7/rex m.

25 NLW MS 9058E, item 99.

26 NLW, Great Sessions 4/802/7. Dorcas Heddin was originally from Wilburton, Cambridgeshire.

Chapter 3

1 NLW, Great Sessions 4/13/2/18; Great Sessions 4/34/6/38 (bearded witch); Great Sessions 21/224/m.19; Great Sessions 19/57/m.22; William Aubrey, *Llyfr Ffynon Elian* (Llanerchymedd, n.d.), 19.

2 *GPC*, *s.v.* 'gwrach'; Melville Richards, 'The supernatural in Welsh place-names', in *Studies in Folk Life: Essays in Honour of Iorwerth C. Peate*, ed. Geraint Jenkins (London, 1969), 309-11. *The First Volume of the Conway Parish Registers . . . 1541–1793*, ed. Alice Hadley (London, 1900), 36, for 'gwrach y gwenniath'.

3 NLW, Great Sessions 22/121/m.43; Powys Record Office (transferred from NLW), Breconshire Quarter Sessions 1690T/21; NLW, Great Sessions 4/783/5/29; 4/718/2/12.

4 NLW, Great Sessions 4/718/2/8. Translated as 'They are all ould strickers and use dildoes'.

5 NLW, Great Sessions 4/719/2/51-2; 4/781/1/37(ii).

6 NLW, Great Sessions 4/800/2/9; Bodl., MS Ashmole 1815, f.1.

7 NLW, Great Sessions 4/781/1/37(ii). The *OED*, *s.v.*, identifies witches' butter as the 'popular name for certain gelatinous algae and fungi, esp. *Tremella Nostoc*'.

8 NLW, Great Sessions 4/719/2/49-9, 55.

9 NLW, Great Sessions 4/800/2/9; Gwynn Williams, 'Witchcraft in seventeenth-century Flintshire, Part Two', *FHSP* 27 (1975–6), 32; Great Sessions 13/16/1/unnumbered. Cf. George Ewart Evans & David Thomson, *The Leaping Hare* (London, 1972), ch.13, esp. 142-77.

10 Bodl., MS Ashmole 1815, f.1. On the invasion of personal space, cf. Robin Briggs, *Witches and Neighbours* (Penguin ed., 1998), 167.

11 NLW, Great Sessions 19/40/m.30; 4/781/1/37; 4/719/2/48.

12 NLW, Great Sessions 4/780/4/16ᵛ; 4/781/1/37; 4/719/2/54 (with 'non p[ro]b' written in the margin).

13 J. Gwynn Williams, 'Witchcraft in seventeenth-century Flintshire [Part One]', *FHSP* 26 (1973–4), 34-6.

14   This was a celebrated but scientifically unresolved incident. See generally, R.T. Gunther, *Life and Letters of Edward Lhwyd* (Early Science in Oxford xiv, Oxford, 1945), 218-25; E. Gibson (ed.), *Camden's Britannia* (London, 1695), col. 659-61.

15   Shropshire Parish Register Society, *The Register of Oswestry, Volume I* (Diocese of St Asaph series, vol. IV, 1909), 194, 199, for John ap David alias 'Weech' or 'Witch'. 16 NLW, Great Sessions 4/9/4/14; NLW MS 9058E, item 99; Great Sessions 4/985/6/19.

17   NLW, Great Sessions 4/781/1/37; 4/886/8/15; 21/104/m.18 & 13/6/5/unnumbered (Agnes ferch Maddock); 4/886/8/15; 4/719/2/48.

18   Cf. Alan Macfarlane, *Witchcraft in Tudor and Stuart England* (London, 1970 & 1999), pt 3; Keith Thomas, *Religion and the Decline of Magic* (London, 1971), 553-9; 'Introduction' in *Witchcraft in Early Modern Europe*, ed. Jonathan Barry et al., (Cambridge, 1996), 8-9, 12, 18-19.

19   NLW, Great Sessions 33/6/6/unnumbered examination.

20   NLW, Great Sessions 4/719/2/55; Bodl., MS Ashmole 1815, f.1.

21   Williams, 'Witchcraft in seventeenth-century Flintshire, Part Two', 31-2.

22   NLW, Great Sessions 4/800/2/9; Bodl., MS Ashmole 1815, f.1. Olly's words were also reported as, '[You] should give some soule with ye bread to expecte p[er]sons, such as she was'. For sowl(e) meaning 'a relish', specifically in Pembrokeshire 'anything eaten with bread or potatoes, as meat, butter, cheese', see *The English Dialect Dictionary* (London, 1898–1905), *s.v.*

23   NLW, Great Sessions 4/719/2/48, 50.

24   NLW, Great Sessions 33/6/6/unnumbered; 4/781/3/37.

25   Williams, 'Witchcraft in seventeenth-century Flintshire [Part One]', 36-7; NLW, Great Session 4/800/2/9; Williams, 'Witchcraft in seventeenth-century Flintshire, Part Two', 34-5. Cf. also (chap. 2, above) Gwen ferch Ellis's neighbours who advised her to leave the district.

26   NLW, MS 9058E, item 99; *Calendar of Wynn (of Gwydir) Papers, 1515–1690* (Aberystwyth, 1926), no. 1009, 159; NLW, Great Sessions 4/719/2/54; 4/886/8/15; 4/781/1/37.

27   NLW, Great Sessions 4/131/4/76; 4/133/2/8A.

28   Madness and witchcraft: NLW, Great Sessions 4/9/4/14b-c; bewitching to love: Great Sessions 4/160/8 and Chirk B/29b/20. These cases are discussed in chap. 4.

29   NLW, Great Sessions 4/977/9/22.

30   Williams, 'Witchcraft in seventeenth-century Flintshire [Part One]', 34-6; NLW, Great Sessions 4/719/2/48, extracts in C. L'Estrange Ewen, *Witchcraft and Demonianism* (London, 1933), 330-32; Great Sessions 4/886/8/15.

31   NLW, Great Sessions 4/13/4/38; 4/17/1/7; 4/19/3/28; 4/151/4/25; 4/31/6/35; 4/150/1/28; 4/797/5/80.

32   NLW, Great Sessions 4/718/3/22, 33 (Thomas John was acquitted); NLW, Great Sessions 33/6/9/unnumbered examination & Great Sessions 4/779/6/27 (indictment).

33   NLW, Great Sessions 4/980/4/24. Jews (because of their reputation for usury) like witches were thought of as fundamentally malicious. Bp. Middleton's visitation of St Davids (1583) enquired if there were 'any that commit usury, sorcery, or any kind of witchcraft', W.P.M. Kennedy, *Elizabethan Episcopal Administration, Volume*

III: *Visitation Articles and Injunctions, 1583–1603* (Alcuin Club Collections XXVII, 1924), 142.

34 NLW, Great Sessions 4/128/5/30. Robert ap Hugh was arraigned for the felony at the Montgomeryshire Great Sessions but refused to plead. The jury found that he stood mute from malice rather than God's visitation.

35 NLW, Great Sessions 4/139/2/27; 4/789/55/30; 4/793/2/42y; 4/18/1/24.

36 NLW, Great Sessions 4/153/2/7-8; 4/785/4/4y; 33/7/1/unnumbered.

37 NLW, Great Sessions, examinations July 42 Eliz., formerly in Wales 28/19-1.

38 'Superstitious Practices Prevailing in Wales in the Year 1589' in John Leland, *Collectanea* (London, 1774), vol. 2, 648-50, reprinted in *AC* I (3rd ser. 1855), 235-7; Erasmus Saunders, *A View of the State of Religion in the Diocese of St. David's* (London, 1721); E. Owen, 'Meini Cred (Creed Stones)', *AC* 14 (5th ser., 1897), 172-75; J. Fisher, 'The private devotions of the Welsh in days gone by', *Trans. Liverpool Welsh National Society* 13th Session (1897–98), 77-117; Geraint H. Jenkins, 'Popular beliefs in Wales from the Restoration to Methodism', *BBCS* XXVII (1976–78), 440-41; Geraint H. Jenkins et al., 'The Welsh language in early modern Wales', in *The Welsh Language before the Industrial Revolution*, ed. Geraint H. Jenkins (Cardiff, 1997), III-12.

39 NLW, Great Sessions 4/131/3/25. Literally, 'God and Mary carry me away'.

40 Lester K. Little, 'Spiritual Sanctions in Wales' in Renata Blumenfeld-Kosinski (ed.), *Images of Sainthood in Medieval Europe* (Ithaca, N.Y., 1991), 67-80; eadem, *Benedictine Maledictions* (Ithaca & London, 1993), 123ff.; Wendy Davies, 'Anger and the Celtic saint', in Barbara H. Rosenwin (ed.), *Anger's Past: the Social Uses of an Emotion in the Middle Ages* (Ithaca, NY, 1998), 191-202; Dorothy Ann Bray, 'Malediction and benediction in the lives of the early Irish saints', *Studia Celtica* XXXVI (2002), 47-58.

41 Glanmor Williams, *The Welsh Church from Conquest to Reformation* (Cardiff, 1962), 332; Henry Walter (ed.), *Doctrinal Treatises by William Tyndale* (Parker Society, 1848), 273.

42 NLW, Great Sessions 4/21/2/23; Montgomeryshire examinations dated Feb. 21 James in fragmentary Prothonotary's Papers formerly in NLW, Wales 13/34; PRO, STAC/18/205/21.

43 Thomas, *Religion and the Decline of Magic*, 507-8. Parts of early-modern Herefordshire and Shropshire were Welsh-speaking.

44 In 1663 the high constable of Bromfield optimistically made a presentment of 'all the scoulds' in Wrexham, numbering twelve named women, but the comprehensive 'all' was subsequently scored through: NLW, Chirk B/19c/m.17.

45 NLW, Great Sessions 4/23/1/7; 4/21/2/21. On scolding, see especially M. Ingram, 'Scolding women cucked or washed', in Jenny Kermode and Garthine Walker (eds), *Women, Crime and the Courts in Early Modern England* (London, 1994), 48-50.

46 NLW, J. Conway Davies Deposit (E.A. Lewis papers), Machynlleth Court Leet transcripts; NLW, Great Sessions 4/780/1/44; Chirk B/38a/12; Great Sessions 4/137/4/13.

47 NLW, Chirk B/19(b)/37; Chirk B/26(c)/18.

48 Notably at Presteigne and Builth. Cf. Thomas, *Religion and the Decline of Magic*, 531-3.

49 NLW, Great Sessions 4/32/4/22; cf. Jenkins et al., 'The Welsh language in early modern Wales', 122.

50   Elias Owen, *Welsh Folk-Lore* (Oswestry & Wrexham, 1896), 223, for text and translation of the Llanddona curse. Cf. T. Gwynn Jones, *Welsh Folklore and Folk-custom* (London, 1930), 136-7.

51   NLW, Chirk B/32(d)/10; Great Sessions 4/34/2/39. See also Suggett, 'The Welsh language and the Court of Great Sessions', in Jenkins (ed.), *The Welsh Language before the Industrial Revolution*, 166.

52   G. Dyfnallt Owen, *Elizabethan Wales: The Social Scene* (Cardiff, 1964), 180-1. Cf. generally Thomas, *Religion and the Decline of Magic*, 220.

53   NLW, Great Sessions 4/155/3/28; 4/137/4/13.

54   J. M. Shuttleworth (ed.), *The Life of Edward, First Lord Herbert of Cherbury written by himself* (London, 1976), 6; Thomas Pennant, *A Tour in Wales, MDCCLXX* (2 vols, London, 1783), II, 93-4.

55   NLW, Great Sessions 4/971/4/18-21.

56   Robert Jones, *Drych yr Amseroedd*, ed. G. M. Ashton (1820; Cardiff, 1958), 48-9; NLW, B/CC/(G)/54 (excommunication of Dorothy Ellis, 1753); Jenkins et al., 'The Welsh language in early modern Wales', 121.

57   NLW, Chirk B/30b/27; Great Sessions 4/985/6/19; Williams, 'Witchcraft in seventeenth-century Flintshire, Part Two', 31-4; Great Sessions 4/137/4/13; 4/780/4/16ᵛ.

58   Thomas, *Religion and the Decline of Magic*, 502-12. See also the comments in *Witchcraft in Early Modern Europe*, ed. Jonathan Barry et al. (Cambridge, 1996), 38.

59   D.L. Davies, 'The black arts in Wrexham', *Trans. Denbighshire Historical Soc.* 19 (1970), 230-33.

60   Williams, 'Witchcraft in seventeenth-century Flintshire, Part Two', 29, 30-5; Bodl., MS Ashmole 1815, f.1; NLW, Great Sessions 4/800/2/9(iii-iv); Ewen, *Witchcraft and Demonianism*, 333.

61   NLW, Great Sessions 4/794/9/45y-46, 49; 4/784/3/14-17.

62   Bodl., MS Ashmole 1815, f.1; Ewen, *Witchcraft and Demonianism*, 334; NLW, Great Sessions 33/6/6/unnumbered.

63   Ewen, *Witchcraft and Demonianism*, 334.

64   Thomas, *Religion and the Decline of Magic*, 552-3.

65   Cf. Ruth Finnegan, 'How to do things with words', *Man* 4 (new ser., 1969), 537-52.

Chapter 4

1   John Penry, *Three Treatises Concerning Wales*, ed. David Williams (Cardiff, 1960), 33.

2   On popular religion, see generally Martin Ingram, 'From Reformation to Toleration: popular religious cultures in England, 1540–1690', in *Popular Culture in England, c. 1500–1850*, ed. Tim Harris (London, 1995), 95-123.

3   Glanmor Williams, *The Welsh Church from Conquest to Reformation* (Cardiff, 1962), 461; idem, *Welsh Reformation Essays* (Cardiff, 1967), 172-6; idem, *Wales and the Reformation* (Cardiff, 1997), 280-3.

4   Alexandra Walsham, 'Holywell: contesting sacred space in post-Reformation Wales',

in Will Coster & Andrew Spicer (eds), *Sacred Space in Early Modern Europe* (Cambridge, 2005), 211-36. Cf. also eadem, 'Reforming the waters: holy wells and healing springs in Protestant England', in *Life and Thought in the Northern Church, c.1100– c.1700: Essays in Honour of Claire Cross*, ed. Diana Wood (Woodbridge, 1999), 227-55.

5 Chap. 6, below.

6 Williams, *Wales and the Reformation*, 325; Dyfrig Davies, 'Siôn Mawddwy', *Llên Cymru* VIII (1964–5), 225-7; J.A. Bradney, *History of Monmouthshire* (4 vols, London, 1904–33), III, 53. The cleric was a cultural traditionalist in the sense that he was a patron of the bards and genealogists. I am grateful to Iestyn Daniel and Dylan Foster Evans for commenting on the poem. On exorcism in the period, see D.P. Walker, *Unclean Spirits* (London, 1981).

7 PRO, E135/8/25, a faded Latin charm for the protection of Gwenllian verch Ho[well], is unfortunately without a context; NLW, Coed Coch & Trovarth Deeds 30 was for the protection of David ap Rees ap Jankyn ap Llywelyn's cattle in the earlier sixteenth century. See chap. I, above.

8 PRO C/1055/64-65 transcribed in E.A. Lewis, 'A Reformation episode in Radnorshire', *Radnorshire Soc. Trans.* IX (1939), 19-22. Cf. also the vicar of Llanrwst accused in 1581 of collecting payments ('comorthas') from parishioners for 'saying new gospels', G. Dyfnallt Owen, *Elizabethan Wales: The Social Scene* (Cardiff, 1964), 225.

9 Ifan ab Owen Edwards, *A Catalogue of Star Chamber Proceedings Relating to Wales* (Cardiff, 1929), 125.

10 Bodl. MS. Ashmole 1815, f. 56, edited by M. T. Burdett-Jones, 'Gweddi Anarferol', *Y Cylchgrawn Catholig* III (1994), 35-6.

11 NLW MS. 9628E, f. 13 (old pagination p. 42). Some elements of the 'little creed' were incorporated in a prayer called *Breuddwyd Mary* ('Mary's dream'). Cf. T. Frimston, *Crefydd yn Mhlwyf Rhiwabon* (Bangor, 1896), 57; J. Fisher, 'The private devotions of the Welsh in days gone by', *Trans. Liverpool Welsh National Society*, 13th Session (1897–98), 103-5.

12 NLW MS. 9628E, ff. 11-12 (old pagination pp. 36-7); *The Welsh Language before the Industrial Revolution*, ed. Geraint H. Jenkins (Cardiff, 1997), 117, 175. Cf. *GPC, s.v.* 'myn'.

13 Penry, *Three Treatises Concerning Wales*, 41-2; Alexandra Walsham, *Providence in Early Modern England* (Oxford, 1999), 128; J.O. Halliwell[-Phillipps], *A Minute Account of the Social Condition of the People of Anglesey* (London, 1860), 37.

14 Penry, *Three Treatises Concerning Wales*, 34: 'Nû waeth genûf dhim am y tad y gwr craûlon hinnû onûd cydymmaith da ûwr mab'.

15 Penry, *Three Treatises Concerning Wales*, 35: 'gwûr cig Dûw'.

16 NLW, Great Sessions 4/131/1/3 (ghostly father); 4/20/2/32 (God's hand); Penry, *Three Treatises Concerning Wales*, 34.

17 Penry, *Three Treatises Concerning Wales*, 33-4.

18 Penry, *Three Treatises Concerning Wales*, 41: 'Beth a wodhon ni pûn eû bod hwû yn dwedûd gwir eû paidio?'

19 Penry, *Three Treatises Concerning Wales*, 34.

20 Cf. Keith Thomas, *Religion and the Decline of Magic* (London, 1971), *passim*, esp. 76-7.

21 Chap. 2, above; my emphasis.

22 NLW MS 10B, pp. 81-2; Penry, *Three Treatises Concerning Wales*, 34. See generally, R.B. Roberts, 'Rhai swynion Cymraeg', *BBCS* 21 (1965), 198-213.

23 NLW, Great Sessions 4/85/20 (ii); 4/21/3/21. William Salesbury, *Llysieulyfr Meddyginaethol*, ed. E. Stanton Roberts (Liverpool, 1916), xxvii, 32, for *llysiau Ifan* gathered by women.

24 NLW, Great Sessions 4/9/4/14r-15v; 4780/4/16v.

25 NLW, Great Sessions 4/719/2/49, 51.

26 NLW, Great Sessions 4/718/1/13-16. The 'disease of the heart' is possibly an early reference to *clefyd y galon*, discussed in chap. 5.

27 Examples of persons styled 'meddyg' or 'feddyg' in T.J. Morgan & Prys Morgan, *Welsh Surnames* (Cardiff, 1985), 164.

28 NLW, Great Sessions 4/4/6/1; 4/20/4/21.

29 Roy Palmer, *The Folklore of Radnorshire* (Logaston, 2001), 67.

30 NLW, Great Sessions 4/14/4/16. On herbals compiled by clerics, including Thomas Wiliems, see Graham C. G. Thomas, 'From Manuscript to Print—I. Manuscript', in *A Guide to Welsh Literature, c. 1530–1700* ed. R. Geraint Gruffydd (Cardiff, 1997), 246-7.

31 *DWB*, 1018, *s.n.* 'Wiliems, Thomas'.

32 Thomas Cooper cited in Owen Davies *Cunning-Folk: Popular Magic in English History* (London, 2003), 67-8. Davies suggests that one cunning-man probably served several communities; Stuart Clark and P.T.J. Morgan, 'Religion and magic in Elizabethan Wales: Robert Holland's dialogue on witchcraft', *JEH* 27 (1976), 38, n.2.

33 Owen, *Elizabethan Wales*, 61-2, citing PRO, STAC Eliz. P. 13/18; Edwards, *Catalogue of Star Chamber Proceedings Relating to Wales*, 124. One of the parties alleged that Powell had killed his sister.

34 NLW, Chirk B/22a/4.

35 Caernarfonshire Quarter-sessions case (1636/7) discussed by J. Gwynfor Jones, 'Y tylwyth teg yng Nghymru'r unfed a'r ail ganrif ar bymtheg', *Llên Cymru* VIII (1964-5), 96-9; NLW, Great Sessions 4/21/3/21.

36 Inducing an abortion was a potentially risky undertaking both medically and legally, not only because it could be physically dangerous but also because it was a felony to kill an unborn child. Information about abortions is necessarily obscure. There was a folk belief that the urine and dung of certain animals were abortifacients, as some rather pathetic examinations disclose. In 1726 in Merioneth taking the 'piss of a dun cow' was recommended for getting 'rid of a burden'. In 1664 a catalogue of complaints against Mary ferch Harry of Llangollen included the allegation that she had procured 'stallion's dung' as well as certain herbs, roots, and other things to destroy an unborn bastard child. NLW, Great Sessions 4/297/5/3; Chirk B/20d/7.

37 NLW, Chirk B/19(b)/20. 'Sauell', so written, is perhaps sau[re]ll or sorrel. The document is endorsed 'not proved'.

38 NLW, Great Sessions 4/129/4/16-25.

39 Garthine Walker, '"Strange kind of stealing': abduction in early modern Wales', in Michael Roberts and Simone Clarke (eds), *Women and Gender in Early Modern Wales* (Cardiff, 2000), 50-74.

40 NLW, Great Sessions 4/136/4/17-19.

41 Great Sessions 4/160/8/37.

42 Great Sessions 4/9/4/10-15; *Rhyddiaith Gymraeg II*, ed. Thomas Jones (Cardiff, 1956), 169.

43 See Thomas's discussion of cunning-men and popular magic in *Religion and the Decline of Magic*, ch. 8.

44 Davies, *Cunning-Folk*, 83, notes this distinction.

45 Great Sessions 4/9/4/10-15.

46 *GPC, s.vv.* 'dyn hysbys' (1740), 'gŵr hysbys' (1772), 'gŵr cyfarwydd' (1718).

47 NLW, Great Sessions 4/151/4/25; 4/15/2/35; Chirk B/42c/45.

48 Jones, 'Y tylwyth teg yng Nghymru', 96-9; NLW, Chirk B/17b/19 (document endorsed 'in gaol').

49 See Thomas, *Religion and the Decline of Magic*, 215.

50 NLW, Great Sessions 4/3/5/12; 7/4/m.10Dʳ.

51 C. L'E. Ewen, *Witchcraft in the Star Chamber* (n.pl., 1938), 16; Thomas, *Religion and the Decline of Magic*, 220; G. Dyfnallt Owen, *Wales in the Reign of James I* (Woodbridge, 1988), 48, citing PRO, STAC 8 James I/136/15.

52 NLW, Great Sessions 4/151/4/25.

53 NLW, Great Sessions 4/800/1/16 (petition), 45 (indictment).

54 J.H. Davies, *A Bibliography of Welsh Ballads Printed in the Eighteenth Century* (London, 1908/9-11), xviii.

55 Arise Evans, *The Bloudy Vision of John Farly* (London, 1653), 39.

56 NLW, Great Sessions 4/993/5/7-8, printed in J. Gwynn Williams, 'Witchcraft in seventeenth-century Flintshire, Part Two', *FHSP* 27 (1975-6), 27.

57 NLW, Great Sessions 4/15/2/35.

58 Caroline A. J. Skeel, 'Social and economic conditions in Wales and the Marches in the early seventeenth century, as illustrated by Harl. MS. 4220', *THSC* 1916-17, 139; NLW, Chirk B/42c/45.

59 NLW, Great Sessions 4/15/4/65-6, 112.

60 Owen Davies, *Cunning-Folk*, 9-14.

61 NLW, Great Sessions 4/3/4/12.

62 1662 Visitation articles by George Griffith, bishop of St Asaph, cited by Williams, 'Witchcraft in Seventeenth Century Flintshire, Part Two', 25.

63 Information on the diocese of Hereford from Llinos Beverley Smith.

64 'The Devil of Mascon', 50, quoted by Clark and Morgan, 'Religion and magic in Elizabethan Wales', 45; John Ballinger, 'Vicar Prichard. A study in Welsh bibliography', *Y Cymmrodor* XIII (1900), 48-9.

65 Cited by J. Gwynn Williams, 'Witchcraft in seventeenth-century Flintshire [Part One]', *FHSP* 26 (1974-5), 22.

66 Henry Evans, *Cynghorion Tad iw Fab* (London, 1683), 57-60 (attributed to a young man from Abergwili, Carmarthenshire).

67 These publications are discussed by Geraint H. Jenkins, 'Popular beliefs in Wales from the Restoration to Methodism', *BBCS* xxvii (1977), 459-62; idem, *Literature, Religion and Society in Wales, 1660-1730* (Cardiff, 1978), *passim*; Clark & Morgan, 'Religion and magic in Elizabethan Wales', 45-6.

68 Rhys Prichard, *Y Seren Foreu, neu Ganwyll y Cymry* (Llandovery, 1841), verses cxiii-cx-

viii, 387-92; *Cerddi'r Ficer: Detholiad o Gerdi Rhys Prichard*, ed. Nesta Lloyd (Llandybïe, 1994), 152-7. On the background, see Nesta Lloyd, 'Late free-metre poetry' in *A Guide to Welsh Literature, c. 1530–1700*, ed. Gruffydd, 114-19.

69   Richard Davies, *An Account of the Convincement, Exercises, Services, and Travels of that Ancient Servant of the Lord, Richard Davies* (London, 1710), 36, 49; NLW, Great Sessions 4/787/3/27, 47-8, 65, the final charge was not witchcraft but poisoning. On Quakers and witchcraft, see generally Peter Elmer, '"Saints or sorcerers": Quakerism, demonology and the decline of witchcraft in seventeenth-century England', in Barry et al. (eds.), *Witchcraft in Early Modern Europe*, ch. 6.

70   NLW MS 128C, f. 67 for verse and translation. The rhyme was preserved because the satirist, Morgan Howell, was apparently converted in 1653–4 and afterwards composed its inversion, praising Cradoc as '*Cenhadwr Duw, hynod yw'r dyn*': 'The messenger of God, a remarkable man'.

71   NLW MS 128C, f. 69. The source is not contemporary but records a tradition probably collected by the Independent minister, Edmund Jones of Transh (1702–93).

Chapter 5

1   See chap.1, above. The relatively late development of the modern meaning of 'conjuring', and related terms for 'stage magic' and legerdemain, is discussed by Philip Butterworth, *Magic on the Early English Stage* (Cambridge, 2005), 1-6, 181-94.

2   Jonathan Ceredig Davies, *Folk-Lore of West and Mid-Wales* (Aberystwyth, 1911), 264.

3   Marcel Mauss, *A General Theory of Magic*, transl. by Robert Brain (London, 1972), 40.

4   *The Life and Mysterious Transactions of Richard Morris. . . Dick Spot the Conjurer* (London, 1799), 28.

5   John Walters, *An English–Welsh Dictionary* (London, 1794), *s.v.* 'Gipsy'; NLW MS 10B, pp.76-8; Bryn Ellis, 'Flintshire quarter sessions rolls, 1752–1830', *FHSP* 36 (2003), 112 (Abraham Wood); Eldra Jarman & A.O.H. Jarman, *The Welsh Gypsies: Children of Abram Wood* (Cardiff, 1991), 36-45.

6   W.H. Jones, *Old Karnarvon* (Carnarvon, n.d.), 76; Edward Pugh, *Cambria Depicta* (London, 1816), 391-2; Ellis, 'Flintshire quarter sessions rolls', 100. References to fortune-tellers in ballads are noted by Siwan M. Rosser, *Y Ferch ym Myd y Faled* (Cardiff, 2005), 217-8.

7   Dafydd Wyn Wiliam, *Llwynogod Môn* (Penygroes, 1983), 64; Rosser, *Y Ferch ym Myd y Faled*, 218-9; *The Diary of William Thomas*, ed. R.T.W. Denning *et al.* (Cardiff, 1995), 84-5 (entry for Sept. 1763); *The Life and Opinions of Robert Roberts a Wandering Scholar as told by Himself*, ed. J. H. Davies (Cardiff, 1923), 40-1.

8   *The Diary of William Thomas*, ed. Denning, 82 (11 Aug. 1763).

9   *Diary of William Thomas*, ed. Denning, 73, 121, 128, 227, 319; Edmund Jones, *The Appearance of Evil*, ed. John Harvey (Cardiff, 2003), 76.

10   *Life and Mysterious Transactions of Richard Morris*, 40.

11   *Diary of William Thomas*, ed. Denning, 203; Glamorgan Record Office, Q/SR/1768A/27;

the inquest on William Griffith records death from visitation of God, NLW, Great Sessions 4/621/4/2. The background is discussed by Morfydd E. Owen, 'The medical books of medieval Wales and the physicians of Myddfai', *Carmarthenshire Antiquary* 31 (1995), 34-43.

12 NLW, Great Sessions 4/47/3/27 (examination of Catherine Tayler); NLW, Cwrt Mawr MS 38B, p, 156.

13 NLW, Great Sessions 4/47/3/11; NLW, Mayberry Collection 4483; Ellis, 'Flintshire quarter sessions rolls', 100; NLW, Castell Gorfod MS 6, p. 117 (misdemeanour for pretending to conjure for lost goods in Monmouthshire).

14 *The Cambrian*, 14.xi.1807; transcript in D. Rhys Phillips, *The History of the Vale of Neath* (Swansea, 1925), 582-3.

15 Jonathan Hughes, *Gemwaith Awen Beirdd Collen* (Oswestry, 1806), 101-4; J.H. Davies, *A Bibliography of Welsh Ballads Printed in the 18th Century* (London, 1908–11), xviii, 134 (no. 402).

16 Edward Hamer & H.W. Lloyd, *The History of the Parish of Llangurig* (London, 1875), 116; Hamer, *Montgomeryshire Collections* VI (1873), 268. Hamer also describes how Old Savage was teased by some local youths who hid his ham and bacon. They were eventually found by accident, Savage exclaiming 'the old books have never let me down yet!'

17 Anthony Munday, *John a Kent and John a Cumber*, ed. Arthur E. Pennell (New York & London, 1980), 119; M. Paul Bryant-Quinn, 'Chwedl Siôn Cent', *Cof Cenedl XX*, ed. Geraint H. Jenkins (Llandysul, 2005), 1-31.

18 Jones, *The Appearance of Evil*, ed. Harvey, 51-3. A. ap Gwynn, 'Introduction', T. Gwynn Jones, *Welsh Folklore and Folk-custom* (1930; London, 1979), xxiv-xxvi.

19 Bodl., MS Willis 36, f. 58 (letter from the diocesan registrar to Browne Willis, 7 Feb. 1720/1).

20 Cardiff MS 4.308, p.13.

21 *The Conjuror of Ruabon: being the life and mysterious transactions of John Roberts* (Ellesmere: n.d. [*c.* 1814 or before]), 2 (NLW copy = XAC909(63)/item 2).

22 Cf. 'The proper dress of Gentleman Magician', a memorandum in red ink made in 1795 by Watkin Powell, a gentleman astrologer, in his 'Complete Astrology', Cardiff MS 4.233, p. 44.

23 David Davies, *Hanes Plwyf Penderyn* (Aberdare, 1905), 91. The incident took place *c.* 1830.

24 Thomas W. Hancock, 'Llanrhaiadr-yn-Mochnant. Its parochial history and antiquities', *Montgomeryshire Collections* VI (1873), 329-30. Hancock places this conjurer *c.* 1825.

25 Edmund Jones, *A Relation of Apparitions of Spirits* [etc.] (Newport, 1813), pp, 66-7.

26 Aubrey, *Llyfr Ffynon Elian*, 85-6.

27 Thomas De Quincey, *Works, Volume VIII: Leaders in Literature* (Edinburgh, 1862), 271-83.

28 Iorwerth, 'Llyfr Cwrtycadno', *Yr Haul* 4 (1839), 142-5. The Cwrtycadno library was extensive; a surviving page from the library catalogue runs from 78 ('Astrologian's Guide') to 89 ('Three Books of Occult Philosophy [by] Henry Cornelius'), NLW MS 11716C. See the discussion by Davies, *Cunning-Folk*, 134-6.

29 UCNW Bangor MS 3212.

30 Kate Bosse Griffiths, *Byd y Dyn Hysbys: Swyngyfaredd yng Nghymru* (Talybont, 1977), 43-5. When described it was in private possession.

31 Philip Yorke, *The Royal Tribes of Wales* (Wrexham, 1799), 6; Ella Mary Leather, *The Folk-Lore of Herefordshire* (Hereford, 1912), 29-31.

32 Flintshire Record Office, D/BC/911, and NLW MS 1591D, pp. 165-7, for Bodeugan; John H. Davies (ed.), *The Letters of Lewis, Richard, William, and John Morris of Anglesey, (Morrisiaid Môn) 1728–65* (2 vols, Aberystwyth, 1907-9), II, 153-6; Jones, *The Appearance of Evil*, ed. Harvey, 51 (Llanllechid), 102-8 (Trwyn or Trewyn).

33 Cf. Douglas Grant, *The Cock Lane Ghost* (London, 1965), esp. ch. 7.

34 Thomas Henry Evans, 'History of the parish of Llanwddyn', *Montgomeryshire Collections* VII (1874), 93; Owen, *Welsh Folk-Lore* (Oswestry & Wrexham, 1896), 21-14.

35 NLW, Great Sessions 4/47/3/27.

36 NLW, Great Sessions 4/73/3/30.

37 NLW, Great Sessions 4/620/3/30. Lloyd, his wife and son, were indicted for the murder but acquitted, and then indicted for conspiracy to accuse one Morgan Williams of murder: Great Sessions 4/620/3/46 & 4/620/4/3.

38 NLW, Great Session 4/382/4/13, 22. Anne David was found not guilty.

39 NLW, Great Sessions 4/47/3/29.

40 See generally, Owen, *Welsh Folk-Lore*, 251-61.

41 Griff. Evans, 'Exorcism in Wales', *Folk-Lore* III (1892), 275-6.

42 Sir Everard Home, 'Observations on certain horny excrescences of the human body', *Philosophical Transaction*, vol. 81 (1791), examined the phenomenon. Cf. chap. I above for the case of Margaret Owen (1588).

43 NLW, Great Sessions 4/529/9/12, 23.

44 *The Conjuror of Ruabon*, 8.

45 NLW, Great Sessions 4/758/1/106.

46 *Diary of William Thomas*, 210, 219, 35, 37, 174, 248, 120, 216.

47 Owen, *Welsh Folk-Lore*, 262-4; *GPC*, *s.v.* 'eryr²' (= 'ridge').

48 W. Kemmis Buckley, 'The skull of St Teilo', *Carmarthenshire Antiquary* XXVIII (1992), 103-4, XXIX (1993), 129; Juliette Wood, 'Nibbling pilgrims and the Nanteos Cup: a Cardiganshire legend', in Gerald Morgan (ed.) *Nanteos: A Welsh House and its Families* (Llandysul, 2001), 219-53.

49 On snake-stones, see Prys Morgan, 'A Welsh snakestone, its tradition and folk-lore', *Folklore* 94 (1983), 184-91; Healing-stones: *Catalogue of Manuscripts, Charms, Remedies . . . Exhibited in the National Museum of Wales* (Aberystwyth, 1928), 7-9; extracts from Iolo's 1802 diary in Davies, *Folk-Lore of Mid and West Wales*, 288-9.

50 Roy Porter, *Health for Sale: Quackery in England, 1660–1850* (Manchester, 1989), 129-30.

51 *Diary of William Thomas*, ed. Denning, 306, 348.

52 *Diary of William Thomas*, ed. Denning, 218.

53 Edmund Jones, *A Geographical, Historical, and Religious Account of the Parish of Aberystruth* (Trevecka, 1779), 71-2.

54 *Diary of William Thomas*, ed. Denning, 203.

55 *Diary of William Thomas*, ed. Denning, 303 (28 March 1781). Cf. the examples in Davies, *Cunning-Folk*, 105-6.

56 'Liveranartegro': Edward Laws, *The History of Little England Beyond Wales* (London, 1888), 420 ('Liver and Hearty Grow'); 'clwyf yr edau wlân': *GPC, s.v.*; 'ymaendwnen': Hancock, 'Llanrhaiadr-ym-Mochnant', 328-9. 'Ymaendwnen' is not noted in *GPC*.

57 Cardiff MS 4.308, pp. 9-11.

58 Cf. *GPC, s.vv.* Both terms are given as spoken forms without literary references.

59 Keith Thomas, *Religion and the Decline of Magic* (London, 1971), 184-5.

60 On yarn measuring, see Davies, *Folk-Lore of West and Mid-Wales*, 290-92; Owen, *Welsh Folk-Lore*, 274-6; Hancock, 'Llanrhaiadr-ym-Mochnant', 328-9.

61 E.A. Williams, *The Day before Yesterday*, transl. by G. Wynne Griffith (Beaumaris, 1988), 283; Owen Lloyd, *Hynafiaethau Llanddona* (Beaumaris, 1910), 28; Pugh, *Cambria Depicta*, 42-4. '*Bwt*' = butt or barrel.

62 *Diary of William Thomas*, ed. Denning, 65-7. For further details of the family, see Brian C. Luxton, 'William Jenkin, the wizard of Cadoxton-juxta-Barry', *Morgannwg* xxiv (1980), 31-60.

63 'Brunton's Book' (John Brunton's autobiography) cited by Stephen Hughes, *The Brecon Forest Tramroads* (RCAHMW, Aberystwyth, 1990), 124; NLW, W.R. Jones MS 258, f. 10; Cardiff MS 4.308, pp. 19-20. Other locally notorious witches included 'Betty'r Bont' of the Ystrad Meurig district, Cardiganshire, and 'Pedws Ffoulk' of Garthbeibio, Montgomeryshire: Owen, *Welsh Folk-Lore*, 236, 240-1, 242. Cf. also Eirlys Gruffydd, *Gwrachod Cymru Ddoe a Heddiw* (Capel Garmon, 1988), 42-54 (narratives from Museum of Welsh Life recordings).

64 E.A. Williams, *Hanes Môn yn y Bedwaredd Ganrif ar Bymtheg* (Llangefni, 1927), 325; idem, *The Day Before Yesterday*, 283.

65 Jones, *The Appearance of Evil*, ed. Harvey, 93-4.

66 Aubrey, *Llyfr Ffynon Elian*, 20 (with Caerfyrddin probably a printer's error for Caernarfon); many other examples in Owen, *Welsh Folk-Lore*, 227-33; Davies, *Folk-Lore of West and Mid-Wales*, 242-45.

67 Assaults on reputed witches in Monmouthshire and Flintshire reported in *The Cambrian* 14 April 1827 (reprinted in *Bye-gones* 1882, 118), and *Notes & Queries* II (6th ser., 1880), 426. C18th threat to scratch a Glamorgan wizard in J.H. Matthews (ed.), *Cardiff Records* (6 vols, Cardiff, 1898–1911), III, p. 203.

68 Griffiths, *Byd y Dyn Hysbys*, 10.

69 NLW, Mayberry Collection 4483-5; John Lloyd, *Historical Memoranda of Breconshire* (2 vols, Brecon, 1901–4), II, 75-6; Powys Record Office (transferred from NLW), Brecs. Q/SR 1789T (true bill found).

70 Transcripts and illustrations of some of these charms have been published in: *Catalogue of Manuscripts, Charms, Remedies . . . Exhibited in the National Museum of Wales*, 26-7; Iorwerth C. Peate, *Guide to the Collection of Welsh Bygones* (National Museum of Wales, Cardiff, 1929), 61-2, 127; Evan Isaac, *Coelion Cymru* (Aberystwyth, 1938), 150-6 with plates; Roy Palmer, *The Folklore of Radnorshire* (Logaston Press, 2001), 110, notes an C18th charm kept in Cefnllys church; Eirlys Gruffydd, *Gwrachod Cymru Ddoe a Heddiw*, 18 (charm at Brecon Museum). See also Ralph Merrifield, *The Archaeology of Ritual and Magic* (London, 1987), 150-4, for finds.

71 Sometimes charms have been found in late-nineteenth-century bottles.

72   W. Ll. Davies, 'The Conjurer in Montgomeryshire', *Montgomeryshire Collections* XLV (1937-8), 170; Owen Davies, *Cunning-Folk* (London, 2003), 134, 159.

73   Peate, *Guide to the Collection of Welsh Bygones*, 61; NLW MS 5563C; NLW MS 1248D; D.R.T., 'Demonology and Witchcraft', *Montgomeryshire Collections* XXXVIII (1915), 147; Isaac, *Coelion Cymru*, 152-6; Pitt-Rivers Museum, Oxford, cat. no. 1925·72·1·1.

74   Hamer, *History of Llangurig*, 114-18.

75   Davies, *Folk-Lore of West and Mid-Wales*, 285-6.

76   Fred. S. Price, *History of Caio, Carmarthenshire* (Swansea, 1904), 57. Photographs of the Harries family: NLW, Objects 7/7. The photograph said to be of John Harries (Junior) is also reproduced by Robin Gwyndaf, *Straeon Gwerin Cymru* (Capel Garmon, 1988), 63. See generally, Richard C. Allen, 'John Harries (*c.*1785–1839)', *ODNB*, vol. 25, 377-9.

77   D. Cunllo Davies, 'Caio and its caves', *Wales* III (1896), 539; Price, *History of Caio*, 56.

78   NLW MS 11,117B, esp. ff. 6, 14-15, 19, 22.

79   Cunllo Davies, 'Caio and its caves', 539; Arthur Mee, *Magic in Carmarthenshire. The Harrieses of Cwrt-y-Cadno* (Llanelly, n.d. [*c.* 1911]).

80   Ronald Hutton, *The Triumph of the Moon* (Oxford, 1999), 93, citing the 'Wonderful Magical Scrapbook' in the Harry Rice Collection, University of London.

81   David Owen (Brutus), *Brutusiana* (Llandovery, 1855), 315-9.

82   NLW MS 11776C.

83   Horoscopes in NLW MS 11,117B, ff. 7, 8, 11v.

84   Price, *History of Caio*, 55; Mee, *Magic in Carmarthenshire*, 17, where the case is said to have been reported in *The Cambrian* about 1830.

85   *The Welshman*, 13.vii.1849. Cf. also the criticisms by the evolutionist Alfred Russel Wallace who encountered Harries's trade-card in the Vale of Neath, A.R. Wallace, *My Life* (2 vols, London, 1905), I, 219

86   *Western Mail*, 3-5.xi.1904; *Morning Leader*, 7.xi.1904: Mee, *Magic in Carmarthenshire*, 17.

87   Davies, 'Caio and its caves', 539.

88   Eirwen Jones, 'A Welsh Wizard', *The Carmarthenshire Antiquary* II (1945–6), 48.

Chapter 6

1   Robert Roberts, *Seryddiaeth, neu Lyfr Gwybodaeth* (Llanrwst, *c.* 1830), 269.

2   Over 200 curse tablets have been found at various Roman temple sites in Britain, notably at Bath, and were often prompted by a theft. R.S.O. Tomlin, 'Tabulae Sulis: Roman Inscribed Tablets of Tin and Lead from the Sacred Spring at Bath', in *The Temple of Sulis Minerva at Bath, II: Finds from the Sacred Spring*, ed. B. Cunliffe (Oxford, 1988), Part IV.

3   R. T. Gunther, *Life and Letters of Edward Lhwyd* (Early Science in Oxford XV, Oxford, 1945), 232.

4   See generally, Francis Jones, *The Holy Wells of Wales* (Cardiff, 1954), esp. 74-5 (Ffynnon Gybi), 104-5 (Ffynnon Degla).

5   Richard Suggett, 'Festivals and Social Structure in Early Modern Wales', *P&P* 152 (1996), 79-112.

6   Ffynnon Elian fed the stream which divided the township of Eirias (Caernarfonshire)—in which Ffynnon Elian lay—from Llaneilian (Denbighshire).

7   'Jac Ffynnon Elian', *Cymru* ix (1895), 112.

8   NLW, Gwrych Castle 294.

9   Bryn R. Parry, 'Ffynnon Elian', *Denbighshire Hist. Soc. Trans.* 14 (1965), 188, 196.

10   NLW MS 2594E (Denbighshire file: Ffynnon Elian). Cf. also Edward Pugh, *Cambria Depicta: a Tour through North Wales . . .By a Native Artist* (London, 1816), 19-20.

11   *Parochialia: Being a Summary of Answers to "Parochial Queries . . ." issued by Edward Lhwyd*, ed. R. H. Morris, *AC Suppl.*, (3 parts, London, 1909–11), I, 37.

12   R. W. Jones, *Bywyd Cymdeithasol Cymru yn y Ddeunawfed Ganrif* (London, 1931), 97, citing Richard Parry, *Dihuniad Cysgadur* (1723), 6.

13   Alexander Borthwick, *Llanelian-yn-Rhos, 1579–1867* (printed for the author, 1922), 7. According to Pennant's informant (NLW MS 2594E: Denbighshire file), the bathing place was constructed about sixty yards south of Ffynnon Elian and supplied with water from the well. The bath was about six yards long and four wide, and enclosed by a wall two yards high. Visitors descended into the well-flagged bath by a flight of steps. A floodgate at the lower end discharged the water when the bath needed cleaning. The structure was evidently substantial but has entirely disappeared.

14   Thomas Pennant, *A Tour in Wales, MDCCLXX* (2 vols, London, 1783), II, 351.

15   NLW MS 2594E (Denbighshire file: Ffynnon Elian) adapted by Pennant, *Tour in Wales*, II, 337; Thomas Pennant, *The History of the Parishes of Whiteford and Holywell* (London, 1796), 159-60; Siwan M. Rosser, *Y Ferch ym Myd y Faled* (Cardiff, 2005), 170-1, citing a ballad attributed to Elis Roberts (d. 1789); Elias Owen, 'Holy wells, or water-venera-tion', *AC* 8 (5th ser., 1891), 8-16.

16   Denbighshire Record Office, PD/53/1/11 (Llanelian Vestry Book). Foulkes, probably writing *c.*1730, says that the 'superstitious box' in which 'strangers offered' had been burnt some years before: NLW MS 10B, p. 84.

17   NLW MS 10B, p. 84.

18   NLW MS 2594E (Denbighshire file: Ffynnon Elian).

19   NLW, Great Sessions 13/6/5/unnumbered. Offering a bent coin had been customary before the Reformation when seeking the intercession of a saint, especially at a shrine or before an image of a saint.

20   The charm 'worn by a person for many years without any visible good effect' is tran-scribed in NLW MS 1591D, p. 71.

21   S. Baring-Gould and J. Fisher, *The Lives of the British Saints* (4 vols, London, 1907–13), II, 437. Edward IV is said to have confirmed the charter in 1465.

22   The detail of the stag with candles on its antlers suggests that the painter was more familiar with the iconography of St Hubert than St Elian.

23   Baring-Gould & Fisher, *Lives of the British Saints*, II, 435-44.

24   NLW MS 2594E (Denbighshire file: Ffynnon Elian).

25   Pugh, *Cambria Depicta*, 392; NLW, St Asaph Probate Records, 1812/78, administration of

Margaret Holland of Ffynnon Elian granted to Jeffrey Holland of Dolbenmaen, clerk, her lawful husband.

26   Peter Roberts, *The Cambrian Popular Antiquities* (London, 1815), 246; William Jones, *A Prize Essay, in English and Welsh, on the Character of the Welsh as a Nation, in the Present Age* (London, 1841), 128-9. Cf. Angharad Lhwyd's note in her copy of *Cambrian Popular Antiquities* (NLW shelf-mark WC 1524, p. 245) that a parson's man-servant (when ill) never recovered from the shock of being told that his initials were seen on a pebble in Ffynnon Elian.

27   Jones, *A Prize Essay . . . on the Character of the Welsh*, 128.

28   Pugh, *Cambria Depicta*, 391. On *clefyd y galon*, see chap. 5 above.

29   *Bye-gones*, 1873, 185-6, reprinting an extract from *The Cabinet of Curiosities*, No. 9, 137. *The North Wales Gazette*, 15.iv.1819, and *The Times*, 16.iv.1819, reported the case. Margaret Pritchard of Y Ro, Caernarfonshire, gave evidence and said she formerly lived at Cefnyffynnon and was known as 'Gwraig y Ffynnon' or the woman of the well. She knew John Edwards but had not seen him for three years.

30   Pugh, *Cambria Depicta*, 20. The preface is dated 1813.

31   Parry, 'Ffynnon Elian', 185-96

32   Roberts, *Seryddiaeth, neu Lyfr Gwybodaeth*, 270-1, gives a prayer of this type to be written on a piece of clean white paper or parchment and kept in the waistcoat pocket. The prayer concludes by asking God to punish the curser, 'may his conscience be painful and his life sorrowful.'

33   Pennant, *A Tour in Wales*, II, 351.

34   Parry, 'Ffynnon Elian', 185-96

35   Roberts, *Seryddiaeth, neu Lyfr Gwybodaeth*, 265-7. For Robert Roberts (1777–1836), see *DWB, s.n.* His 'book of knowledge' (Llanrwst, 1830), which included information allegedly from *llyfr Dic Smot* or 'Dic Spot's book', may have become something of a cunning-man's vade mecum. A well-thumbed copy now in the NLW (shelf-mark XBF 1701.R64) has a note recording that it belonged to a Carmarthenshire cunning-man (*dyn hysbys*).

36   Two pin-pierced cursing corks ('*corcyn melltithio*'), recovered in 1920 from a well at Llanddwyn, Anglesey, are in Ceredigion Museum, Tre'r-ddôl Collection T359 (information from Michael Freeman, curator). *Notes & Queries* 9 (4th ser., 1872), 55-6, reports the discovery of a 'cursing-pot' by a labourer when removing a fence at Penrhos Bardwyn Farm, Holyhead, Anglesey. The black pipkin contained a frog impaled with pins and was sealed with a slate inscribed 'Nanny Roberts' (Fig. 15). The cursing-pot, now at Gwynedd Museum, Bangor, is also illustrated in Eirlys Gruffydd, *Gwrachod Cymru* (Caernarfon, 1980), pl. 2.

37   Samuel Lewis, *A Topographical Dictionary of Wales* (3rd edn, 2 vols, London, 1845), II, 5; NLW MS 3290D.

38   NLW MS 3290D; E. Neil Baynes, 'Ffynnon Eilian', *Trans. Anglesey Antiquarian Soc.* 1925, 115-16; Eirlys & Ken Lloyd Gruffydd, *Ffynhonnau Cymru, Cyfrol 2* (Llanrwst, 1999), 100-102. The cursing slate is now at Gwynedd Museum, Bangor.

39   Roberts, *Seryddiaeth, neu Lyfr Gwybodaeth*, 259-71.

40 *Llyfr Ffynon Elian* (Llannerch-y-medd, n.d. [1861]), 83-4.

41 Pugh, *Cambria Depicta*, 20; Roberts, *Cambrian Popular Antiquities*, 247; NLW, Plas yn Cefn MS 2553; M. L. L[ouis], *Gleanings of a Tour in North Wales* (Liverpool, 1824), 10-12.

42 Edmund Hyde Hall, *A Description of Caernarvonshire (1809-1811)*, ed. Emyr Gwynne Jones (Caernarvonshire Historical Society Record Series No. 2, 1952), 47, 321-2.

43 Indictment of John Edwards in NLW, Great Sessions 4/1019/5/9.

44 Charlotte Wardle, *St. Aelian's, or the cursing well. A poem* (London, 1814), 110 (holly overhanging the well was thought to have a special virtue which proceeded from its roots: *Powysion . . . Llyfr II* (Bala, 1826), 203, n.4; M.L. L[ouis], *Gleanings of a Tour in North Wales*, 9-10. A newspaper report of 1831 says: 'A few years ago the magistrates of the county prosecuted one of the high priests of the well, who, in consequence, was . . . put into prison and his well of holy waters destroyed', *Folk-Lore* I (1890), 131.

45 *Powysion . . . Llyfr II*, 202, n.3; T. Parry & T. M. Jones, *Hanes Dechreuad a Chynydd y Methodistiaid Calfinaidd yn Ngholwyn Bay a'r Cylch* (Dolgellau, 1909), 12-17.

46 Parry & Jones, *Hanes . . . Methodistiaid Calfinaidd yn Ngholwyn Bay*, 16-17; cf. 'Ffynnon Elian' (letter from D. Davies, Colwyn), *Y Dysgedydd* IX (1830), 141.

47 The chronology is not exactly clear, but it seems that Jac probably constructed his well after the prosecution in 1818, and the 1829 destruction of the well enhanced its reputation.

48 Indictment in PRO, ASSI 64/2.

49 Case reported in *The North Wales Chronicle*, 16.viii.1831 (summary in *Bye-gones*, 1888, 178); *The Times*, 13.viii.1831; *The Lincoln Herald*, 19.viii.1831, reprinted in *Folk-Lore*, I (1890), 131-3.

50 NLW, tithe schedule for Llandrillo-yn-Rhos dated 9 Oct. 1846.

51 *AC* I (1846), 54; Parry, 'Ffynnon Elian', 188.

52 Deeds in NLW Gwrych Castle Collection, Box 15, Parcel 97. Jac sold 'Meddiant' to Evan Evans of Bryn-y-gwynt who re-sold it in 1861 to Rev. R.H. Jackson, vicar of Llanelian, whose heir sold it on to the Gwrych Castle Estate in 1867 for £15. The cottage was subsequently demolished.

53 'Hanes Ffynon Elian, a'r twyll a arferwyd trwyddi. Gan John Evans (Jack Ffynon Elian', *Y Nofelydd* I (1861); 'Hanes Bywyd J. Evans, fel y dywedai ef ei hun' in *Llyfr Ffynon Elian*, 5-12, abridged in *Hanes Ffynon Elian*, 11-12.

54 Marcel Mauss, *A General Theory of Magic*, transl. Robert Brain (London, 1972), 25-44.

Chapter 7

1 Bengt Ankarloo & G. Henningsen (eds.), *Early Modern European Witchcraft: Centres and Peripheries* (Oxford, 1993); Robin Briggs, '"Many reason why": witchcraft and the problem of multiple explanation' in Barry et al. (eds.), *Witchcraft in Early Modern Europe* (Cambridge, 1996), 55.

2 My estimate based on the surviving gaol files. See generally, Richard Suggett, 'The

Welsh Language and the Court of Great Sessions,' in Geraint H. Jenkins (ed.), *The Welsh Language Before the Industrial Revolution* (Cardiff, 1997), ch. 4.

3   J. Fisher (ed.), 'Wales in the time of Queen Elizabeth. De presenti statu totius Walliae', *AC* 15 (6th ser., 1915), 237-48.

4   Christina Larner, *Enemies of God: the Witch Hunt in Scotland* (London, 1981); Brian P. Levack, 'State-building and witch hunting in early modern Europe', in Barry et al. (eds.), *Witchcraft in Early Modern Europe*, ch. 4. See also the correctives in Julian Goodare (ed.), *The Scottish Witch-hunt in Context* (Manchester, 2002).

5   Peter Burke, 'The Comparative Approach to European Witchcraft', in Ankerloo & Henningsen (ed.), *Early Modern Witchcraft*, 441; Carlo Ginzburg, *The Night Battles: Witchcraft and Agrarian Cults in the Sixteenth and Seventeenth Centuries* (London, 1976).

6   Keith Thomas, *Religion and the Decline of Magic* (London, 1971), 576; Robin Briggs, *Witches and Neighbours* (London, 1996), ch. 9; James Sharpe, *Instruments of Darkness: Witchcraft in England, 1550–1750* (London, 1996), ch. 9.

7   Cf. Willem de Blécourt, 'On the Continuation of Witchcraft', in Barry et al. (eds.), *Witchcraft in Early Modern Europe*, ch. 13; Bengt Ankarloo & Stuart Clark (eds), *The Athlone History of Witchcraft and Magic in Europe, Volume 5: The Eighteenth and Nineteenth Centuries; Volume Six: The Twentieth Century* (London, 1999); Owen Davies, *Witchcraft, Magic and Culture, 1736–1951* (Manchester, 1999).

8   Peter Burke, 'The Comparative Approach to European Witchcraft' in Ankerloo & Henningsen (ed.), *Early Modern Witchcraft*, 441.

9   Cf. Mary Douglas (ed.), *Witchcraft Confessions and Accusations* (London, 1970), xxvi-xxxvi.

10 See generally, Glanmor Williams, *Wales and the Reformation* (Cardiff, 1997); B. Bradshaw, 'The English Reformation and identity formation in Ireland and Wales', in B. Bradshaw & P. Roberts (ed.), *British Consciousness and Identity* (Cambridge, 1998), 72-88; K.S. Bottigheimer & U. Lotz-Heumann, 'The Irish Reformation in European Perspective', *Archiv für Reformationsgeschichte* LXXXIX (1998), 268-309; Felicity Heal, *Reformation in Britain and Ireland* (Oxford, 2003), esp. 128-9.

11 As Glanmor Williams has noted, the number of recusants in Wales was very small. Presentments of those not attending church (not necessarily recusants, of course) were routinely made at the Court of Great Sessions.

12 Cf. E.R. Leach (ed.), *Dialectic in Practical Religion* (Cambridge, 1968). The term 'practical religion' seems preferable to 'popular religion'. Eamon Duffy, *The Stripping of the Altars* (New Haven & London, 1992), 3, uses 'traditional religion' in preference to 'popular religion' to indicate the dimension of shared belief between clergy, elites, and people. 'Practical religion' conveys the lack of explicit doctrine, and the necessary accommodation with authority.

13 George Gifford, *A Briefe Discourse of certaine points of the Religion which is among the Common Sort of Christians* (London, 1581).

14 See generally the discussion of religious art and artefacts in Peter Lord, *The Visual Culture of Wales: Medieval Vision* (Cardiff, 2003).

15 Erasmus Saunders, *A View of the State of Religion in the Diocese of St. David's about the beginning of the 18th Century* (1721; Cardiff, 1949), 16-24.

16 Saunders, *View of the State of Religion*, 4-5, 23-4.

17 Saunders, *View of the State of Religion*, 35.

18 Saunders, *View of the State of Religion*, 35-6; Robert Jones, *Drych yr Amseroedd*, ed. G. M. Ashton (1820; Cardiff, 1958), 22.

19 Saunders, *View of the State of Religion*, 17-37.

20 Jones, *Drych yr Amseroedd*, ed. Ashton, 27.

21 NLW MS 9628E, p. 78 (old pagination).

22 Edmund Jones, *The Appearance of Evil: Apparitions of Spirits in Wales*, ed. John Harvey (1780; Cardiff, 2003), 46.

23 Jones, *Appearance of Evil*, ed. Harvey, *passim*, esp. 68, 114.

24 Most felicitously by Godfrey Lienhardt in *Divinity and Experience* (Oxford, 1961).

25 David Williams, *The Rebecca Riots: a Study in Agrarian Discontent* (Cardiff, 1971); D.J.V. Jones, *Rebecca's Children: a Study of Rural Society, Crime, and Protest* (Oxford, 1989).

26 N. Tyacke (ed.), *England's Long Reformation* (London, 1998).

27 A point made by Peter Burke, *Popular Culture in Early Modern Europe* (London, 1978), 238-9; cf. also Prys Morgan, *The Eighteenth Century Renaissance* (Llandybïe, 1981), ch. 1.

28 Jenkins, 'Popular Beliefs in Wales from the Restoration to Methodism', 459-62.

29 NLW MS 10B (fair copy); NLW MS 9628E (drafts); NLW, SA/Lett/821 (letter from Foulkes to the Bp. of St Asaph). I must thank Mary Burdett-Jones for discussing her work on Foulkes with me.

30 Cf. Chap. VI above for the rood-screen and chest at Llanelian.

31 Bodl., MS Gough Wales 7, f. 24. Cf. also William Harris, 'Observations on the Julia Strata [etc.]', *Archaeologia* II (1771), 13.

32 A theme explored by E.P. Thompson in *Customs in Common* (London, 1991).

33 'Fairy Legends of Wales' included in *Fairy Legends and Traditions of the South of Ireland. The New Series*, ed. T. Crofton Croker (London, 1828), 205. For the context, see Morfydd E. Owen, 'A Cambro-Hibernian alliance: Maria Jane Williams and Thomas Crofton Crocker', *AC* CXLIII (1994), 1-36.

34 Jones, *Appearance of Evil*, ed. Harvey, 47.

35 Jones, *Appearance of Evil*, ed. Harvey, 94; my italics.

36 Jones, *Appearance of Evil*, ed. Harvey, 56-7; Richard Baxter, *The Certainty of the World of Spirits* (London, 1691), 135-46.

37 Jones, *Appearance of Evil*, ed. Harvey, 124-5.

38 Jones, *Drych yr Amseroedd*, ed. Ashton, esp. 22-8.

39 A reference to a printed broadside supposedly reproducing a letter by Christ. There are versions in English, French, and Welsh. See W. Garmon Jones, 'A Welsh Sunday epistle', in *A Miscellany Presented to J. M. Mackay, LL.D.*, ed. O. Elton (Liverpool, 1914), 233-42, for MS (1665) and printed (1779) versions of the letter in Welsh.

40 Jones, *Drych yr Amseroedd*, ed. Ashton, 25.

41 Richard Suggett, 'Festivals and Social Structure in Early Modern Wales', *P&P* 152 (1996), 79-112.

42   William Howells, *Cambrian Superstitions* (Tipton, 1831), 161.

43   *Fairy Legends and Traditions*, ed. Croker, 208.

44   NLW MS 10B, p. 208.

45   Jones, *Drych yr Amseroedd*, ed. Ashton, 27; William Williams, *Observations on the Snowdon Mountains* (London, 1802), 14; Trefor M. Owen, *Welsh Folk Customs* (Cardiff, 1968), 174; Edmund Hyde Hall, *A Description of Caernarvonshire (1809–11)*, ed. E. Gwynne Jones (Caernarvonshire Historical Society Record Series II, 1952), Appendix I, esp. 321.

46   See chap. 6 above.

47   *Powysion, Llyfr II. Awdlau, Cywyddau, ac Ynglynion, a ddanfonwyd i Eisteddfod Trallwng, Medi, 1824* (Bala, 1826), iii, 193-232. Cf. also the poetic attack on the belief in corpse-candles (*Cân y canhwyllau cyrff*) by Theophilus Davies (1838) cited by Huw Walters, *Canu'r Pwll a'r Pulpud* (Denbigh, 1987), 281. The poet concludes by pointing out that the fiery corpse-candles would have reduced villages (of the Aman Valley) to ashes had they appeared during the cholera epidemic.

48   *Powysion, Llyfr II*, 203 (poem by Samuel Evans, Caerwys, Flintshire).

49   Information from E. Wyn James, Cardiff, citing Robert Owen, *Hanes Methodistiaeth Gorllewin Meirionydd* (Dolgellau, 2 vols, 1889-91), I, 23-4, 200. This conjurer it may be noted was the grandfather of a prominent Congregational minister, Hugh Pugh (1803-68), 'Mostyn'.

50   William Jones, *Nodweddion y Cymry fel Cenedl* (London, 1841), 307. The rebuke seems to have been too embarrassing a matter to include in the English version of the pamphlet, *The Character of the Welsh as a Nation, in the Present Age* (London, 1841).

51   Prys Morgan, 'From Long Knives to Blue Books', in *Welsh Society and Nationhood: Historical Essays Presented to Glanmor Williams*, ed. R.R. Davies et al. (Cardiff, 1984), 199-215.

52   *Reports of the Commissioners of Inquiry into the State of Education in Wales* (3 parts, London, 1847), II, 64.

53   Cf. the analysis of this passage in Gwyneth Tyson Roberts, *The Language of the Blue Books: the Perfect Instrument of Empire* (Cardiff, 1998), 187-8.

54   *Reports of the Commissioners of Inquiry into the State of Education in Wales*, II, 64.

55   Ibid.

56   *The Life and Opinions of Robert Roberts*, ed. J.H. Davies (Cardiff, 1923), 24-9.

57   On the background, see Russell Davies, *Hope and Heartbreak: A Social History of Wales and the Welsh, 1776–1871* (Cardiff, 2005); Gareth W. Williams, 'The disenchantment of the world: innovation, crisis and change in Cardiganshire c. 1880–1910', *Ceredigion* IX (1980–83), 303-21.

58   John Cule, *Wreath on the Crown* (Llandysul, 1967); Siân Busby, *"A Wonderful Little Girl"* (London, 2003); *The Welsh Fasting Girl* (London & Pencader, 1904), esp. 182.

59   *Tuchan-gerddi i Glwyf yr Edau Wlan: sef Tair Can Wobrwyedig yn Nghyfarfod Cystadleuol Talerddig, Llanbrynmair, Mawrth 10fed, 1876* (Bala, 1876; NLW copy = shelf-mark XAC 909 (424)). I am grateful to Angela Bennett for drawing my attention to this pamphlet and discussing the text with me. The woollen-yarn cure is still practised in parts of Montgomeryshire, primarily as a remedy for depression: S. Philpin, 'Wool measure-

ment: community and healing in rural Wales', in *Welsh Communities: New Ethnographic Perspectives*, ed. Charlotte Aull Davies & Stephanie Jones (Cardiff, 2003), 117-34.

60 John Jones, *Llef yn erbyn Ofergoeledd ac Ysbrydegaeth* (Llandyssul, 1901; NLW copy = shelf-mark XBF 1042. J77). The pamphlet also has an attack on spiritualism, which it contrasts with the old belief in ghosts. Alwyn D. Rees refers to Ioan Lenydd's pamphlet in his classic *Life in a Welsh Countryside* (Cardiff, 1950), 135-6.

61 'Buchedd' was a term used in Welsh community studies to describe status differences: Elwyn Davies and Alwyn D. Rees (ed.), *Welsh Rural Communities* (Cardiff, 1960), x-xi, 12-23. See the discussion of 'buchedd' in Graham Day, *Making Sense of Wales: a Sociological Perspective* (Cardiff, 2002), 148-51.

62 'Ofergoelion Cymru', *Y Dysgedydd* XLVI (1867), 185-94.

63 On 'chapel civility', see Prys Morgan, 'Wild Wales: civilising the Welsh from the sixteenth to the nineteenth Centuries', in P. Burke et al. (eds), *Civil Histories* (Oxford, 2000), 279-83; Matthew Cragoe, *Culture, Politics, and National Identity in Wales, 1832–1886* (Oxford, 2004), 174-81, discusses chapel discipline.

64 Judith Devlin, *The Superstitious Mind: French Peasants and the Supernatural in the Nineteenth Century* (New Haven and London, 1987).

65 *Tuchan-gerddi i Glwyf yr Edau Wlan*, 12.

66 NLW MS 3290D (Ffynnon Elian, p. 20); John Rhŷs, *Celtic Folklore, Welsh and Manx* (2 vols, Oxford, 1901), I, viii; T. Gwynn Jones, *Welsh Folklore and Folk Custom* (London, 1930); D. Parry-Jones, *Welsh Legends and Fairy Lore* (London, 1953), 1-5.

67 Text and translation in *The Physicians of Myddvai; Meddygon Myddfai*, ed. John Williams 'Ab Ithel' (The Welsh MSS. Society, Llandovery, 1861), xxviii. The stanza concluded the legend of Llyn y Fan Fach, as written down in 1841 by William Rees of Tonn from the oral recitation of several named informants. Cf. also *A People's Poetry: Hen Benillion*, translated by Glyn Jones (Bridgend, 1997), 19; Parry-Jones, *Welsh Legends and Fairy Lore*, 13.

LIST OF ILLUSTRATIONS

INDEX